Historical Distillates

Historical Distillates

CHEMISTRY AT THE UNIVERSITY OF TORONTO SINCE 1843

ADRIAN G. BROOK
AND
W.A.E. (PETER) McBRYDE

THE DUNDURN GROUP
TORONTO

Copyright © Adrian G. Brook and W.A.E (Peter) McBryde, 2007

All rights reserved. No part of this publication may be reproduced, stored in a retrieval system, or transmitted in any form or by any means, electronic, mechanical, photocopying, recording, or otherwise (except for brief passages for purposes of review) without the prior permission of Dundurn Press. Permission to photocopy should be requested from Access Copyright.

Copy-editor: Jennifer Gallant
Design: Alison Carr
Printer: Tri-Graphic Printing Limited

Library and Archives Canada Cataloguing in Publication

Brook, Adrian G. (Adrian Gibbs)

    Historical distillates : chemistry at the University of Toronto since 1843 / Adrian G. Brook and W.A.E. (Peter) McBryde.

Includes bibliographical references and index.
ISBN 978-1-55002-709-9 (bound).--ISBN 978-1-55002-724-2 (pbk.)

    1. University of Toronto. Dept. of Chemistry--History.
I. McBryde, W. A. E., 1917- II. Title.

QD49.C33T67 2007   540'.71'1713541   C2006-906842-9

1 2 3 4 5   11 10 09 08 07

   Conseil des Arts   Canada Council   Canada
             du Canada   for the Arts

We acknowledge the support of the Canada Council for the Arts and the Ontario Arts Council for our publishing program. We also acknowledge the financial support of the Government of Canada through the Book Publishing Industry Development Program and The Association for the Export of Canadian Books, and the Government of Ontario through the Ontario Book Publishers Tax Credit program, and the Ontario Media Development Corporation.

Care has been taken to trace the ownership of copyright material used in this book. The author and the publisher welcome any information enabling them to rectify any references or credits in subsequent editions.

J. Kirk Howard, President

Printed and bound in Canada.
Printed on recycled paper.

www.dundurn.com

Dundurn Press	Gazelle Book Services Limited	Dundurn Press
3 Church Street, Suite 500	White Cross Mills	2250 Military Road
Toronto, Ontario, Canada	High Town, Lancaster, England	Tonawanda, NY
M5E 1M2	LA1 4XS	U.S.A. 14150

To Peg — for surviving the last four years

Contents

Foreword   9
Acknowledgements   13
Introduction: Chemistry Comes to Upper Canada   17

PART I: GENTLEMAN PROFESSORS FROM BRITAIN (1843–1920)
1 Father of Toronto Chemistry: Henry Croft (1843–1879)   27
2 William Pike and Undergraduate Research (1880–1900)   50
3 Gentleman and Officer: W.R. Lang (1900–1920)   65

PART II: EARLY CANADIAN LEADERS (1920–1960)
4 Builder and Skeptic: William Lash Miller (1920–1937)   85
5 Frank B. Kenrick and War Research (1937–1944)   102
6 A.R. Gordon and Postwar Expansion (1944–1960)   110

PART III: LASH MILLER'S LEGACY (1960–2005)
7 Expansion and Retrenchment (1960–1974)   129
8 Broadening the Base (1974–1993)   151
9 Chemistry in the Suburbs (1964–2005)   164
10 Probe and Measure: Instruments and Keepers (1960–2005)   175
11 Transforming the Lash Miller Building (1993–2006)   189

Appendix: Chemistry Club Skits and Songs   209
Notes   231
Index   245

Foreword

This is a family history, a century and a half of lives and deaths, parenthood and offspring. It happens to be my family, so I find it absorbing.

I am mindful, nonetheless, of Tolstoy's remark at the opening of *Anna Karenina* that "All happy families resemble one another, each unhappy family is unhappy in its own way." I take comfort, therefore, from the fact that this account of our beginnings resembles that of other chemistry departments that have achieved much. Fundamentally, it is, therefore, the story of a happy family.

What is remarkable is that such a family can be forged out of a group of ambitious individualists and eccentrics. But the evidence is here. The secret is the existence, beneath the turbulent surface, of a commonality of purpose. Each individual in this enterprise wishes to shine; indeed, ignoble as it may seem, each wishes to outshine. But through it all there is a consciousness that each is a part of a process that is forging a tradition. That is the subtext of our department's story, and of this book. That is its claim to our attention.

The story begins, naturally, with such recollections as we have of our earliest chemical ancestors. The earlier, the more colourful they appear, as, no doubt, will we. The first professor of chemistry, Henry Holmes Croft, aged twenty-three, began lecturing in 1843, the year the university opened. The timing was propitious since England, and consequently its colonial possessions in what is now Toronto, was undergoing a culture change — a delayed consequence of the Enlightenment.

The country, and hence this minor outpost, was emerging from theocracy in the direction of secular democracy. (As I write, in 2006, democracies view with impatience countries only now embarking on this transition, forgetting how recently we ourselves made it.)

Though the president of the university was, of course, an Anglican, and in our case a bishop, it was no longer obligatory for the professor of chemistry to be an ordained clergyman. It was only required that he be male and British, and preferable that he be Scottish.

Further changes followed. In the course of a century the world capital for science shifted first to Germany (all chemists were required to study German when I joined the staff here) and then to the United States. Of these two seismic shifts, the ascendancy of North America resulted in the most visible changes. The department ceased to be subject to its "Head" (as had been the case in both Britain and Germany) and began a slow evolution in the direction of consultative meritocracy.

The way was therefore open to change, at the very time that immigration was bringing a fresh breeze of new thinking. Early in this period the professoriate increased from a single eminence, the prof, to more than a dozen professors. Their names remained at first evocative of the British Isles. Joining the faculty in 1956 the writer was the first to require the dubious letter y to be displayed on an office door. It would be years before x and z brought fresh unknowns.

A more profound culture change was yet to come, as I soon learnt. On arrival I enquired of Mrs. M.A. (Robin) Thomson, secretary to the head of department as well as supervisor of the single employee in the departmental office, whether it would be possible to obtain secretarial assistance and access to the departmental telephone. I was assured that there would be no problem with this, provided, of course, that I did not use either for personal purposes. "What," I asked cautiously, "would constitute a personal use?" "Anything to do with research," came the reply.

This too was to change, as Professor Donald LeRoy, acting as assistant to the head of department and later as "Chair" (a new designation for a new age), insisted that research, rather than being a personal indulgence, constituted a part of a university teacher's responsibilities ensuring that he, and much later she, was situated at the forefront of the field.

A further culture shift to which my generation was witness was the slow march of chemistry toward physics as the twentieth century unfolded. This is today being followed by the equally important and fruitful melding of chemistry with biology.

Accompanying this there has been a burgeoning sense of social responsibility. This is not new, but in the present stage of our fragile tenancy of the globe it presents itself with unprecedented urgency.

While responding to this need, we should seek to protect what a century and a half of endeavour has brought into being: a community of teachers and learners in which each of us shares. That community must continue to provide its members with the freedom to explore ideas for the single good reason that understanding gives meaning to our sojourn on earth.

Betterment of the circumstances of our existence, vital as it clearly is, must take second place. Otherwise the history set out in this volume, and the further story of the blossoming of discoveries only hinted at here, will have come to an end. That would be a sorry outcome to the great adventure on which we are embarked. It would leave us — as can happen in societies under siege — having forgotten what it is we are protecting.

In 1843 the Department of Chemistry consisted of a lone twenty-three-year-old Englishman. By 2043, in this favoured land, it should have become a mecca for scientific sages from all corners of the earth, rivalling the best to be found anywhere. In times ahead we shall need this example of achievement to show what can be built when people from around the world join hands in an extraordinary endeavour.

Nobel laureate John C. Polanyi
Professor, Department of Chemistry, University of Toronto
October 2006

Acknowledgements

W.A.E. (Peter) McBryde started the research that led to this book in the early 1980s. He attended schools in Toronto and obtained his BA and MA degrees in chemistry at the University of Toronto. He then went to the University of Virginia, where he completed a PhD in analytical chemistry and taught for several years. He returned to Toronto as an assistant professor in 1948. He served at Toronto until 1960, when the new Waterloo University in Guelph invited him to be the head of its chemistry department. He later became dean of science there, and then served a second term as head of chemistry. During this period as administrator, he also conducted research in analytical chemistry.

At some stage, his interest in laboratory research diminished, giving way to fascination with the life of the remarkable Toronto chemist William Lash Miller. Miller had been in the department at Toronto from 1890 to 1937, serving for years as de facto head and becoming a major force in the university. This interest led McBryde to research and write several papers on Miller, the growth of the university, and the city of Toronto. His knowledge grew, and he

W.A.E. (Peter) McBryde.
Courtesy Department of Chemistry, University of Toronto.

ultimately began writing a history of the department from its beginnings in 1843.[1]

McBryde did a huge amount of research in the University of Toronto Archives and numerous other sources and also corresponded with many knowledgeable people. This research serves as the basis for the first three chapters of this book. While working on the chapter on Lash Miller, he developed an illness that halted his efforts. Nothing happened to the manuscript from about 1988 until 2002, at which time his Waterloo colleagues realized that he would make no further progress.

They sent the collected material to the chairman of the Toronto department, David Farrar, who had visited McBryde several times. Shortly after its arrival, Farrar asked me if I would complete the history, and I agreed to try. I warned him that I was no historian, although I had recently helped to proofread Martin Friedland's *The University of Toronto: A History*. McBryde and I had been very good friends when he was in Toronto, had served together on a major building committee, and had kept in touch after his move to Waterloo.

I began writing, making as much use as possible of McBryde's material and other sources, in addition to my own personal knowledge of the department, which I had entered in 1943 as a freshman in mathematics and physics. My studies led to a BA in physics and chemistry and a PhD in 1950 in organic chemistry. There followed a year teaching at the University of Saskatchewan and one-year post-doctoral appointments at the Imperial College of Science and Technology, London, and Iowa State College of Agriculture and Mechanic Arts (now Iowa State University). I then returned to Toronto and have been active in the department ever since, with only minor breaks, as a faculty member or retiree. Sadly, McBryde died on October 30, 2004, before he could see this volume, to which he contributed so much.

When I accepted this challenging project, I advised the chairman and faculty that I would be less a researcher-author, as McBryde obviously had been, and more a compiler of input from whatever source. This approach seemed particularly necessary since the chairman had told me that he hoped to see the book before his term ended in 2004.

Apart from McBryde's major contributions, many people in the Department of Chemistry and elsewhere responded magnificently to my requests for information. (This was crucial: I found that after the 1940s the university archives had virtually no material about the department. I learned that a super-keen student whom the department had hired one summer to tidy a room had thrown out much of the archival material that it had carefully collected and stored.) Particularly helpful were many of my colleagues in organic chemistry, especially Bryan Jones, Ron Kluger, Mark Lautens, Stewart McLean, Tom Tidwell, and Keith Yates, whom I quote and cite in the text. Alex Harrison also contributed extensively — for example, proofreading most chapters and suggesting changes. Cynthia Goh, Martin Moskovits, Tony Poë, John Polanyi, Bill Reynolds, and Stan Nyburg (who is now at King's College, London) also gave me material that I use below. Professor Byron Lane of Biochemistry provided an insightful article on Andrew Gordon. My many interviews collected valuable information; for example, John Valleau and Stuart Whittington helped me clarify some historical details about the department's computers, and Scott Mabury explained the background of its ANALEST facility. Revealing insights about some of its equipment for X-ray diffraction came from Dr. Alan Lough and Dr. Srebri Petrov.

Several former students submitted often-poignant reminiscences, particularly Bob Stobie and Ron Fawcett, and Christina Schwarz and Rob Webster informed me about the current Chemistry Club. Also, the department's annual publication *Distillations* contains much useful material by various authors.

There are numerous stories, many unverifiable, about some of the department's "characters." When they appear reliable, I include them.

The staff at the University of Toronto Archives, particularly Harold Averill and Marnee Gamble, guided me to documents, pictures, and photographs. Patricia Meindl, the librarian of the Chemistry Library, directed me to useful books and to sites in the university archives with information about the department. Trevor Levere of the Institute of History and Philosophy of Science and Technology provided helpful suggestions.

Throughout the project, Penny Ashcroft Moore, the department's indefatigable secretary, provided a host of details about the faculty and other matters, and she, Fiona Gardiner, Armando Marquez, and Ken Jones (Scarborough) assisted me in dealing with many of the photographs. Sue McClelland, who eventually became the department's first development officer, provided great encouragement, shared memories of past events (particularly the four Nobel Lectures series), passed on various interesting bits of information, urged various former faculty members to make submissions, communicated with numerous people on my behalf, and helped me with secretarial tasks. Without her efforts, much would be missing from this account.

Finally, I want to thank John Parry, recently chosen as editor, for his many helpful suggestions about organization and selection of the material in the book and its style of presentation, which greatly improved the manuscript. Similar appreciation is due Jennifer Gallant and other staff of The Dundurn Group for their efforts guiding me in preparing the manuscript for publication.

Adrian Brook
Toronto, October 2006

Introduction

CHEMISTRY COMES TO UPPER CANADA

John Graves Simcoe and a Provincial University

In 1793 Upper Canada's new administrators built a British fortification at the strategic location where Toronto now stands. Its natural harbour was the best on the north shore of Lake Ontario. In August, Lieutenant-Governor John Graves Simcoe named the place York.[1] Simcoe's very English ideas were to help shape the small Anglican King's College founded in 1827 in York, as did those of the Scots science teacher–turned–Anglican bishop John Strachan. As well, English university practice, German research ideals, social democratization, and industrialization influenced chemical education at what was to become the University of Toronto.

Simcoe was British, class-conscious, and Anglican, and he put a powerful imprint on the new province and its education system. First, he was intensely pro-English and anti-American, having served with the British army in the War of Independence. He feared for this new British society and culture in Upper Canada in the face of its much larger U.S. neighbour. Second, he was rigidly class-conscious — an attitude abhorrent to most of the new colonists, many of whom had fled Britain's system of rank and privilege. Third and finally, he wanted the Church of England dominant in the colony. He surrounded himself with like-minded people, ignoring the views of the majority of settlers.

Simcoe sought to establish a provincial university, and — although he left the province in 1796 and died in 1806 — his efforts apparently influenced the British Crown's eventual granting of such a charter in

1827. The resulting University of Toronto has named its principal administrative building after him.

Some months before his departure for Canada, Simcoe wrote to Sir Joseph Banks, president of the Royal Society: "Schools have been shamefully neglected. A College of a higher class would be eminently useful and would give a tone of Principles and Manners that would be of infinite support to the Government." The next year he wrote to Home Secretary Henry Dundas suggesting (for the proposed permanent capital of Upper Canada, London) "a University with a Head and professors in the Capital all of whom should be of the Church of England and, the medical professor perhaps excepted, Clergymen." Dundas served the ball back: "The Country must make the University, and not the University the Country." Dundas wanted at least one good school, which the British government might assist, but not a university.[2]

John Strachan, Science, and a University

Late in 1799 a twenty-one-year-old schoolteacher named John Strachan arrived from Scotland bound for Kingston, Upper Canada.[3] His mother had wished him to enter the Presbyterian ministry, but his father's early death and his limited means had steered him into teaching. He had a three-year contract to teach the children of several people in Kingston, including those of Richard Cartwright, a businessman and member of the province's upper house, the Legislative Council. In about 1802 Strachan decided to enter the ministry in the Church of England. It was common in Britain for grammar schools and universities to draw teachers from the clergy.

Strachan was gifted in mathematics and natural philosophy, which embraced classical physics. In 1796 Dr. James Brown, who had known him at St. Andrews University, had proposed him as his lecture assistant when he became professor of natural philosophy at the University of Glasgow. Instead, however, Brown took early retirement from Glasgow. In 1803, when Strachan moved to his first parish at Cornwall, Upper Canada, he also opened what quickly emerged as the province's outstanding grammar school. There he wrote a textbook on arithmetic, which was published in Montreal.

In 1806 the provincial House of Assembly — probably at Cartwright's suggestion — voted £400 to "some person in education" for instruments to illustrate the principles of natural philosophy. The government handed the entire sum to Strachan. "The collection included an air pump, an electrical machine, and contrivances for illustrating the laws of motion, the elasticity of bodies and the equal velocity of heavy and light substances falling in a vacuum." Strachan was probably the only Upper Canadian who could put such equipment to good use. The apparatus followed him in 1812 to York, where he continued to teach for some time.[4]

Because of his educational endeavours, Strachan in 1823 became president of Upper Canada's Board for the General Superintendence of Education; three years earlier he had joined the Legislative Council. In 1826 Lieutenant-Governor Sir Peregrine Maitland, believing the time ripe to reopen the question of a university, sent Strachan to Britain to negotiate with the colonial secretary on the matter. King George IV issued a royal charter dated March 15, 1827: "His Majesty has been pleased to grant a Royal Charter by Letters Patent, under the Great Seal, for the establishing at or near the Town of York, in the Province of Upper Canada, one College, with the style and privileges of a University."

The document gave the Church of England considerable control over the new King's College, of which Strachan became first president. One British MP pointed out that "in a country where the majority of the people do not belong to the Church of England, the Professors must all subscribe to the Thirty-Nine Articles; so that if Adam Smith were alive he could not fill the Professor's chair of Political Economy; and if Dr Black were alive, he would be excluded from the chair of Chemistry."[5]

In 1828 King's College found a site on the northwest outskirts of York. This 168 acres of parkland included rights of way for roads leading to it westward from Yonge Street (along present-day College Street) and northward from Lot (now Queen) Street (along University Avenue). The tract included today's Queen's Park, which houses the provincial legislature, and the main (St. George) campus of the University of Toronto. Political events halted further development until 1842, when the university started construction where the provincial parliament now stands.[6] In that same year the university sought half a dozen professors, aided by the new governor general, Sir Charles Bagot. A graduate of Christ Church, Oxford, and with a brother who was bishop of Oxford, Bagot had excellent academic connections.

The Act of Union created in 1841 a single government for the united Province of Canada, which consisted of the southern parts of present-day Ontario and Quebec. Kingston became the first, temporary, capital, so the university, instead of moving into Queen's Park, took temporary occupation of the vacant parliament building[7] on Front Street at John, where classes began in 1843. On June 8, President Strachan, bishop of Toronto since 1839, spoke about the history and intended purposes of the new institution. On the following day four of the professors — including twenty-three-year-old, English-born Henry Holmes Croft, the university's first professor of chemistry and experimental philosophy — delivered inaugural lectures. That autumn students began instruction; twenty-six candidates had enrolled the previous June.

Themes and Domestic Variations

Both imported models (for example, the English professorship and German research) and traditions (such as traditional English ambivalence towards science and technology) and domestic practices and aspirations (democratization, resource extraction, and industrialization) helped shape chemical education at Toronto. The tremendous growth and excellence of American scientific research and education has long provided a stimulus for and a challenge to Canadian universities, a launching pad for many Canadians' careers, as well as many superb personnel for Canadian universities. The expansion of Canadian government support for research in the last half of the twentieth century also had a profound effect. The emergence of relativity and quantum physics not only changed humanity's understanding of the universe and its own role, and of matter, but also revolutionized chemistry, even if Toronto was never in the vanguard of that change. And the awesome developments in instrumentation have transformed chemistry throughout the world. All these themes — and their domestic variations — appear in the book that follows.

The reader may wonder what role the already-influential Scottish science teacher John Strachan played in fostering chemistry at King's College. The Scottish Enlightenment of the eighteenth century held science in great esteem, and that country had produced some of the great figures of the Industrial Revolution. South of the border Sir Isaac Newton, the first scientific knight, had reworked European physics, and industry — inspired often by "dissenters" (non-Anglicans) — was transforming that "green and pleasant land." In the early nineteenth century, science was advancing in England's three universities — Cambridge, Oxford, and the newcomer London.

It was perhaps with Prince Albert, the German-born first cousin whom Queen Victoria married in 1840, that science and technology began to reach the popular consciousness in England and find acceptance in elite circles. His greatest feat, the Exhibition of 1851 — in its magnificent, sprawling Crystal Palace — presented the wonders of modern science and technology from all over the world to an enthralled populace and attracted visitors from every continent. A swath of west-central London, south of Kensington Palace and Hyde Park, bears his imprint: the Royal Albert Hall, the Victoria and Albert Museum, the palatial British Museum of Natural History, and the Imperial College of Science and Technology, one of the finest science schools in the world and home usually to about half a dozen Nobel laureates.

Scholarships from the proceeds of the Exhibition of 1851 were to finance study in Britain for the best students from all over the Empire for decades to come. Administration of those awards was to provoke heated controversy in the Chemistry Department at the University of Toronto, as we see below. Britain was to be a mecca for Canadian science students well into the twentieth century and in fact provided the first three professors/heads of chemistry at Toronto — H.H. Croft (1843–79), W.H. Pike (1880–1900), and W.R. Lang (1900–20).

If English models and ideals inspired the creation of King's College, Toronto, as we saw above, so did the English tradition of professors as all-powerful heads of departments. In the early decades at Toronto, the chemistry professor *was* chemistry — its sole figure and its public face to the university and the world. Later in the century the practice began of hiring demonstrators and other assistants to help the professor. At Toronto modern "departments" began to emerge late in the nineteenth century, with the appointment of other "professors" of lesser rank soon following. When the department leader William Lash Miller (acting head, 1898–1900 and 1914–37) had a certain *idée fixe* — his aversion to atomic theory — the effect was powerful and widespread.

The other powerful external influence was the German tradition of university research. W.H. Pike had studied in Germany and made changes in the undergraduate curriculum at Toronto to reinforce and expand undergraduate research, which became a hallmark of Chemistry at Toronto. William Lash Miller held two German PhDs!

The pressing needs of a growing industrial economy in Ontario and Canada and the imperative of resource extraction also fostered the development of "practical" and "applied" science and technology — profoundly influencing the chemistry curriculum at Toronto and leading to a proliferation of new colleges in Canada, including Toronto's School of Practical Science (SPS), home to the university's Chemistry Department in the late nineteenth century. Chemistry professors began to emerge in closely related, even overlapping, fields — most notably W.H. Ellis at SPS.

The gradual expansion and diversification of the Chemistry faculty forms a major theme of this study, as does the slow democratization of its governance — especially through the university's Haist Rules (implemented in the 1960s), which replaced indefinitely serving "Heads" with fixed-term "Chairmen." Today the department has about fifty professors of varying rank. Chemistry has had a number of homes at Toronto (and sometimes more than one): the University College "roundhouse" (now the Croft Chapter House), the School of Practical Science, the Chemistry Building (the "Old Chemistry Building") on King's College Road, part of the Mining Building, part of the McMaster University building on Bloor Street, and the Wallberg Building. Since the early 1960s, some four decades in the Lash Miller Building, and its recent expansion, suggest a rather more secure place for Chemistry in today's University of Toronto.

Outline of This Book

This book has three parts. The first covers the long era (1843–1920) of the British gentleman professors — Croft, Pike, and Lang — from the nomadic days of King's College, through University College, the School of Practical Science, and the Old Chemistry Building. The second looks at the period (1920–60) of Canadian heads, beginning with William Lash Miller and his successors, Frank B. Kenrick and Andrew R. Gordon, as they built a highly influential department. Gordon orchestrated the department's move in 1949 to the Wallberg Building. Part III considers the era (since 1960) of the eight post-Haist chairs in the Lash Miller Chemical Laboratories. Subjects that it explores include the department's relations with new branches at Scarborough and Mississauga, the vast array of increasingly sophisticated technology available for chemical research, and the breathtaking transformation of the Lash Miller Building as the department prepares for the new millennium.

In the heart of a burgeoning, multicultural city of 3 million people, the department has students from all over the world. Heirs of Croft's King's College laboratory, launched seventeen years before Europe's chemists agreed on standard atomic weights for elements, these eager researchers now explore chemical questions in fields ranging from the environment and DNA to the invisible, sub-microscopic "nanoworld" at their very fingertips.

Part One
Gentleman Professors from Britain
∽ (1843–1920)

Chapter One

FATHER OF TORONTO CHEMISTRY: HENRY CROFT (1843–1879)

Introduction: Historical Context

In 1834 Upper Canada incorporated the Town of York, with a population of 9,256, as the City of Toronto. The next fifteen years saw a political struggle for responsible government and for the elimination of privilege, especially special status for the Church of England. In this contest, the city's provincial university (King's College) became a focus and a forum, where reformers sought to break the stranglehold of the establishment (the Family Compact). Soon prominent among the reformers was Henry Croft, the first professor of chemistry and experimental philosophy in King's College, who arrived in Toronto from England in January 1843.

By the time he retired as professor and department head in 1880, the discipline and the institution (by then the secular University of Toronto) had changed dramatically, and the reforms for which he and others fought in the 1840s had become part of the fabric of daily life in the new province of Ontario and the new Dominion of Canada. Croft and his immediate successors, also British-born — William Pike (head, 1880–1900) and William R. Lang (head, 1900–20) — were to serve seventy-seven years between them, up to and after the First World War and into the days of relativity, quantum mechanics, and Nobel Prizes.

What was Toronto like when Henry Croft first arrived? "By 1842 houses extended along King and Queen Streets [west] to Garrison Creek.[1] Bathurst Street and Spadina Avenue showed scattered houses as far north as College Street, and along Yonge Street they extended to the cemetery on Bloor Street. The main development had been toward the north-west.... To the east, Queen Street was broken by the swamps of Moss Park, but extended to the sole bridge over the Don [River]."[2]

Charles Dickens visited the city in the spring of 1842 and commented, "the town itself is full of life and motion, bustle, business, and improvement. The streets are well paved, and lighted with gas; the houses are large and good; the shops are excellent. Many of them have a display of goods in their windows, such as may be seen in thriving county towns in England; and there are some which would do no discredit to the metropolis itself. There is a good stone prison here; and there are, besides, a handsome church, a court-house, public offices, and many commodious private residences, and a government observatory." At the university, "The first stone of a new college had been laid but a few days before by the governor-general. It will be a handsome, spacious edifice, approached by a long avenue, which is already planted and made available as a public walk."[3]

And what about chemistry in 1842? Berzelius in Sweden had brought a high degree of accuracy to chemical analysis, which led to reliable tables of atomic weights for many elements. His modern symbols for elements and formulae for chemical compounds made it easy to represent chemical reactions. Electrochemistry had sprung from the discovery of Galvanic electricity and led to the discovery of the alkali and alkaline-earth metals as well as of the elementary nature of the halogens; Faraday's work led to laws governing the amounts of chemical substances produced by measured quantities of electricity. Moreover, the evidence of electrochemistry led to Berzelius's electrically based theory of chemical combination and affinity. Wöhler's conversion of ammonium thiocyanate into urea destroyed the notion of a "vital force" as a requirement for the creation of organic compounds. Thus synthetic organic chemistry emerged; by 1842 it had recognized substitution reactions and double decompositions. Also, Alexandre Dumas's theory of chemical types proposed for the first time a relationship between formula (structure) and chemical behaviour.

New university schools of chemistry, mainly in Germany, offered instruction and opportunities for research under distinguished professors — most notably, Liebig at Giessen and Wöhler at Göttingen. The tradition of German training would help shape "Toronto chemistry."

Croft: A Well-Rounded Young Man, 1820–43

Croft's involvement with chemistry began with a letter of January 24, 1837, from Michael Faraday to Eilhardt Mitscherlich, a former pupil of Berzelius's and now professor of chemistry at the University of Berlin: "I write at present for the sake of introducing you, either by letter or personally, to Mr Crofts, a friend of mine, who may have occasion to consult you on a matter relating to chemical study."[4] Born on March 6, 1820, Henry Holmes Croft was not yet seventeen.

Historians usually associate Faraday mainly with his brilliant professorship at the Royal Institution, London, but for twenty-two years he also lectured in chemistry (for a very substantial £200 per annum) at the Royal Military Academy in Woolwich.[5] He received this payment through Deputy Paymaster of the Ordnance William Croft, who lived in Gower Street in Bloomsbury, London. Croft's son, Henry, had acquired a keen interest in science, especially chemistry, while at school at nearby Tavistock House.[6] Later he attended several lectures at University College, also close by. Despite the family's long record of public service, young Henry soon found his first job, as a junior clerk in the Tower of London, uninspiring, and he yearned to do chemistry instead. His father spoke with Faraday, who advised him to send Henry to Germany to further his education.

So Henry studied German intensively for a year and then set off for Prussia, where he spent three and a half years at the well-endowed University of Berlin. Mitscherlich advised him not to over-specialize, so he took anatomy and physiology, botany, entomology, German metaphysics, mineralogy and geology, physics, zoology — and, of course, chemistry. His resulting diversity of interests influenced Croft's career and outfitted him well for a new colonial university. Croft left Berlin without taking any degree; he said later that ready availability had trivialized the German PhD.[7] Its absence proved no hindrance to his career.

Croft returned to London in the autumn of 1841 and soon entered a partnership with young chemist William Francis, a recent PhD from Liebig's school at Giessen. These two launched the *Chemical Gazette*, published by Richard and John E. Taylor.[8] Before the first volume had run its course, however, Croft had accepted a post in Toronto. For several years he contributed articles to this journal, of which Francis remained editor. Francis eventually became a publishing partner; Taylor and Francis still publishes scientific monographs and textbooks, as well as the famous *Philosophical Magazine*.

In Canada, Governor General Sir Charles Bagot was seeking a chemistry professor for Toronto and knew William Holmes, who was Croft's godfather. Holmes inquired among his scientific acquaintances, including Faraday, who endorsed Croft from personal knowledge.[9]

The remaining four sections of this chapter look at Croft's long career in Toronto: the university's nomadic years (1843–59), in which Croft taught chemistry, fought Anglican hegemony, and became the first vice-chancellor of the secular University of Toronto; his years (1859–78) in the University College "roundhouse" (now the Croft Chapter House); his long-time service to the university and community; and his final years (1879–83), when Chemistry moved to the new School of Practical Science, from which he retired.

University on the Move, 1843–59

Once in Toronto, Croft set up in the former parliament building, on the north side of Front Street between Graves (now Simcoe) and John streets, the temporary site of King's College.[10] The first chemical laboratory and

The houses of parliament at Front and John streets, Toronto, home of the Chemistry Department, where Croft started work in 1843.
Courtesy Department of Chemistry, University of Toronto.

lecture room occupied a new wooden structure at the west end,[11] where chemistry and anatomy each had a room about sixteen feet by fourteen feet. From three rows of tiered benches students could observe experiments or dissections.

On June 8–9, 1843, four professors gave inaugural lectures at public opening ceremonies for the new university. Croft made his address dramatic and memorable by adding demonstrations. He was exhibiting the reaction between water and metallic potassium when an ignited fragment of the latter flew out of the vessel and onto the robes of Bishop John Strachan, president of the university council. The burning metal set fire to his linen sleeve. Many people, including Croft, later regarded that incident as an ill omen, for he and Strachan were soon in stormy conflict over secularizing the new university.

Also at the opening, Croft created great mirth with several experiments, including one with nitrous oxide, or laughing gas: "Several of the students offered themselves as subjects for experiments with this gas, and as the polka was at the time a new and fashionable dance in Canada, and was the subject of conversation among young and old persons, it was natural enough that the minds of some of these subjects while under the influence of this gas should run upon the new accomplishment, with the result that they unwittingly gave the audience an exhibition of their skill in this dance" — particularly the toe-and-heel, then the principal step of the polka. An observer commented: "nitrous oxide 'has well earned for itself the name of laughing gas, not so much perhaps from the effects it produces on the patient, as from the roars of laughter elicited from those who witness its inhalation.'"[12]

There is abundant evidence that Croft was a remarkably skilled

Henry H. Croft.
Courtesy University of Toronto Archives.

teacher: "Professor Croft's lectures were always most attractive. He had a facile delivery, and I never knew him to fail in any experiment that he ever attempted"[13]; "Professor Croft was amiable and popular. He was a brilliant teacher of Chemistry"[14]; "Croft, Professor of Chemistry, was far in advance of his colleagues in knowledge of scientific progress."[15]

W.J. Loudon, nephew of future university president James Loudon, has given a vivid account of a lecture on oxygen, with which Croft opened each new session. Croft evidently made ample use of demonstrations, emphasized the practical importance of his subject matter, had a charismatic lecturing style, and commanded respect and affection from many students.[16]

In this era, science did not figure significantly in the schools of Upper Canada/Ontario. Despite the efforts of people such as John Strachan and Egerton Ryerson to create a free public school system, the province had insufficient teachers of the experimental sciences to provide even a basic preparatory course. This situation severely limited the university curriculum.[17]

Some of Croft's activities made him a bothersome adversary to Bishop Strachan. In this he allied himself frequently with Professor of Anatomy and Physiology William Gwynne. Strachan's council fended off any encroachment on the Anglican college's monopoly on public funding. However, during 1843 Croft and Gwynne petitioned Attorney-General Robert Baldwin to reduce the de facto majority that Church of England clergymen held on this council. (In 1837 the legislature of Upper Canada had amended the charter to provide for more public appointments to the university council and had almost completely eliminated religious tests.)

The same two professors consistently opposed this majority. In 1844 they took to absenting themselves from council meetings, thereby preventing a quorum (some politically appointed members had to remain in Kingston, then the seat of government). This tactic drew a rebuke from the chancellor, Governor General Sir Charles Metcalfe, but not disciplinary action. Later the same two men gave evidence to a commission of inquiry into the sale of the land bank that the Crown had initially set aside to support the university. Their evidence was critical of the actions of the president and his friends. Early in 1844 another fracas developed: professors were to start receiving their pay in a provincial currency worth only 90 percent of the value of sterling, the currency in their contracts. Croft's opposition to such powerful forces was bold for a young man of twenty-three or twenty-four who was also new to the country.[18]

In August 1844 Croft married Mary Ann Shaw, daughter of the late Captain Alexander Shaw of the 35th Regiment and granddaughter of the late Major General Aeneas Shaw, a member of Lieutenant-Governor John Graves Simcoe's executive council.[19] Rev. Henry Scadding performed the ceremony. This marriage appears to have been happy and may have helped Croft to gain prompt and easy acceptance into Toronto society. Both he and his wife were accomplished musicians, and they held musical soirees and happy parties, with music and dancing. They, along with several other university families, lived in Abbotsford Place, where Mt. Pleasant now passes under Bloor Street.[20] They eventually had seven children, with Croft a caring father.

In 1850 the agitation of Croft and many others finally resulted in a secular university at Toronto, where he acquired a high profile. As we saw above, controversy over control of King's College had become chronic, as reformers sought to lessen Anglican hegemony. In the late 1840s, reformer Robert Baldwin obtained support in the Parliament of the United Province of Canada for a new University Act, which completely secularized King's College, renamed it the University of Toronto, and abolished all religious tests and teaching there.

John Strachan resigned as president of King's College in January 1848, rallying support and obtaining a charter for the University of Trinity College, which stayed close to his original ideas. It built a home on Queen Street, west of the city, and federated with the University of Toronto only in 1903.

Its founding legislation gave the renamed University of Toronto a senate, and on May 25, 1850, the new body elected Henry Croft — whom someone nominated from the floor — vice-chancellor,[21] and hence chairman of the senate. He continued by re-election until 1853, when amendments to the act provided for the government to appoint the vice-chancellor. At the time of his first election, the university awarded Croft the honorary degree doctor of civil law (DCL). In 1857, in recognition of his service, it accorded him lifetime membership in the senate, where he long remained influential.

In 1853 Croft gained a colleague and frequent ally in university politics in the new professor of history and English. As Daniel Wilson recalled after his friend's death, Croft "had set his face very courageously against abuses and stupidities in College management before I reached Canada, and I found myself at one with him from the first in most College matters." Wilson added, "I recall him thirty years ago, when I landed a stranger in Toronto: young, bright, gay, his wife equally so, both excellent musicians, their house a centre of gaiety, their family a bright young circle." The Wilsons settled in Abbotsford Place near the Crofts, and the two men became close friends. Already a distinguished academic in Scotland, Wilson became "perhaps the best Canadian example of the well-rounded nineteenth-century scholar" — an interesting parallel in the humanities and social sciences to Croft's scientific breadth.[22]

Accommodating students at the university proved problematic. The building for King's College, started in 1842 in Queen's Park, lay empty for two years and then became a residence. In 1849 the government requisitioned back the parliament building on Front Street, forcing the university to offer all its instruction in the new structure in Queen's Park — one wing of the projected building.

King's College, Queen's Park, home of the Chemistry Department, 1850–53.
Courtesy University of Toronto Archives.

But the peripatetic game did not end there. In 1853 the government requisitioned the Queen's Park building and relocated the university to Front Street while Parliament met in Quebec City. The following year it needed the legislative edifice again and sent the university back to Queen's Park, where the Board of Works had partially gutted its home. Two years later, the government appropriated the building for a mental institution, which became popularly the "University Lunatic Asylum." For the academic year 1856–57 the university had only a small brick edifice, later named Moss Hall, built in 1850 on the east side of Taddle Creek.[23] It put up some makeshift wooden structures, and there University College operated until it opened its present home in 1859. There Croft, as we see in the next section, taught chemistry for almost twenty years.

What about chemistry instruction in the 1840s and 1850s? "Experimental Philosophy" was part of Croft's professorial title, implying that he was to teach botany and non-medical parts of zoology. In addition he also taught geology — the first geology examinations in the possession of the present Geology Department were set by Croft. When William Hincks became professor of natural history in 1853, Croft found himself limited to chemistry.

In the 1840s, the degree program lasted three years and entailed a fixed curriculum, with a year's course of chemistry and one of natural philosophy. After 1853 it expanded to four years and provided a limited choice of subjects. A second course in practical chemistry became available in third year. Various "departments" (today's programs) recognized classes of honours, including chemistry with natural history or with mineralogy and geology, and by 1859 students in honours programs could specialize to some extent. Examination papers for 1858 disclose the relatively unsophisticated level of instruction:[24]

University of Toronto

ANNUAL EXAMINATIONS 1858

FIRST YEAR.

ELEMENTARY CHEMISTRY

Examiner: Henry Croft, D.C.L.

1. What is the meaning of chemical affinity?
2. What is meant by double decomposition? Give instances.
3. What peculiarities are observed during the union of chemical substances.
4. In what respect does chemical attraction differ from all other kinds of attraction?
5. What is meant by the specific gravity of a body?
*6. How may the specific gravity of a body be ascertained?
*7. What is meant by the boiling point of a liquid, and what circumstances cause it to vary?
8. Describe fully the preparation and properties of hydrogen.
9. What is the percentage composition of water, and how is this ascertained?
*10. What impurities usually exist in water, and how may they be detected?
*11. Explain the nomenclature of the acids, oxides, and salts, and give the proper names for the following substances: Fe^2O^3, S^2O^2, SO^2, S^2O^5, SO^3, MnO, SnO^2, $KO.CO^2$, $KO.2CrO^3$.
12. Describe the preparation and properties of carbonic acid, and of carbon dioxide.
*13. Describe the preparation and properties of olefiac gas.
14. From what sources are the salts of potassium obtained?
15. What is common salt, and how is it obtained? What is the action of sulphuric acid upon it?

16. Give an account of the most important compounds of iron?

*17. Mention the proximate elements of plants and their formulae.

*18. What is the composition of alcohol, whence obtained, and how acted on by oxygen?

---

*Honor Questions.

University of Toronto

ANNUAL EXAMINATIONS 1858

THIRD YEAR.

APPLIED CHEMISTRY.
HONORS AND SCHOLARSHIPS.

Examiners {Henry Croft, D.C.L.
{Michael Barrett, M.A., M.D.

---

1. What is the action of hard water upon soap, and how may this be prevented?

2. Describe the ordinary method of filtration.

3. In what form is carbon best adapted for decolourizing, and how may this property be stored when diminished by the absorption of colouring matter; as in the purification of sugar?

*4. What gases are evolved during the destructive distillation of coal, and which of them are useful as illuminating agents; and which are injurious and require removal?

*5. Describe the general process of purification, and the method of separating the ammonia.

6. How are sal-ammoniac and carbonate of ammonia prepared, and from what sources?

7. What technically useful substances are obtained from the tar as produced by the distillation of coal?

8. Describe the manufacture of wax candles.

9. Describe the manufacture of stearine candles.

10. Mention the principal fats used in the manufacture of soaps and candles, and their sources.

*11. By what means are they purified?

*12. Compare the composition of potatoes, wheat, peas and rice, as regards their nutritious power.

13. Explain the fermentation of bread.

*14. Explain the action of mordants in dyeing.

*15. Give an account of the different ways in which colours can be communicated to textile fabrics.

---

*Honor questions.

A list of the equipment available in 1854 for instruction in physics and chemistry is revealing. "Chemistry" teaching included some material that today would be considered part of physics — fairly typical of the times.

Apparatus

(1) Illustrative of Natural Philosophy: the number of Instruments, etcetera, is about One hundred and eighty: - of these Thirty-nine are illustrative of Statics, Fourteen of Dynamics, Fifty of Hydrostatics, Ten of Acoustics, Thirteen of Heat, Twenty of Optics, Sixteen of Physical Optics, and Sixteen of Geodesy and Astronomy.

(2) Illustrative of Chemistry and Chemical Physics: The number of Chemical products is about Twelve hundred, and of Minerals

used in the Arts, etcetera, about Four hundred. This collection includes also a large number of instruments illustrative of Electricity, Galvanism, Electro-Magnetism, Magneto-Electricity, Thermo-Electricity, Heat, Light, etcetera. Technology and Metallurgy, etcetera. Although these Collections are both valuable and extensive, yet it is most desirable that additions should be made of newer Instruments; and the Council respectfully suggest an appropriation of funds for the purpose.

∽ At University College, 1859–78 ∾

Croft and the university moved into the new University College building in 1859. What of Croft's discipline and his adoptive city at this stage? The next year, through the persistent efforts of Cannizzaro at a first-ever conference of European chemists, practitioners finally agreed on methods of assigning atomic weights to the elements. Thereafter standard formulas would represent compounds. Kekulé and Couper, building on the work of Frankland and others, showed how to interpret the constitution of a growing multitude of organic compounds by two simple principles: the universal "atomicity" (or "valency") of four for carbon, and the catenation of carbon atoms. This opened the way to structural representation by the chemist's formulas. Perkin and Griess in Britain, from quite different starting points, were laying the foundations of a valuable synthetic dye industry, and an industry that depended on the refining of crude petroleum had arrived, hard on the heels of one based on the distillation of coal, to revolutionize domestic illumination.

Chemistry and "natural philosophy" were beginning to converge in certain areas. The spectroscope facilitated chemical analysis and identification of new chemical elements. The kinetic-molecular theory of gases, which Maxwell and others developed in mathematical form, would soon explain experiments on the rates of chemical reactions.[25] In the almost twenty years since Croft's arrival in Toronto, chemistry had grown, not just in the number of identified substances, but through the emergence of unifying theoretical bases for understanding and predicting reactions.

Toronto had expanded in extent and in population; the 1861 census gave the latter as 44,821. The economy had surged, and many fine buildings had gone up. "Churches, cathedrals, market, post-office, colleges, schools, Mechanics Institute, rise in imperial dignity over the city."[26] The arrival of the railways had spurred manufacturing and brought temporary prosperity. Toronto was becoming a centre for forwarding and wholesale business, with numerous banking and other financial institutions.[27]

How had University College come to have its splendid new home — seat of the provincial university and one of the grandest structures in British North America? It was four hundred feet across its south façade, had stone and brick construction, and looked on to three sides of a quadrangle. The chemistry laboratory was in the spacious roundhouse at its southwest corner — since 1915 the "Croft Chapter House." In 1856, the combined efforts of the chancellor and the governor general, Sir Edmund Walker Head, secured government authorization and a grant for a new building and museum for the university. On February 7, 1856, the university senate appointed architects Frederic Cumberland and William Storm and a building committee that included the vice-chancellor, John Langton — Croft's successor in that office and his neighbour in Abbotsford Place.[28] Langton did most of the committee's work, and apparently Croft and Daniel Wilson advised him — perhaps on space requirements.

"As preparation for the building, Cumberland had visited England at a rather momentous time in the history of the Gothic revival. The most important building in England in 1856 was the Oxford Museum. The architect was Benjamin Woodward, but John Ruskin became interested and hoped to get the whole pre-Raphaelite brotherhood to work on [stone] carving." Apparently "Cumberland knew Ruskin, and there is every reason to believe that he was profoundly affected by what he saw and heard at Oxford. The silhouette of the [University] College is markedly similar to the Museum's — even to the chemistry department, isolated in a chapter house because of its intrusion on a building sacred to the humanities."[29, 30]

The chemistry laboratory itself "is the circular room at the southwestern corner of the building. It is very lofty, being furnished with a lantern roof, and is one of the most beautiful rooms in the college. Here again we meet with a large number of bottles, and in addition electric machines, galvanic batteries, retorts, iron stoves, stands, and the thousand various articles necessary to the experimental chemist."[31] Croft himself had provided a number of the items.

In the laboratory, "the benches are arranged in a semicircle, rising as they recede from the position to be occupied by the speaker." In the contiguous (Professor Croft's) lecture room, in the main building, "The seats are placed in the same way, and will accommodate one hundred and fifty persons." In addition to the lecture room, Chemistry had an apparatus room, a storeroom, and a washroom. The storeroom contained chemicals for experiments.

The moderately capacious laboratory would certainly have permitted instruction in practical chemistry. Indeed, in 1860 Croft published *Course of Practical Chemistry as adopted at University College Toronto*.[32] A revised edition appeared in 1870. Yet the facts appear otherwise. Professor and President James Loudon recalled, "Croft's time was mainly spent in the Chemical Laboratory ... but students had no access to it, instruction being given entirely by experimental lectures."[33] His nephew W.J. Loudon is more generous: "No professor, if he could avoid it, lectured in the afternoon, which was reserved for recreation and walking. The exception was Professor Croft, who, being a scientist, used to take his students into his laboratory in the Roundhouse, and show them some of the wonderful experiments in the science of Chemistry."[34] Despite the seeming lack of scheduled practical work, Croft encouraged students to visit his laboratory and help him there. Laboratory teaching in chemistry began only in the late 1870s, in the School of Practical Science.[35]

Croft's 1860 laboratory manual is essentially a guide to qualitative and some quantitative analysis. He acknowledges that he bases it somewhat on Odling's *Course on Practical Chemistry*.[36] He explains that readers might have to make some of the apparatus required, as Canada did not

Croft Chapter House.
Courtesy University of Toronto Archives.

have much available. He gives directions, for instance, for constructing an alkalimeter (burette) able to deliver one thousand grains of water and divided into one hundred divisions. He apologizes for "old habits and predilections" — for instance, citing NO^5, SO^3, and PO^5 instead of HNO^3, H^2SO^4, and H^3PO^4, respectively. (Croft's manual came too early to benefit from Cannizzaro's rationalization of chemical formulae in 1860.) As well as being an excellent teacher, Croft kept abreast of the literature and contributed at least eighteen publications — no mean accomplishment, given the conditions and isolation. Several report on his own investigations — for instance, a study of the double salts of cadmium that he had begun in London.[37]

But his greatest renown in Canada came in toxicology and the chemistry and detection of poisons. As early as October 1843, a committee on which he sat and that was planning a medical school for King's College had recommended lectures in forensic medicine.[38] Croft's work led to improvement and simplification of many methods for detecting and determining poisons, and his court appearances involving suspicious deaths became quite famous. "In this branch of his profession he was unsurpassed. His clear intelligence, his wide knowledge, his careful attention to details, and his absolute devotion to truth, were shown equally in the laboratory and in the witness box."[39, 40]

As early as 1861 Croft worked on identification of blood stains, even some said to be fifteen months old, and in 1877 he reportedly determined gender from blood stains, although he later abandoned the method.[41] Courts in Ontario first accepted evidence concerning identification of blood stains in 1878 — three years before Conan Doyle had Sherlock Holmes in *A Study in Scarlet* lamenting the lack of reliable tests.[42] Incidentally, Croft's laboratory manual of 1860 dealt with the recognition of poisons — something that would be most unusual today — and some of the directions may have embodied Croft's own findings.

Croft also worked as a consultant to James Miller Williams of Hamilton, a pioneer in the Canadian petroleum industry.[43] Williams had acquired property at Oil Springs in Lambton County, probably in 1857, and there had dug and drilled for oil. He distilled this material to produce an illuminating oil and some lubricating oil. Earlier in the 1850s James Young in Scotland, and then Abraham Gesner (a Canadian) in the United States, had distilled soft coals or shales to produce lamp oils — variously "coal oils," "paraffine," or "kerosene" — which were revolutionizing domestic lighting. The opportunity to market a similar local product spurred Williams to find a way to remove the objectionable smell of Lambton County oil. He evidently turned to Croft, who adapted chemical methods for treating coal oil to refine and deodorize the distillate, by agitating it with sulphuric acid, then with alkali. News of Croft's success emerged before the drilling of Pennsylvania's first oil well in 1859, but it attracted very little recognition.[44]

Until 1884 University College did not admit female students, but a few interested women prepared for university examinations privately. During the 1870s the university arranged extramural lectures through the Ladies' Educational Association of Toronto. In 1874–75, for instance, it offered four series of such lectures; Croft gave eighteen lectures entitled "Chemistry and the Collateral Sciences as Applied to Modern Life."[45, 46]

Wider Service

Through his long career Croft contributed in many ways to the life of Toronto — via the Mechanics and Canadian Institutes; through his interest in other sciences: entomology, agriculture, and veterinary medicine; and by service in the militia. These undertakings, like his forensic and consulting work, reveal a remarkably versatile and public-spirited man. They added to his reputation, thereby helping to solidify favourable public views of the university. The Mechanics Institutes, as developed in Britain from 1823 on, promoted adult education for a growing number of artisans and skilled tradesmen. In 1848, members of Toronto's Institute (founded 1830) asked Croft to offer a course in chemistry. He gave a number of lectures there between 1848 and 1851. The titles reveal his broad interests: "Application of Chemistry to Manufactures," "Calico Printing and Dyeing," "The Earth," "Entomology," "Gas Illumination," and "Meteorology." Fellow lecturers included Frederic Cumberland, the architect; Sanford Fleming, the engineer; and Henry Youle Hind, professor of chemistry and geology at Trinity College, Toronto.[47]

The Canadian Institute, established in 1849, was a society of architects, engineers, and surveyors; it first met in the Hall of the Mechanics Institute in the upper storey of the Toronto Fire Hall. Attendance and participation did not live up to expectations, so the society began to admit persons interested in the arts and sciences. It invited many guests to its second annual *conversazione* on April 3, 1852, including Attorney-General Robert Baldwin and Professors Croft and Cherriman (natural philosophy). Thirty-five of the guests, including these three, signed a paper to express their desire to become members, and the following week the Institute granted them membership.[48] It soon invited Croft to serve on council, which he did for many years, including his presidency, 1866–68.

In 1852 the Institute began to publish the *Canadian Journal (of Industry, Science and Arts)* — which later became the *Proceedings*, and eventually the *Transactions of the Canadian Institute*. The first eighteen volumes constitute a repository of early Canadian scientific publications, and Croft was a fairly regular contributor.

Canadian entomologists knew Croft's name as well as Canadian chemists did. "Botany and entomology and, in fact, all branches of 'Natural History' had throughout his life been great charms for Croft, as he was by taste and inclination rather more a naturalist than a philosopher."[49] He was a great collector of plants and insects, and his collection of dried plants formed the nucleus of University College's original Biological Museum.[50] He collected all orders of insects, especially Hymenoptera (ants, wasps, and so on) and Coleoptera (beetles) — "the finest in the Province."[51]

Through the Canadian Institute, Croft put budding young entomologist C.J.S. Bethune in touch with William Saunders, a pharmacist in London. These two enthusiasts gathered the names of thirty-six entomologists in Canada, published the list in a journal, and then, with Croft, invited them to a meeting to form an association. The gathering took place in September 1862 at Croft's residence in Yorkville.[52] The group met again the following April at the Canadian Institute and launched the Entomological Society of Canada. Its first president was Croft (1863–64 and 1868–71); its members included William Osler.[53] The society was soon providing farmers with information about harmful and beneficial insects. In gratitude, the Ontario legislature set up an annual grant for it and in 1871 incorporated it as a provincial body — the Entomological Society of Ontario.

Croft's wife's family had farmland northwest of the city, which may be the basis for some historians' claim that Croft was active in early agricultural and horticultural societies near Toronto.[54]

The University of Toronto had a professorship in agriculture from 1851 until 1885, held by George Buckland, a genial Englishman who arrived in Canada West in 1847 with a reputation for the use of scientific methods in agriculture. Late in 1851 he and Croft selected the site of a fifty-acre experimental farm (with six acres as a botanical garden) at the north end of the university park. Buckland planted wheat there and studied the performance of English seeds, in order to select and recommend suitable species for use in the province. The university's program in agriculture attracted few students, even when it added prizes and scholarships. Only a handful of candidates qualified for the diploma, yet they described Buckland as a well-informed, popular teacher. The experimental farm languished and in time became garden land and pasture.[55]

The university's impractical program in agriculture led the government to provide alternatives. In 1870, Sir John Carling, first commissioner of agriculture for Ontario, proposed two schools, for agriculture and for mechanic arts. The outcome was the founding of the School of Practical Science (SPS) in Toronto and the purchase of six hundred acres for a School of Agriculture at Mimico, west of Toronto. Buckland helped launch the new agriculture college and selected its motto.

A more visible product of Croft and Buckland's relationship appears in Croft's association with the Toronto (later Ontario) Veterinary College, established in 1862. As secretary of the Board of Agriculture for Canada West, Buckland helped bring the college's first director to Canada and pressed the province for support. The college's annual reports list Henry Croft as professor of chemistry from 1864 until 1879.[56]

During the U.S. Civil War, the *Trent* Affair stirred up anti-American fear in Canada and sentiment in favour of a defensive force. In December 1861, at a public meeting of students and graduates at the university, which Croft or President McCaul had initiated, many volunteers resolved to form a University Rifle Corps. Croft was instrumental in its formation and became its first captain[57]: "Singularly unsoldierly in appearance, with spectacles and long hair and beard that were the despair of the adjutant, he was nevertheless a first-rate officer. He had the happy gift of making his men eager to do his bidding, and the company was never more efficient or more popular under his captaincy."⁵⁸ The corps later became No. 9 Company of the Queen's Own Rifles of Toronto.

In 1866 this company was part of a force dispatched to the Niagara area to repel a raid by Fenians from the United States. In a battle at Ridgeway, near Fort Erie, the invaders failed to achieve their purposes and withdrew, but not before killing three of Croft's men and wounding several others.⁵⁹ A stained glass window in the East Hall of University College commemorates the fallen, as apparently did memorial windows in a church that Croft's children built in San Diego, Texas, where he retired.

∽ Winding Down, 1878–83 ∽

In the late 1870s, Henry Croft led Chemistry across the Front Campus into the School of Practical Science and almost immediately retired. SPS had been a long time in gestation. Despite the university's making provision as early as 1857 for a diploma in civil engineering, the program had attracted neither enough students nor much public confidence. The provincial government in 1871 took steps to develop a non-university School of Technology in Toronto.⁶⁰,⁶¹ Notwithstanding controversy, the school appointed staff and advertised classes in the spring of 1872. Frederic Cumberland's Mechanics Institute (1854) at Adelaide and Church streets served as its home.⁶² The following year, the bill of incorporation referred to the School of Practical Science. After much study and debate, the government moved the school near University College, to allow for shared teaching. The senate approved erection of a building in June 1877, and Professors Croft and Loudon chose the site on the south side of the Front Campus.⁶³ Generations of engineering students knew the structure as the "Little Red Schoolhouse." Croft became the first chairman of its board.

The teaching of chemistry at the university moved to and consolidated in the new building. By the 1870s a budding chemical industry and government regulatory bodies needed trained chemical analysts, both qualitative and quantitative. Providing instruction would have overburdened the facilities at University College, and by 1875, at SPS, W.H. Ellis was offering a course in chemical manipulation and qualitative analysis.

SPS Building, 1904, home of Chemistry, 1878–95.
Courtesy University of Toronto Archives.

In the summer of 1878 Ellis and Croft moved their equipment, furniture, and supplies from downtown and from the University College roundhouse, respectively, to new laboratories in the west wing of the new SPS. Croft became professor of chemistry in SPS, with Ellis as his assistant. The evidence available suggests that hands-on experimental work became a regular feature of instruction.

The loss of four of his beloved children in rapid succession in the 1870s brought Henry Croft intense grief and led eventually to a nervous breakdown, forcing his resignation from the university at the end of 1879. He retired on a pension amounting to two-thirds of his annual salary ($2,800).

In leaving the academic world, Croft acted with great foresight and generosity, as two main elements of his departure reveal. First, at its last meeting of 1879 Croft informed the board of SPS of his intention to convey to the school much of his library — some three hundred volumes, as it turned out, a number of them still in the university library — together with a collection of minerals.[64] In March 1880 Croft wrote, offering to sell to the school a supply of apparatus and chemicals that he had personally bought "for the illustration of his lectures." The school later did purchase some chemicals from Croft; some of his apparatus is still in the Department of Chemical Engineering.

Second, between April 1878 and April 1881, Croft donated his books on entomology, and a collection of foreign plants and insects, to the Toronto Entomological Association (later the Natural History Society of Toronto).[65] This body, in gratitude, named him president, later honorary president. The group eventually merged into the Canadian Institute.

And so in the spring of 1881 Croft and his family left Toronto for the southernmost part of Texas, not far inland from Corpus Christi. His son William owned a ranch at Las Hermanas and had a large wool company in nearby San Diego. W.H. Ellis, Croft's closest friend, said years later that they moved because of Croft's concern for his wife's health.[66] In less than two years Croft died, on March 1, 1883; his wife followed a few years later. As a memorial, their children built a Protestant Episcopal (i.e., Anglican) church in San Diego. The Church of the Atonement apparently had three windows in memory of the three students in their father's militia company who died at Ridgeway in 1866.

Looking back more than a century, and in the absence of much archival documentation, we may find it difficult to make a thorough assessment of Croft's importance to Canadian science and education. However, he was probably the most respected scientist in Canada West/Ontario during his three and a half decades as professor. Dr. P.-J.-O. Chauveau, first premier of Quebec and long-time minister of education, observed, "In Forensic Chemistry he is without an equal in the Province" (the pre-Confederation Province of Canada).[67] A succession of chemists at the University of Toronto has sustained this tradition of excellence for over a century.

Science had no secure place in a university based on British traditions in the nineteenth century, yet Croft, by the authority and breadth of his knowledge, managed early to establish a scientific tradition at Toronto. His successors, and others, have since raised it to great heights of achievement. His early and daring standing up to John Strachan over church control certainly catalyzed the province's eventual creation of a secular institution.

One commentator observed that, at Strachan's death in 1867, "Professor Croft's voice was the first raised in emphatic assertion that he at least would do what in him lay to pay his tribute of respect. It was a characteristic speech. Professor Croft was in his best days, before sorrow and sickness broke his spirits, the soul of generosity and kindliness, interested in everything, brimming over with hope and energy, and one of the most popular figures in the University." He was exceptional even among professors: "The ruthless progress of specialization may give us in the future greater savants and chemists for professors, but it is very unlikely to give us more well-balanced and many-sided men than Professor Croft."[68]

His close friend Daniel Wilson, by now president of the university, said of Croft, "I have rarely met a man of whom it could be more truly said that in him there was no guile. He was by no means judicious in all that he said or did; and I never saw his name to a letter in the public prints without fear. But he was most generously transparent, honest, and straightforward, said and did many unwise things, but never did a mean or ungenerous act."

Croft's chemist colleague W.H. Ellis wrote, "He was a most delightful companion, steeped with the love of nature, full of dry humour, thinking strongly and speaking fearlessly, but brimming over with kindness."[69]

In 1915, the University of Toronto renamed the roundhouse at University College, where Professor Henry Croft had laboured so long and effectively. The Croft Chapter House stands as an elegant and lasting tribute from the university he served so well.

Chapter Two

WILLIAM PIKE AND UNDERGRADUATE RESEARCH
(1880–1900)

Introduction: Historical Context

The 1881 census shows Toronto's population at 86,415.[1] The Canadian depression of the second half of the 1870s gave way in the 1880s to a healthy recovery. Prosperity, municipal annexation, immigration, and local migration caused Toronto's population to more than double and its boundaries to spread. W.H. Russell, who had visited Toronto in 1861, found himself twenty years later "not prepared for such very fine buildings and such a great array of wharves and quays on the lake, and the great fleets of craft alongside them."[2]

Local hero Ned Hanlan was the toast of the sculling world, and a grateful city gave him a block of free-lease land — now Hanlan's Point on Toronto Island. During summers in the 1960s many University of Toronto graduate students would head out to the Island after long days in offices or laboratories to relax and enjoy wonderful views of the rapidly expanding skyline; the particularly energetic headed out further to relax, swim, and barbecue. Sadly, swimming is not so common today, thanks to pollution of the lake.

Toronto in 1878 launched an Industrial Exhibition in Garrison Common, which became an annual event — now the Canadian National Exhibition — that would display many of the world's new technological marvels. Alexander Graham Bell had invented the telephone in nearby Brantford in 1876; by 1879 Thomas Edison had developed electric light bulbs in the United States, as Joseph Swan had earlier done in Britain. By 1882 arc lamps lit the grounds of the Toronto Exhibition, to the wonder of the patrons.[3] The following year visitors saw an electrically driven locomotive moving on rails.

In 1879 Sanford Fleming presented to the Canadian Institute his ideas for a worldwide system of time zones based on the meridian at Greenwich; five years later "standard time" was an accomplished fact.

Also in 1879 Hart Massey, an implement manufacturer in Newcastle, Ontario, moved his father's business to Toronto, where it became in time a national, then an international, corporation — Massey-Harris, later Massey-Ferguson. The Massey family was to give to Toronto many wonderful amenities, such as Massey Hall, and, to the University of Toronto, Burwash Hall, Hart House, the Lillian Massey Building, and Massey College. For almost a century many members of the Chemistry Department have found sustenance, recreation, and pleasure through these Massey gifts.

In 1880 the province tabled plans in the legislature for a new parliament building in Queen's Park — virtually on the site of the original King's College.[4]

Chemistry in 1879 was beginning to use mathematical and physical principles to interpret experimental phenomena. The subject was slowly transforming itself from an art, based mainly on experience and intuition, to a science, which could explain or interpret events by a limited set of principles. Physical chemistry ultimately became a distinct subdivision of the whole subject.

One of the leading architects of this movement was J.H. van't Hoff, who in 1874 had recognized (simultaneously with J.A. LeBel) the three-dimensional attribute of valency embodied in the "tetrahedral" carbon atom. When van't Hoff moved to the University of Amsterdam in 1877, he began to use calculus to interpret data on reaction rates, thereby anticipating chemical kinetics. His work also brought recognition for Guldberg and Waage's earlier studies (1867) in Norway on the so-called law of mass action.

In the United States, between 1874 and 1878, J. Willard Gibbs, a professor of mathematical physics at Yale University, evolved a highly mathematical application of thermodynamics to chemical processes. Thermodynamics dealt with the relationships between heat and work, as men such as Carnot, Helmholtz, Joule, and Kelvin had formulated it to account for the efficiency of heat engines. Gibbs's "chemical thermodynamics," with terms such as "free energy" and "chemical potential," could explain the long-puzzling "affinity" of elements.[5] Gibbs was to influence Toronto chemistry for a long, long time.

Organic chemists were discovering new reactions and reagents, which required cataloguing. Friedrich Beilstein, a Russian of German extraction, published the first edition of the *Handbuch der organischen Chemie* (two volumes, 2,201 pages, 1880–82). Today this vast, indispensable compendium is also available electronically. In 1877, C. Friedel and J.M. Crafts's famous reaction for performing substitutions of aromatic compounds came into widespread use. Many other reactions for the synthesis of other organic compounds appeared, including the Hofmann degradation, the Reimer-Tiemann reaction, and the Schotten-Baumann reaction. These endeavours helped facilitate the dramatic syntheses of naturally occurring compounds — the sugars, purines, terpenes, and others — during the 1880s and 1890s.

In 1877, discovery of the first diazo dye began to reduce the need for a mordant to directly dye cotton and linen. Again, as theoretical ideas advanced, such notions as the relationship between colour and chemical constitution provoked discussion, and in the late 1870s such terms as "chromophoric groups" and "bathochromic shifts" emerged. Chemists synthesized indigotin (indigo blue), which — before commercial production became economical — heralded use of "synthetic" materials for traditional purposes.[6]

Pike: A Man of Means

At the University of Toronto, both Henry Croft and University College Principal John McCaul retired in 1879. Professor Daniel Wilson noted in his diary for July 7 that year, "Hon. A. Crooks, Minister of Education, starts tomorrow with the Vice-Chancellor, Chief Justice Moss, for England, where it is to be hoped they will find a pair of professors to fill the vacant chairs and maintain the reputation of our University and College."[7] On October 1, he added, "College opens with McCaul reinstated as President [principal], Croft resuming the chemical professorship, and to complete our incapacity for the real work of the College, the chemical assistant and practical teacher, Dr Ellis, prostrate under most dangerous hemorrhage of the lungs."[8] In the event, Crooks and Moss found William Herbert Pike, lecturer in natural science at Merton College, Oxford, and a man of some means.

Pike was born in Brixton, England, on July 5, 1851, son of Warburton Pike, a London barrister, and his wife, Eliza (née Gaskell).[9] His uncle was John William Pike, a wealthy landowner in Wareham, Dorsetshire, whose fourth son, Warburton Mayer Pike, moved to British Columbia[10] and became an entrepreneur and gentleman adventurer. Warburton Pike wrote two books describing canoe trips through Canada's northwest.

William H. Pike.
Courtesy University of Toronto Archives.

At the age of eight, young W.H. Pike entered Cholmondeley School, Highgate; at fifteen he entered the famous Rugby School, where he spent three years. In 1869 he entered King's College, London, where he studied chemistry with W.A. Miller and then C.L. Bloxam and physics with John Tyndall. At the Royal School of Mines, South Kensington, he worked under Frederick Guthrie.

Pike went to the Polytechnikum (later the Technische Hochschule) in Vienna in 1870 and studied organic chemistry for a year with Professor A.E.A. Bauer. Then followed two years of study and research in organic chemistry in Berlin under A.W. Hofmann. Finally, in the autumn of 1873 he enrolled at Göttingen, where on November 22 he received a PhD for his thesis — "Contributions to the Chemistry of Urea and Its Derivatives."[11] Pike acquired immense respect for German education, which thereby helped shape chemistry at Toronto.

Returning to London, Pike worked briefly, probably as an assistant, with Henry Armstrong at the London Institution in Finsbury Circus. In 1874 he became a Fellow of the Chemical Society and, possibly that autumn, an assistant in the Chemical Laboratory at Oxford under

Professor William Odling. In 1876 Merton College appointed him lecturer in natural science.[12]

Pike's resignation from Merton was reported on December 4, 1879. Five days later, Pike matriculated into Merton College, and on December 11, just before he left for Canada, Oxford conferred an MA on him.[13] Perhaps Crooks and Moss convinced him that an Oxford degree would impress Torontonians. In January 1880 he took up his new duties.

The rest of this chapter explores Pike's struggle to control Chemistry in SPS, his introduction of undergraduate research, the resulting new Chemistry Building of 1895, and the man and his legacy.

Who Rules at SPS?

Pike immediately began to reorganize the chemical facilities and instruction according to his own ideas and extensive experience. In November 1880 the *Varsity* reported that "the long expected apparatus for volumetric analysis, the determination of vapour densities, &c, has arrived, and Professor Pike has been using it to illustrate his lectures." The following month "Professor Pike has just received a collection of alcohols, aldehydes, ethers and acids, in a wonderful state of preservation, from Germany." By January 1881, "several additions have been made to Professor Pike's laboratory. New water, gas, waste pipe, and steam fixtures have been put in; and a large boiler for distilling water has been so arranged as to provide steam and distilled water to the lecture room. New draught cupboards have been built; and a large down-draught pipe has been fitted into the lecture table. Two sets of copper water baths have just arrived."[14]

Instruction (now including laboratory work) began in the new SPS building, across the South Lawn (Front Campus) from University College. Facilities there included the lecture and demonstration room and the department's first teaching laboratories. In the autumn of 1879, enrolments in chemistry had been as follows: 137 candidates from University College, 38 from Toronto Veterinary College, 24 from Toronto School of Medicine, and 12 from SPS.[15] Apart from increases in SPS figures, numbers remained fairly constant through the 1880s. According to SPS's annual report in 1881, the laboratory had proven "scarcely adequate" for classes this size.[16]

Pike joined the SPS board on January 6, 1880, and the school reported directly to the minister of education. On November 6, 1889, a new university act affiliated SPS with the University of Toronto.[17] A principal (John Galbraith) and a council of instructors now governed the school. Administrative control of the science departments (Botany, Chemistry, Physics, and Zoology) switched from University College to a university council, but SPS remained home to Chemistry.

During his first three years on the SPS board, Pike provoked some rather touchy debates. In these he appeared to be the odd man out, and some commentators have cited this as a factor for his failure to become chairman of the board. Some people believed that the minister had promised him this position, possibly at Oxford in 1879.[18] Daniel Wilson eventually took the chair in October 1880, which displeased several members.[19]

However, Pike had already challenged the instruction in analytical and applied chemistry that SPS students received. He perhaps questioned its content and funding, which Croft and Ellis had amicably worked out. He claimed in March 1880 to have no funds for this teaching and sought its deletion, but the board blocked this move.

By November 1880 the board faced controversy over Ellis. The school's report listed him as assistant professor of chemistry, even though the government had appointed him instructor. Was he an assistant to Pike or an instructor "whose primary duties were those required for the School of Science, thus relieving the Professor of Chemistry therefrom"? Pike viewed his own role as entitling him to prescribe and administer all chemistry instruction in SPS and therefore regarded Ellis as a subordinate.

Here was a classic academic dispute. Pike was twenty-nine, the new professor, with confidence because of his family standing at home and his impressive education. Ellis, almost six years his senior, had acted as principal of the School of Technology and had applied for the chair that Pike now occupied.[20] Pike may have considered Ellis's education and qualifications in chemistry "colonial," old-fashioned, and inadequate. Yet Ellis was probably far more aware of the chemical instruction appropriate to Ontario's young economy.

In April 1881 the board recognized Ellis "as an independent teacher of the School of Science and member of the Board, while Dr. Pike in his independent position as a Professor of University College is required to carry out his part in fulfilling the agreement between the College and the School of Science." Pike contested this resolution for almost two years, even asking the minister to intervene, but the board's united and decisive action blocked such a move. Finally, in December 1882 the board learned that the University College council, perhaps at Pike's urging, had named "a committee for the purpose of considering and reporting on certain impediments to Prof. Pike's teaching which had arisen in consequence of a resolution of the Board of the School." In response, the board politely admonished the college council to mind its own business. Later the same month the minister, acting on Galbraith's recommendation, appointed Ellis professor of applied chemistry at SPS and gave him appropriate authority and resources. More than a century later, the university still has a department entitled "Chemical Engineering and Applied Chemistry" within the Faculty of Applied Science and Engineering.

The SPS report for 1884 states that "an additional practical laboratory has been fitted up and placed at the disposal of Dr. Pike; and the upper laboratory set apart for the exclusive use of Dr. Ellis in carrying out the work of his department and the practical instruction of his pupils in the school as Professor of Applied Chemistry."[21] The chemical facilities were on SPS's main and second floors (at its northern end after its enlargement in 1890). The reports for 1886 and 1887 show serious overcrowding there, which reinstitution of the university's Faculty of Medicine in 1887 worsened.[22]

Relief came in three stages. In 1889 Biology moved from the third floor to a new edifice nearby. The 1890 expansion of SPS generated new space: the second-floor drafting room became a new laboratory for practical instruction to engineering and medical students, with the old laboratory reserved for chemistry specialists. Yet the lecture room for chemistry, with two hundred seats, could barely accommodate the first-year classes, and so SPS added a new chemical laboratory in 1894–95.

Introducing Undergraduate Research

Thanks to the persistent efforts of William Mulock and James Loudon, which in the 1870s had led to SPS, the university and the school could offer hands-on experimental work for undergraduates. After 1880, Pike applied his experience of German research at Toronto. Although

Croft had offered students some laboratory experience, Pike sought to increase and modernize such practical work. In hiring additional, non-professorial personnel to supervise it, he launched the modern "Department" of Chemistry.

Remodelling of the Faculty of Arts in the late 1870s allowed undergraduates to specialize more. The original program had had a fixed curriculum, but by the 1850s it had permitted a range of options and four years of study. In the 1870s the senate committee on degrees advocated division of the arts program into pass (three-year) and honours (four-year) courses. The former combined breadth and flexibility in content, while avoiding intense specialization; this so-called fixed course in time became less rigid. The latter offered European-style specialization and demanded excellent ("honours") standing each year — a distinction long unique to Toronto.

Students could enter one of five honours "departments" (programs): Classics, Mathematics (and Physics), Mental and Moral Science with Civil Polity, Modern Languages with History, and Natural Sciences. Chemistry was linked with Natural Sciences and remained so for almost seventy years. What made Toronto's honours courses distinctive in North America was the extent of specialized study. The honours "department" in Natural Science embodied instruction in biology, chemistry, and geology (with mineralogy), and the courses included work in mathematics and physics.[23]

However, laboratory instruction created a lot of extra work for professors and, especially in chemistry, considerable extra expense. This burden became more and more apparent between 1875 and 1900 as enrolment grew rapidly in University College and later in the Faculty of Arts. Various disciplines, including chemistry, named assistants to professors — the launch of modern "departments."[24] In 1882 the University College council, with the support of the university senate, increased the fees of all matriculated students from $10 to $20 per annum, with the added revenue to pay fellowships to assistants in selected departments.

An announcement of the first such appointment in chemistry (at SPS) appeared in the *Varsity* of November 11, 1880; thereafter the names of fellows in chemistry (and also in applied chemistry) appeared annually. In 1891 Chemistry had its first demonstrator — William Lash Miller, who became lecturer in 1893. It named a second lecturer, F.J. Smale, in 1895. In 1892 "Lecture Assistant" began to appear. The annual reports from 1892 on list Ellis as demonstrator in chemistry in the Faculty of Arts, as well as holding appointments in the Faculty of Medicine.[25]

Under Croft in the 1870s, lectures and examinations covered general, organic, and analytical chemistry (the latter two in fourth year). Pike developed the full range of the honours program in chemistry in the 1880s, with assistance from only one "Fellow." University calendars are very revealing.[26] In 1889–90 the courses of lectures in chemistry were:

- an introductory course for first-year students;
- inorganic chemistry for medical students and for the second-year pass examination;
- inorganic chemistry for second-year students;
- organic chemistry for third-year students; and
- chemical theory for fourth-year students.

Laboratory practice included qualitative analysis in second and third years and quantitative analysis in third and fourth.

By 1893, both staff and program had grown. The honours course involved:

- first year: elementary inorganic chemistry (also taken by the pass course);
- second year: inorganic chemistry, physical chemistry, and laboratory practice;
- third year: organic chemistry and laboratory practice; and
- fourth year: advanced inorganic chemistry, advanced organic chemistry, stereochemistry, history of chemical theory, theory of chemical affinity, physical chemistry, and laboratory practice.

Laboratory practice consisted of:

- second year: qualitative and quantitative analysis and the preparation of a selected number of inorganic substances;
- third year: quantitative analysis (volumetric) and the preparation of organic substances; and
- fourth year: a selected research project (introduced in 1892–93).

The calendars of those days listed required text and reference books. With one exception (Ira Remsen), all were British or continental European, and they included authors such as Fresenius, Ostwald, Roscoe and Schorlemann, Wurtz, and many other classics, some even in German.

The introduction of undergraduate research was clearly Pike's way of injecting his practical experience in Austria and Germany into the Canadian system. Although some American universities had introduced experimental research, Johns Hopkins being one of the first, they did so in *postgraduate* programs. To the best of our knowledge, there was no North American precedent for undergraduate research. Pike's initiative at Toronto became standard practice in later years in most Canadian university departments of chemistry for honours or specialist programs.

During Pike's professorship the honours courses, including chemistry, attracted a number of excellent students, many of whom achieved prominent chemistry positions in Canada and the United States. He encouraged a number of these students to pursue postgraduate work, mostly abroad. Before Pike left Toronto, the university senate (in 1897) established the research degree Doctor of Philosophy (PhD),[27] and chemistry enrolled its first candidate, F.B. Allan, a teaching fellow. Allan, whom we discuss below, received this degree in 1901.

Six male graduates in chemistry at Toronto, of whom five had begun under Pike, studied and received PhDs at Leipzig under Wilhelm Ostwald (to whom Toronto awarded an honorary LLD in 1906).[28] These were W.L. Miller (1892), F.G. Smale (1892–95), F.B. Kenrick (1894–97), W.G. Smeaton (1898–1901), W.C. Bray (1902–05), and J.W. McBain (1904–05). Several studied abroad thanks to a scholarship that the commissioners for the Exhibition of 1851 (London, England) placed at Toronto's disposal. The Prince Consort's industrial exhibition created a surplus that the trustees invested in scholarships throughout the British Empire in "those branches of science such as physics, mechanics, and chemistry, the extension of which is specially important for our national industries."[29] Canadian science owes much to their far-sighted wisdom and benevolence.

Chemistry was growing into a necessary and respectable occupation, and under Pike the program at Toronto was able to prepare candidates for a successful career in this new profession. Other distinguished graduates included brothers Charles E. and A.P. Saunders — sons of William Saunders, first director of the Dominion Experimental Farm in Ottawa[30] — who earned PhDs in chemistry at Johns Hopkins University.

William and Charles's efforts to develop a strain of wheat for the Canadian climate led to the famous Marquis wheat, for which Charles received a knighthood. His brother spent much of his life as professor of agricultural and general chemistry, and also as dean, at Hamilton College, in Utica, New York. F.T. Shutt — undergraduate laboratory demonstrator to these brothers — became chemist at the Dominion Experimental Farm, where, over forty-six years, he earned international regard.[31] E.B. Kenrick — Shutt's classmate and a cousin of the F.B. Kenrick discussed below — became government chemist in Winnipeg and a professor at the University of Manitoba.[32] Robert Kennedy Duncan achieved numerous advances in U.S. industrial chemistry.[33]

The new SPS of 1878 provided space for laboratory instruction in chemistry, biology, and geology and mineralogy, while physics replaced chemistry in University College's roundhouse. During the 1880s, increasing enrolments in arts rendered all this laboratory space inadequate. In 1888 the university erected a new Biology Building east of SPS, roughly on Moss Hall's site of thirty-eight years, and two years later it added to that structure. The new Biology Building housed three "departments" — biology, physiology (originally in Arts), and anatomy (in the Medical Faculty) — as well as the Mineralogy Museum. The university report for 1890 pleaded for new space for chemistry instruction in view of "the termination ... of the mutual relations established by the late Minister of Education and the School of Practical Science."[34]

Early in 1881 Pike had reported to the senate that want of space and resources left him unable to offer laboratory work for almost a quarter of the arts students taking chemistry. He urged a new building for chemistry, whose size would depend on who the students would be. In due course the university decided to erect a structure able to handle arts and medical students. Work started in 1894, and the edifice was ready in the autumn of 1895.

The Chemistry Building of 1895
(The "Old Chemistry Building")

The new Chemistry Building stood just north of the eastern end of the present Wallberg Building. Though utilitarian, it generated respect from three generations of staff and students, perhaps because of its seeming

The "Old Chemistry Building" in 1907, from the north.
Courtesy University of Toronto Archives.

indestructibility, or perhaps because of association with the activities inside. Many former graduate students will swear that the place had a ghost, of unknown identity.

The structure was "a commodious Building of red pressed brick and Credit Valley stone.... It consists of a ground floor, upper storey, and basement, and is constructed in the form of a hollow square, with central Courtyard for light and ventilation, the west side being occupied by the large lecture-room, and the east by the Students' Laboratories while the north side is devoted to the entrance, staircase, and approaches, and the south to the Storerooms, Caretaker's Residence, private Laboratories, Library, and Professors' Rooms."[35] The building had electric lighting, steam-heated air, and large fans for thorough ventilation. Exposed wires and pipes facilitated repairs, and four separate hydrants provided water in case of fire.

The spacious, two-storey lecture theatre "is fitted with Chairs for an audience of three hundred and eighteen, and is lighted altogether from the top, either by the skylight (which may be closed by curtains from above), or by means of groups of electric incandescent lamps suspended from the ceiling, thus avoiding all confusing reflections in the glass part of the Lecture Apparatus."

The structure's east wing had student laboratories. The ground floor consisted of "a suite of three large Rooms, fitted with work

Early 1900s undergraduate laboratory in the Mining Building.
Courtesy Department of Chemistry, University of Toronto.

places for in all 100 men. Each Student has for his own use about five feet of Table, two gas Taps, a Water Tap, a Sink, and a set of Reagent Bottles (there are nearly 5,000 of these in the Laboratory)." Connections with the ventilation system in front provided each student with a simple fume "duct." The first room was for "beginners, — the test-tubers of the lower years, — the second for those more advanced — doing quantitative work — and the third for practical work in organic chemistry. Conveniently accessible from the Quantitative Laboratory is the Balance-room, with twelve delicate Instruments, on independent brick piers." The upper storey had a small lecture room and "a large Laboratory, capable of accommodating ninety-six men at one time. It is here that the large class of medical students receive their practical instruction."

The building's total floor area was 19,558 square feet (1,820 square metres), and it cost about $80,000. Its air-circulation system attracted favourable comment.[36] The caretaker's residence was an apartment at the southwest corner of the top floor. In this lived E.J. Repath (long-time steward for the laboratory) and then his successor, R. Fortescue. This area became research space about 1948.

Pike was active in planning and equipping the laboratory. He "preferred to spend his leisure in mechanical rather than chemical experiments. His chief delight was … in making apparatus and machinery, and the new chemistry building which he planned and the erection and fitting of which he superintended, contains many mementos of his industry and ingenuity."[37]

∽ Pike: The Man and His Legacy ∽

Pike's few publications suggest little skill or interest in experimental work; an explosion in March 1890 that cost him his right eye is the only evidence of his laboratory research at Toronto. Rather, he concentrated for two decades on building an up-to-date school of chemistry, mostly on his own. Moreover, he inspired many of his graduating students to pursue research. His published comments on German science[38] and his introduction of undergraduate laboratories at Toronto clearly reveal his emphasis on research.

As his pupil William Lash Miller said, Pike "did not seek the limelight."[39] Yet, despite his fractious start in SPS, he apparently developed a fine reputation. In the autumn of 1880 and again in 1881, he was a judge at the university's annual field day. In 1881–82, University College's staff and students put on Sophocles' *Antigone* in its Convocation Hall; Pike sat on the production's ways and means committee and managed the stage and properties.[40] Pike appears to have been a cricketer and was vice-president in 1886–87 of the Toronto University Cricket Club, which had played five matches the previous season.[41]

Like his cousin Warburton Pike, the professor was fond of exploring and hunting in wilderness areas and reportedly went annually to Labrador or Newfoundland. After the loss of his right eye in 1890 he had his hunting rifle fitted with special sights and continued his outdoor life.

University President James Loudon considered Pike "something of an authority in the matter of investments." Pike purchased 93.5 acres near then-suburban Davisville in 1895 and arranged surveys for two streets there, which he named Merton and Balliol, after colleges at

Oxford. He was able to discharge outright a $25,000 mortgage on this property four years later.[42]

In September 1898 Pike indicated his wish to resign. After a year's leave of absence, he left office in September 1899. With the minister of education's consent, William Lash Miller, whom Pike had endorsed as his successor, managed affairs during Pike's leave and for another year until a new professor arrived.

Pike meanwhile settled as a country gentleman in Salcombe, in south Devon, where he rebuilt his machine shop from Toronto. He wrote to Miller: "Tell Repath that I have just got my workshop in order & even now there are many belts to be laced & that I wish I could tell him to lace them & go out until they were done."[43] He died in Salcombe on February 8, 1921.

At Toronto, Pike had been very controversial. Some commentators have portrayed him as almost draconian: "He drove everything before him, winning his victories at the point of a bayonet"[44]; "Certainly a troublesome gentleman enough"[45]; "Dr Pike, however, was the special bête noire of the Vice Chancellor [Mulock] and his medical friends."[46]

Yet other comments place him in a very favourable light. L.F. Barker — a medical student who had worked two years in a drugstore — helped to interpret Pike's lectures for his fellow students. He observed, "Professor Pike, an Oxford man and an excellent chemist, was a very enthusiastic teacher, but unfortunately his lectures on chemistry work too far above the heads of the first-year medical students to be understood by the majority of them."[47] John Cooper wrote, "His latch-string was always out when he was not in the lecture room, and no student ever sought his advice or assistance without reward; none ever performed a bit of original work without being highly commended."[48] Pike was as good as his word. "He was never afraid to say what he thought. He never told a lie because he was not afraid to tell the truth. A promise made by him in his private room could be relied upon just as absolutely as if his name were appended to that promise in a legal document."[49]

In his revealing sketch, John Cooper concludes: "It is doubtful if he ever felt contented with either social or professional life as he found it in Canada, though he gave to Canadian education the best years and best efforts of his life."[50]

Chapter Three

Gentleman and Officer: W.R. Lang (1900–1920)

Introduction: Historical Context

By the time William R. Lang took the chair of Chemistry at Toronto in 1900, the city had grown: the 1901 census found 208,040 residents in 24 square miles. Electricity now powered illumination for most of the city's streets, larger and faster streetcars, and suburban radial carlines that already or soon reached Newmarket, Port Credit, West Hill, and Weston. Electricity from Niagara Falls powered these amenities and a growing manufacturing sector. Newspapers focused on the South African War (1899–1902) — Toronto was very British, and a contingent of Canadian militia volunteers had gone to serve in that theatre, in effect putting part of the country "at war."

Toronto was gaining important new structures: the Legislative Building in Queen's Park (1892), city hall at Queen and Bay streets (1899), and several university buildings during James Loudon's presidency (from 1892 on). On the Front Campus, University College had long occupied the north side, and the School of Practical Science was on the south; the Library (1893) opened on the east side, and the Medical Building (1904) immediately to the south. South and east of that stood the Biology Building (1888–90). At the southwest corner, Convocation Hall (1906) joined them, and just south of it, the Physics Building (1907). The "Old Chemistry Building" (1895) was on the west side of King's College Road, site today of Metallurgy, and Chemistry and Mining (1904–05), today just Mining, went up along College Street.

East and north of University College stood the Gymnasium (1892–93), which expanded in 1894; it gave way to Hart House

(1914–19). North of it stood Wycliffe College (1891). After federation with Toronto, Victoria University finished its main building (1892) on the northeast corner of Queen's Park. McMaster University opened its home (1890) — now the Royal Conservatory of Music — on the south side of Bloor Street.

In 1901, the Nobel Prize began to be awarded in chemistry; the first four awards were as follows:

- 1901: Jacobus Henricus van't Hoff (laws of chemical dynamics and osmotic pressure in solution);
- 1902: Hermann Emil Fischer (work on sugar and purine syntheses);
- 1903: Svante August Arrhenius (electrolytic theory of dissociation); and
- 1904: Sir William Ramsay (discovery of the inert gaseous elements in air and determination of their place in the periodic system).

Physicists' and chemists' interests had overlapped little in the nineteenth century. Physics (or natural philosophy) was older, and its mathematical predisposition made it quite rigorous and quantitative. Chemistry had its origins among artisans, had picked up a lot of mystique during medieval times, and became a rational science probably in the 1790s. The tradition of "pot-boiling" prompted the view that there was an *art chimique*; this notion prevailed well into the twentieth century and made many chemists highly empirical.

Nowhere is the nineteenth-century gap between chemical and physical thinking clearer than in approaches to atoms and molecules. Despite John Dalton's chemical theory of atomism (c. 1800), chemists agreed on how to assign relative masses to the postulated atoms only in 1860.[1] In theorizing about how atoms grouped into molecules, many chemists denied any physical reality to their deductions. Edward Frankland, an advocate of valence, could write in 1866, "It must be carefully borne in mind that these graphic formulae are intended to represent neither the shape nor the supposed relative positions of the constituent hypothetical atoms."[2]

Yet by 1860 Maxwell had applied statistical methods to the distribution of speeds of gaseous molecules, and Clausius was discussing "mean free paths" for individual molecules in a gaseous assembly and "energy exchange" between translational and rotational motion of colliding molecules.[3] Such sophisticated mathematical analyses suggest untypical confidence in the descriptive model and reliance on quantitative inferences from evidence.

Studies of the conduction of electricity through gases at low pressure, begun in 1859, had led to identification of cathode rays. In 1897 J.J. Thomson (at Cambridge) confirmed that these rays consisted of negatively electrified particles travelling at about one-tenth of the speed of light and showed that each gram of particles carried almost two thousand times as much electrical charge as the lightest known particle — the hydrogen ion. Thomson inferred that the new particle was very light, and therefore subatomic; the particle received the name "electron." In 1895 W.K. von Roentgen (at Würzburg), experimenting with cathode rays, discovered penetrating radiation that would darken photographic plates and cause certain substances to glow in the dark. He called them "X-rays," and medical applications soon followed.

In 1896, A.H. Becquerel (in Paris), almost by accident, discovered "radioactivity" (a name that Maria Sklodowska-Curie, a.k.a. Marie Curie, coined) and thereby launched a chain of discoveries that transformed the chemist's understanding of atoms. And, finally, in 1900 Max Planck (in Berlin), seeking to explain the colour and intensity of the radiation emitted by glowing hot bodies, proposed that matter gives out or takes up radiant energy in tiny "quanta," with a magnitude inversely proportional to the radiation's wavelength. Five years later Albert Einstein (in Berne, Switzerland) incorporated and extended Planck's idea to explain the photoelectric emissions of electrons from metals. Thus started quantum theory, the basis of "modern" physics.

In the twentieth century, chemistry too would go "modern" and incorporate many concepts of the new physics to interpret its own mysteries. Many chemists did not yet realize how ideas from physics would transform their own science.

Lang at Glasgow

Twenty-nine-year-old Dr. William Robert Lang, a graduate of the University of Glasgow, became professor of chemistry in the University of Toronto in 1900. He was born on July 29, 1870, in Lenzie,

Lanarkshire, northeast of Glasgow. He was the youngest son of John Lang, a local manufacturer, and his wife, Janet Stuart (née Kennedy). He started his education at Kelvingrove Academy, Glasgow. He entered the city's university at age fifteen to take medicine but instead studied physical sciences, graduating with honours in chemistry in 1891. In 1889, while still a student, he became private assistant to the professor of chemistry, and three years later he succeeded Dr. George G. Henderson as tutorial assistant. His duties included tutorials and demonstrations and occasional lecturing. In 1897–98 his series of lectures on organic chemistry attracted seventy students. The professor proposed making Lang a lecturer; the university court created the position in 1898 and appointed Lang. He also gave a course of extramural lectures in agricultural chemistry.[4]

In his application for Toronto, Lang claimed to have performed original investigations by himself or with others and to have published some of these, but much of this work appears rather trivial.[5] Glasgow, like many British universities, did not have a strong tradition of chemical research. Toronto professors Croft and Pike had studied chemistry in Germany, as did many British chemists of that period.

One observer describes the situation at Glasgow in 1870: "The University's curricula still concentrated on the Humanities, Philosophy, and Divinity. The study of law, medicine and certain branches of science was carried out but under difficulties. Professor William Thomson (later Lord Kelvin) was grudgingly granted laboratory facilities. And although [Anatomy] Professor Allen Thomson ... was chairman of the Building Committee, he still had to struggle to obtain a dissecting room and museum for his department."[6]

Clearly the Chemistry Department was a teaching school, but not a centre of experimental investigation — as Lang well knew. Professor John Ferguson (appointed in 1874) worked very ably on the history of chemistry, alchemy, and the occult.[7,8] Most candidates took medicine or engineering, and "a certain body of students [were] preparing for a career in teaching or technical work."[9] Lang defensively informed Toronto that he had "endeavoured to enlarge [his] knowledge of continental methods of teaching and investigation by visits during vacations."[10] He spent part of the summer of 1899 in Paris in Professor L. Troost's laboratory at the Sorbonne, where he participated in some experimental research later published.[11] For three weeks in October of the same year he went to Ramsay's[12] laboratory in London "to pick up ideas." Probably his deepest interests lay elsewhere. While still an undergraduate, Lang had joined the army. He served with the Scottish Air Line Company within the Lanarkshire Royal Engineers, a voluntary militia corps. The unit consisted largely of science and engineering undergraduates at Glasgow. Lang passed a couple of summer vacations with the militia in England at Salisbury Plain. By the time he left for Canada he held a captaincy in the Imperial Reserve Army. As we see below, he soon joined the Canadian militia, which occupied much of his life.

In the spring of 1899 Glasgow conferred on Lang a DSc degree, which resembled the MA that Pike had received at Oxford twenty years earlier — an award to graduates for accomplishments and/or simply for payment of a fee.

Picking the Professor: Uneasy Lies the Head

As we saw in Chapter 2, William Pike, when he resigned as head of Chemistry at Toronto, received a terminal leave of absence for 1898–99, and William Lash Miller, with permission from the minister of education, took charge. The authorities made no effort to fill the professorship during that year. Perhaps Miller was serving unofficially on probation; also, a new minister took office.[13]

Evidently a decision to have a competition was made in the autumn of 1899. In November an advertisement announced the vacancy and invited applications; Pike, now living in England, was to so inform interested parties in Britain.

By early 1900 nine applications had arrived from Britain, and at least one from the United States. As far as we know, none of the British applicants received an interview. Three went on to distinguished careers: all three eventually gained fellowship in the Royal Society (FRS); two, knighthoods (Jocelyn F. Thorpe and Gilbert T. Morgan); and one, the Nobel Prize (Frederick Soddy).[14, 15] Soddy applied and, without waiting for a response, set out for Canada. En route to Toronto by train from New York, he read about a farewell dinner for Pike, where President Loudon reportedly commented, "Professor Pike came to us from Oxford, but thank God his chemistry was 'made in Germany'!" Soddy concluded that he had no chance and, after a few days in Toronto, decided to return to England via Montreal. There he visited McGill University to see the new, well-appointed Macdonald laboratories for physics and chemistry.[16, 17] B.J. Harrington, the professor of chemistry, received him graciously and soon offered him a demonstratorship, which he accepted. This is how Soddy and Ernest Rutherford (professor of physics at McGill) came to meet and collaborate for a couple of years. They hypothesized the spontaneous disintegration of atoms to explain the phenomenon of radioactivity.[18]

In fact, Toronto reviewed Soddy's application like all the others but downgraded it because of his youth. He was just twenty-two, had graduated BA from Oxford the previous year, and possessed no teaching experience. Harrington's offer at McGill was more commensurate with his experience.

In his unpublished memoirs, President Loudon indicated that no one consulted him concerning the appointment at Toronto.[19] However, he made considerable effort to secure opinions, directly or indirectly, about the British applicants. As late as May 1900, Professor Ramsay Wright (Biology), evidently on leave in Europe, wrote him from Heidelberg with an offer to inquire about the candidates "after returning to England." Perhaps the minister made the final selection — Lang — without consulting the president.

The department, and especially Pike, had encouraged William Lash Miller to think of himself as the heir apparent. However, once the university advertised a competition, his succession was no longer automatic. When he heard about Lang's appointment, he began investigating other options, as we see below.

In August or September 1900, Professor Lang arrived in Toronto. He proved to be "possessed of a genial disposition which has already won him many friends in our midst."[20] He and Miller met in September and divided the work of the department. Indeed, on October 20, the university offered to appoint Miller associate professor of physical chemistry; after some negotiating, he accepted. However, on November 16 Lang ordered Miller to vacate the "private laboratory" — about four hundred square feet on the top floor of the Chemistry Building. Miller had used this room (because Pike did little experimental work) ever since the new structure opened, and F.B. Kenrick had joined him there on returning from Germany in 1897. Miller counter-proposed that Lang share the space, which, he said, was large enough for all their needs.

In Britain, people rarely questioned "the professor" — especially one obsessed with military protocol. The next month saw a flurry of letters and memoranda among these two men and Loudon, including some melodramatic passages: "You are my tenant-at-will in my building and I can put you out if I want to."[21] Loudon probably had to support Lang, whereupon Miller insisted that the matter go to the university council. Finally in December, W.H. Ellis, on behalf of the council, negotiated an agreement on the sharing of departmental responsibilities and resources. A storeroom area in the basement was to become a laboratory for Miller, and Lang took over the "private laboratory."

Lang, undoubtedly within his rights, handled matters poorly. Miller throughout argued that the phrase "of Physical Chemistry" gave him a certain independence and virtual equality. He was almost certainly wrong in this assumption, but the term "associate professor" was new and still open to interpretation.

Adapting the Professor's Role

The rest of this chapter examines Lang's interpretation of his role as professor, the major academic changes at Toronto in his era, his applied work in chemistry and his outreach to the community, and his full-time military career from 1914 to 1925.

As professor, Lang sought to be a spokesman, cheerleader, and fundraiser for his department, representing it to the public and the world of chemistry, even if research played little part in that activity. For example, he quickly became "a popular Lecturer and Demonstrator."[22] "He was a good lecturer, clear and direct, simple, and students could easily follow him. For them the foundations of this science were well and truly laid."[23] Especially early on, Lang — trying to be a conscientious professor — did much public lecturing and popular writing on pure and applied science. His papers included "A Century of Chemical Process," "Chemistry in the Nineteenth Century," "Conceptions of Matter — Ancient and Modern," and "Lord Kelvin,"[24] and his public lectures, "Combustion," "The Development of the Modern High Explosives," "The Gases of the Atmosphere," and "Matter at Low Temperatures." He presented a series of public lectures at the university to raise money for the proposed new Convocation Hall and gave others to groups such as the Canadian

Institute and the Canadian Manufacturers' Association.

Lang set out to procure donations of chemicals, raw materials, intermediates, and metals to build up a chemical museum in the department. He evidently worked his connections in Britain in the Society of Chemical Industry. In all, more than five hundred substances were in this collection by early 1903.[25] The Chemistry Building had no room for their proper display, and Lang housed them in showcases in the main-floor balance room. A published account states that they were in daily use in the lecture room. But within a generation they had largely disappeared — victims in part of a switch to principles rather than descriptive chemistry.[26]

Lang worked hard and used his personal contacts to enrich the teaching of chemistry. Toronto and its university were attracting distinguished visitors. In a great coup for the city, in 1897 — the year of Queen Victoria's Diamond Jubilee — the British Association for the Advancement of Science had held its prestigious annual meeting in Toronto.[27] The American Chemical Society did the same in 1907. Such occasions allowed many well-known scientists to acquaint themselves with the university's facilities and faculty. As well, numerous individuals (for example, Wilhelm Ostwald in 1904) visited, but usually during the long vacations, when students could not benefit. However, Lang arranged a lecture, primarily for undergraduates, by Sir William Perkin, who spoke of developing the dye industry in Britain[28] — undoubtedly an inspiration to many in his audience.

Lang also wrote or co-wrote two laboratory manuals of qualitative and quantitative analysis published by the University Press.[29] These were recipe books, clear and practical. Contemporary textbooks showed little interest in theoretical interpretations of group separations and tests, which Ostwald championed.

The minutes of the university's Chemical Society (April 1906–March 1909) indicate a visit by Lang. The group's elected participants were staff members and students in Chemistry and in Applied Chemistry. It met almost every week during term, in the evenings. Members presented and discussed papers — the forerunner of group seminars? — and good humour abounded. Topics included material from current journals and how to teach specific topics (for example, how to define a solution).

Lang and William Lash Miller developed a quiet modus vivendi, but it seemed to collapse in 1908. Recurring entries in Lang's diaries show that he found Miller, Kenrick, and Allan a combined source of discomfort. That these three "locals" ("Miller's gang") would, on provocation, close ranks against the "outsider" is easy to imagine.

Whatever the cause — perhaps the reorganization under Ellis that made Miller professor of physical chemistry — Lang decided in the summer of 1908 that he wanted to leave Toronto. He wrote to President Robert Falconer from London, asking for a testimonial to use with applications to some British universities. He asked that the document emphasize his "organizing and administrative ability, his power of control over students, and his qualifications as a lecturer."[30] Falconer did supply such a testimonial.

Lang called on Sir William Ramsay (a good friend and staunch supporter), and also on Sir William Dewar, Sir J.J. Thomson, W.A. Tilden, and others, to discuss "chairs" for which he might apply. Nothing came of this overture. Lang's lack of research or scientific accomplishment would have handicapped his prospects. He would not accept anything less than a professorship and found himself trapped in Toronto. In October 1913 he noted a vacancy at Dundee advertised in *Nature*, but we do not know whether he applied.

Academic Changes at Toronto

During Lang's headship, developments in the university and its Faculty of Arts affected the Department of Chemistry. Physicist James Loudon's term as president (1892–1906) saw further university federation, major construction on campus, and transformation of postgraduate education. His influence ensured strong science programs, a clear mandate of research, and a postgraduate school,[31, 32] all reforms that benefited the Chemistry Department. The tenure of his successor, Robert Falconer (to 1932), brought further institutional growth and maturation in which Toronto at last became a world-class university.

Loudon's presidency also witnessed a few mishaps, including a student strike in the late 1890s and attacks on the university in Toronto newspapers.[33, 34] In the sciences, in 1900 and 1904 there were charges of lack of probity in the award of 1851 Exhibition Scholarships,[35] which may have started the long feud between physicist J.C. McLennan and William Lash Miller (see Chapter 4).

In the early years of the new century, the Faculty of Arts was restructuring academic programs and practices. For instance, in 1904 it laid out a common first year for all honours science courses, delaying specialization until the final two years. From about 1910 on there was increasing pressure for it to introduce a higher matriculation standard for admission, to which it agreed in 1912. It added joint honours programs in biology and physics (1904) and in physiology and biochemistry (1910), offering parallel pathways towards the first three years of the medical program, leading to a BA in four years and an MB in a further three.

The Faculty of Arts began to offer credit courses in the summer and later in evenings. It started a pass course for teachers in 1907, and that summer F.B. Allan and John A.M. Dawson (a junior assistant) offered three chemistry courses.[36] In the summers of 1905 and 1906 it presented courses in chemistry[37] for high school teachers who were helping students meet new university requirements for matriculation and departmental examinations.[38] The instructor was F.B. Allan, aided by F.B. Kenrick in 1906, when one of the topics was practical glassblowing — a skill that the laboratory program in physical chemistry still required in 1946.

Soon after Falconer took office as president, prolonged study and revision began of Arts courses, starting with the four-year general course. This process led to the introduction of laboratory work in several science subjects, thereby adding to the workload in chemistry. Skirmishes occurred during the planning stage. Professor A.B. Macallum proposed to faculty council, and later to the senate,[39] a prohibition on original research in undergraduate courses — a direct repudiation of Pike's practice. Lang voted against the proposal and had earlier tried to dissuade Macallum. The motion lost in council, and its sponsors withdrew it in the senate.

Earlier, in 1909, there had been an attempt in council to limit students' required number of hours per week in scheduled classes. Such a constraint would have affected only science courses, especially chemistry. Staff members in science departments defeated the motion, although Lang, in a written submission, argued for more leisure for the students.

Between 1912 and 1914 there was a prolonged controversy over introducing the BSc degree for certain programs. Entries in his diary suggest that Lang favoured this suggestion but faced strong resistance within his own department. It was not the first such proposal: as early as 1874, Henry Croft and Daniel Wilson had tried to persuade the senate to establish the BSc and the DSc.[40] As we see below, it was not until 1960 that the Faculty of Arts added "and Science" to its title and introduced the BSc.

By 1900 SPS had become almost unmanageably crowded, thanks to increased enrolment and the remarkable growth of industrial technology in Ontario. Consequently the university and the government decided in 1901 to erect the Chemistry and Mining Building (1905), to accommodate Applied Chemistry, Assaying, part of Chemistry, Electrochemistry, Metallurgy, and Mining, as well as the Arts departments of Geology and Mineralogy.

Applying Chemistry and Reaching Out

Professor Lang had other scientific interests, mostly in practical applications of chemistry. He found W.H. Ellis, in Applied Chemistry, a much more compatible colleague than the men in his own department. Lang's interest in application derived probably from his contacts with medical, military, and manufacturing people in Glasgow. His early published investigations include "Experiments on Pot Ale — Its Acidity and Action on Metals," "Note on Analysis of Human Gastric Juice," and "The Secondary Products of the Combustion of Gunpowder."[41] In Glasgow, Lang had joined the Society of Chemical Industry (SCI), founded in 1882 for applied chemists. The SCI maintained local sections in major centres such as London and Liverpool and by 1900 had a section in New York.

In early 1901 W.H. Ellis and Harold van der Linde (of Gutta Percha Rubber Co.) had considered a Canadian section, which Lang keenly supported and mentioned at the SCI's general meeting in Glasgow in July 1901. The new section was Canada's first professional organization of chemists. It met first on March 6, 1902,[42] and chose Lang as chairman, Professor G.P. Girdwood (McGill) and van der Linde as vice-chairmen, and Ellis and F.J. Smale (now in industry) for the executive. In 1945 it merged with three other groups to form the Chemical Institute of Canada. The country's SCI sections also joined but continued to offer annual awards within the profession.

Lang recorded his vision of a flourishing chemical industry in Canada, and he compiled an inventory of chemical firms.[43] Following the First World War the federal government published an official directory, using Lang's records.

Lang's visit to the Sorbonne in 1899 was probably his first experimental work in an active research laboratory with others to inspire and guide him. Unlike the simple analytical measurements he had made in Glasgow, covering a wide range of unrelated materials, here he used special apparatus and incorporated physico-chemical principles. One of the two resulting publications upheld conclusions reached by Henry Croft in 1842[44] on the ammines of cadmium halides. At Toronto Lang continued research on the ammines of metal halides and produced six short articles for scientific journals. His name appeared, usually with those of students and assistants, on nineteen publications in all. The last appeared in 1911; in his diary for May 4 he entered: "Lab. Wrote short paper on $CuSCN.N(CH_3)_3$ for J.C.S. *'Pot boiler'.*" The piece occupied eleven lines in the *Journal of the Chemical Society*, but Lang fully grasped its status.

Lang became a popular and respected member of the university. At both Glasgow and Toronto he was active in campus life. According to the *Glasgow University Magazine* "he took a lively interest in S.R.C. [Student Representative Council] doings and the university magazine, in the University Volunteers, and in fact in all the student institutions." At Toronto, the *Varsity* reports his involvement with the Natural Science Association, where he once performed in a musical program with students.[45] He wrote for the *Varsity* and the *University of Toronto Monthly*.

Until 1939, professors at Toronto, like their Scottish counterparts,[46] had a long, relaxed summer vacation, and until the First World War Lang went "home" to Scotland each summer. While in Britain, he would attend the annual SCI meetings and call on his former cronies. In 1909, in addition to joining its council, he married Edith Hollington, youngest daughter of A.J. Hollington, JP, of London. In the next few years the Langs had three daughters. Following the summer of 1912 his wife remained with her family in England, and Lang joined her the following January, on a few months of leave he had coaxed from President

Falconer[47] to visit German universities and scientific institutions. This he did between February 17 and July 11, 1913, "picking up ideas."

By all accounts "Scotty" Lang was a genial, sociable man. Probably because of his military connections he soon joined Toronto "society." For example, he was a friend and frequent visitor to Henry (later Sir Henry) Pellatt, who built the palatial Casa Loma. He kept a horse, stabled on College Street, and rode on weekends. He had always had an interest in music, and after the war he worked on behalf of the Canadian Operatic Society, of which he was president at the time of his death.

War and Military Studies, 1914–25

On arrival in Toronto in 1900 Lang had immediately rejoined the militia; every year from 1901 to 1914 he left Toronto at the close of lectures for spring military exercises at Niagara. By 1901 he established a volunteer militia company of university engineers, which formed the guard of honour when the Duke and Duchess of Cornwall and York (later King George V and Queen Mary) attended a special convocation on October 11, 1901. He had already joined the Second Field Company, Canadian Engineers, where he became major in 1902 and lieutenant-colonel ten years later. In 1911 he commanded the infantry troops and served as adjutant of the Canadian Corps at the coronation of King George V.

His military activities became full time during the war. In his diary at year's end of 1913, Lang wrote, "We are heartily sick of Canada. I am particularly sick of Toronto University's Chemistry Department of which I am Head. The three 'legacies' of my predecessor W.H. Pike — Kenrick, Allan, and that extraordinary man Lash Miller — who were here before I came, do not tend to making one of my nature happy. I like to *love* all my fellow workers, for to work with them is distasteful. We long to return to London, home and beauty."

The war saved Lang. When the conflict broke out in August 1914, he immediately volunteered — "ready to serve anywhere." He soon went on leave for military service (at full pay), and Miller began to run the Chemistry Department, although Falconer did secure Lang's pro forma approval of appointments or committee memberships. Lang's wartime letters to the president were almost wholly military. Lang was to pay for a substitute lecturer; he employed W.S. Funnell — a 1912 graduate in

William R. Lang.
Courtesy University of Toronto Archives.

chemistry and mineralogy and an MA candidate in physical chemistry — who started as an assistant but became a lecturer in 1916–17.

The military authorities quickly perceived in Lang a capable educator and an experienced soldier. In September 1914 they appointed him to the Canadian General Staff and gave him charge of military instruction in Military District No. 2 (in Central Canada). From 1914 to 1917 he directed, as lieutenant-colonel, the Provisional School of Infantry, at Niagara-on-the-Lake and later at Camp Borden, where prospective infantry officers trained and qualified for commissions in the Canadian Expeditionary Force.

When the university reopened for autumn 1914, there was sentiment to establish a 1,000-man-strong Canadian Officers' Training Corps (COTC) on campus. The federal Militia Department authorized its formation in October 1914, and in November it named Lang its colonel. More than 1,500 men participated. Classes stopped daily at four o'clock for drill and other military instruction. The university cut three weeks off the academic year so that COTC members could attend training camp at Niagara and qualify for proficiency certificates.

The Chemistry and Mining Building gave the COTC considerable space to store arms and equipment and turned Miller's office (for electrochemistry) into its orderly room. Indeed, the university made its facilities available for Lang's Infantry School and for Major (later Lieutenant-Colonel) Vincent Massey's School of Musketry.

During the war, Massey's unfinished Hart House became the site of military training and a military hospital. The neo-Gothic structure — going up around a quadrangle, just northeast of University College — was to subsume existing campus facilities for the Student Christian Movement (SCM) and the Young Men's Christian Association (YMCA). Massey planned for it to offer a full range of extracurricular activities; the university completed it after the war, and it opened formally on Armistice Day 1919 — a lasting tribute to the soldiers who never returned. Ian Montagnes's history of Hart House, *An Uncommon Fellowship*,[48] tells of the Gallery Grill's "caricatures of the scholars and eccentrics who taught at the university when Hart House was conceived" — among them, Lang (scholar or eccentric?). Generations of chemists at the university have enjoyed Hart House, under the watchful gaze of their former head.

Two members of Lang's "gang" joined the COTC. By 1915 Kenrick was a lieutenant and corps paymaster. Miller, almost fifty, joined as a private, "performed cheerfully all the menial duties of camp life," and "astounded the military authorities by writing the best paper on tactics they had ever seen."

On December 6, 1917, two ships collided in Halifax Harbour, one of them heavily loaded with explosives and chemicals. The enormous loss of life and destruction of property that followed threatened military operations in that crucial port city and eastern coastal defences. Early in 1918 Colonel Lang took charge of Military District No. 6, based in Halifax. There he remained for more than a year.

As the war ended, Lang's days as de jure head of the Chemistry Department began to wind down. In January 1919, he wrote to President Falconer: "I presume it will not be until the session 1919–20 that you will wish me back to my old work though immediately on my return it will be a great delight to me to re-assume my duties as Director of Military Studies under you." There had been a proposal to create, within the Faculty of Arts, an academic department of Military Studies, with Lang as director. Lang would also resume command of the peacetime COTC corps.

The president failed to make clear to Lang that he must in exchange relinquish headship of Chemistry — a huge loss of face for a proud man. Before the war he had loved teaching medical students, so in March 1920 he counter-proposed that he might serve, with appropriate assistance, as professor of chemistry in the Faculty of Medicine (where he had good friends), but the president said no. Finally, in two blunt letters dated May 14 and 17, 1920, following a meeting of the university's board of governors, Falconer put the matter very directly: Lang must resign the professorship but could continue to give lectures in chemistry to first-year medical students. This offer shocked Lang, who called the first letter "extraordinary."

From March till May 1920, Lang repeatedly sought comfort and advice from his confidant and neighbour, W.H. Ellis, who had retired in 1919. Another confidant was Professor J.J.R. Macleod in Medicine.

By October 1920 Lang had resigned from the SCI and was offering his chemical journals for sale. At the end of that year he allowed his fellowship in the Royal Society of Canada (FRCS) to lapse. Though mentioned in dispatches and thanked by the Imperial Army Council in London for his war service, he was bitter that the university did not award him an honorary degree and that Canadian regulations prevented a civil honour from the sovereign. "Here ends 1920. I came to Canada in August 1900. I've given the best 20 years of my life to what has proved an ungrateful country."[49] His headship was over.

However, Lang soon began to savour his new role. His new department was in a house on College Street. His courses of instruction, with assistance from Brigadier-General G.S. Cartwright (retired), proved popular. His COTC contingent blossomed: following inspection in 1925, the chief of staff of the Canadian militia, Major-General J.H. MacBrien, applauded: "This is the largest O.T.C. inspection I have ever seen — and also the best."

In his diary for 1920, Lang had mentioned trouble with his heart, but things seemed on the mend. However, in the days following the 1925 Armistice Day service at the new Soldier's Tower next to Hart House, Lang complained about feeling poorly. He was en route to his physician on Friday, November 20. The doctor happened to pick Lang and his wife up in his car, but during the short trip Lang died of a heart attack at Bay and Bloor streets.[50]

The funeral at Convocation Hall had full military honours, with the officers and men of his corps making up the funeral cortège and firing party. Falconer paid generous tribute, singling out his distinguished military career: "But all through those years before the war if chemistry was the subject of his chief attention, military affairs were an engrossing avocation. Almost by nature, and certainly by devotion, he was a soldier. He was at home among officers; he moved among them as one who understood the life. So Colonel Lang trained good soldiers because he was himself a soldier by instinct. He loved the life and what its duties signified."[51]

A brief entry from Lang's diary for 1917 captures his situation: "The following appears in Book I (see XXXIV) near the end of the Autobiography of Benvenuto Cellini (ca. 1530 A.D.) written by him after the defense of Rome, in which he took a very active part, and was highly successful. 'There have been times when I have been more inclined to the profession of arms than to the one of my choice, and with such goodwill did I give myself to it now that I did better in it than in my own art.' How nearly this resembles my own case (19 vii 1917)."

The *Varsity* reported on Lang's death: "Men of all faculties loved and respected him for the precision with which he discharged his duties, for his amiability, and for the fact that under all circumstances he was a gentlemen in the truest sense of the word."[52]

Conclusion

The powers-that-be had appointed Lang in 1900 evidently without thought for his small department. If an external appointee was essential, it should have been someone who could forge a harmonious group. The cognoscenti already recognized Miller as a very gifted scientist. He was stubborn and stayed at Toronto, and, by virtue of the respect he acquired from the faculty, he prevented Lang from reshaping the department. He hung on and gradually built a highly respected school, but he and Lang failed to unite their talents for the collective good.

Yet the "gang" apparently did not reciprocate Lang's discomfort or distaste vis-à-vis its members. Miller himself prepared a gracious obituary for the *Journal of the Chemical Society*.[53] Also, F.B. Allan wrote to the president to complain about a slur on Lang in a gag issue of the *Varsity* in March 1925.[54]

Many people are unaware of Lang's lengthy headship. Recently a respected historian of science, writing about Soddy's abortive visit in

1900, wrote, "He even ventured to Toronto uninvited, but the appointment had been awarded ... [to] Miller even before he arrived."[55] Even some present members of the department think the same. Lang simply failed to gain a lasting place in the annals of Chemistry. He took too limited a view of his role as professor. He enjoyed teaching, talking, and writing about chemistry. Despite his ouster in 1920, he did continue to lecture — a task that he clearly enjoyed.

However, he seems never to have *done* much chemistry. And while he undertook and directed some research, the resulting publications are not memorable. His interests lay elsewhere, in his military activities and in the company that they brought him. This distraction denied him the scientific recognition that he might have liked, but it became his major contribution.

Part Two
Early Canadian Leaders
∞ (1920–1960)

Chapter Four

Builder and Skeptic: William Lash Miller (1920–1937)

William Lash Miller was a pioneer of the Chemistry Department at the University of Toronto. As this chapter shows, during his forty-seven years there, from 1890 to 1937 — twenty-five of them (1898–1900 and 1914–37) as de facto head — he helped to shape its growth, research activities, and international reputation. At the same time, his disbelief of atomic theory distorted chemical instruction at Toronto — and, through its influence on curriculum, Ontario's high schools — for half a century. This skepticism and isolation from the mainstream continued under Miller's successor, Frank B. Kenrick (1937–44). Also, some of Miller's own research was rather unusual for the times. His controversial personality perhaps hampered and complicated his meteoric rise in the department where he so long had such a powerful influence.

Miller: A Typical Canadian?

Miller was in some ways a typical Canadian of his time. His Ulster-born great-great-grandfather William Miller arrived in Canada as a loyalist and settled in Niagara in the early 1780s. Many of his descendents lived there too, but gradually the family dispersed throughout Ontario. Miller's grandfather, also William, was appointed to the bench in Galt (now part of Cambridge) about 1850, and numerous references to him appear in the local press. Miller's father, William Nicholas, became a lawyer, practising first in Galt and Brantford and then moving to Toronto, where he became a partner successively in two prestigious legal firms.

Miller himself entered the world in Galt in 1866. His family background suggests that his sharp, analytical mind and his dialectical approach to teaching and debate may have owed something to inheritance.

Furthermore, he used family connections during some of his quarrels with the government and the university authorities.

Miller matriculated into the University of Toronto in 1883, with honours in classics. Perhaps he intended to follow the family tradition and enter law. But after a mediocre first year, and even though he carried classics for yet another year, he switched to natural science and graduated in 1887 at the top of his class, earning a medal from the Department of Chemistry.

For the next three years Miller studied at several universities in Europe — a common phenomenon in those days. William Pike, for example, had studied in Vienna and Berlin, then spent a semester at Göttingen, where he earned his PhD. Miller spent about a year each with Hofmann at Berlin, Victor Meyer at Göttingen, and Claisen at München. While at München he submitted a doctoral thesis on certain derivatives of acetone oxalic esters ("Über einige Derivate des Acetonoxalesters," 1890). He next went for the summer of 1890 to Leipzig, where he fell under the spell of Wilhelm Ostwald. He joined the staff at Toronto later in 1890, but spent the summer of 1892 again with Ostwald, producing a second thesis and earning a second PhD in a different field of chemistry.

Ostwald introduced the young Canadian to the exciting domain of physical chemistry, which he, van't Hoff, and Arrhenius had just defined, and specifically to J. Willard Gibbs's thermodynamics — a new strategy for interpreting physical and chemical properties and processes. Gibbs was a reclusive professor of mathematical physics at Yale College. Between 1873 and 1883, his series of papers in the *Transactions of the Connecticut Academy of Arts and Sciences* laid the foundations of thermodynamics. Unfortunately, these abstruse, highly mathematical articles failed to reach most chemists, and so Ostwald and many of his pupils moulded their ideas into more practical terms.

Miller's research with Ostwald showed that the electromotive force of a cell incorporating a fusible metallic electrode (mercury, tin, or lead) was independent, at the metal's melting point, of whether the electrode was solid or liquid.[1] Since the chemical potentials, or "Gibbs free energies," of the two metallic phases are equal at the melting point, Miller's work revealed how the free energy determined the electrode potential.

By 1912, Perrin's study of the Brownian movement had convinced Ostwald of a particulate theory of matter. But his Toronto disciples —

Miller and his colleague and eventual successor, Frank Kenrick — never spoke of "atoms" and "molecules," and their department came to think the same way.

As this chapter reveals, Miller, though a highly effective researcher and teacher, often had troubled relations with people and groups at the University of Toronto, and his rejection of atomic theory kept his department (and Ontario schools) out of the chemistry mainstream for decades! The chapter's remaining four sections deal with Miller's almost half a century at Toronto — his towering reputation, which emerged very early; his decades of research in thermodynamics, electrochemistry, and "Bios"; his roles as long-time teacher and prickly administrator; and the influential yet isolated department that resulted from his leadership.

A Powerhouse

In the autumn of 1890, Miller returned to the University of Toronto, and by 1898 his brilliance as a chemist had made him the likely next head of Chemistry. He started in autumn 1890 as a departmental fellow, received a three-year term as demonstrator in 1891, and became lecturer in 1894 at term's end. The department in those days consisted of Miller, Pike as head, and one demonstrator.

At about this time the university removed its teaching of chemistry from the School of Practical Science Building to the new Chemistry Building (1895). Pike, with the university's agreement, had introduced fourth-year research in chemistry — at first, the "repetition of a selected research," and from 1892–93 on, "a selected research." Honours and specialized chemistry programs have continued the practice, and many other Canadian universities have followed suit. The resulting stimulation and excitement soon helped make Toronto a major centre of chemistry research.

We saw in Chapter 2 that Pike had in 1898 announced his intention to resign, having obtained the minister's approval of Miller as his interim successor. The minister selected Lang in 1900, and awkward consequences followed (see Chapter 3).

On June 5, 1900, Miller wrote to Professor B.J. Harrington at McGill University: "I have just heard today that the provincial government has appointed a Mr Lang of Glasgow Professor of Chemistry here in place of Dr Pike; they have offered to make me Associate Professor, but under the circumstances I would prefer to leave the University if there is an opening at McGill. Etc."[2] A reply has not surfaced. But Miller also knew well two professors at Cornell University[3] and by early July had received the offer of a position there. He rented a house in Ithaca, New York, in anticipation of a move, but decided to stay in Toronto.

Miller wrote frankly to the minister.[4] He pointed out that Lang was four years his junior and had very little chemical experience. He had remained as demonstrator only because of his affection for the university and his hope of replacing Pike. His two years as de facto director had satisfied the authorities, yet they failed to appoint him, so he concluded that his prospects at Toronto were hopeless. Yet he decided to stay and fight!

William Lash Miller.
Courtesy University of Toronto Archives.

The president and the minister appointed Miller associate professor of physical chemistry — one of six in the university, each running a sub-department, Physical Chemistry in Miller's case. The proposal offered Miller some autonomy and saving of face.

In 1914 Miller became the recognized senior professor in the department, after W.R. Lang took up military duties (Chapter 3). Miller — clearly the strongest of the department's three faculty members, who included Allan and Kenrick — took over its running. When Lang returned in 1919, the university created a Department of Military Studies for Lang, leaving Miller in charge of Chemistry.

Miller had long stirred up strong feelings within the university. Don LeRoy stated, "Apparently, the possibility of making Miller Head had come up on a number of occasions but, presumably because of the Miller–Lang controversy, Miller's case was not supported. Professor Beamish of the Chemistry Department told me [he heard that] Professor Burwash had threatened to take Victoria University out of federation if the University made 'that atheist' Head of the Department of Chemistry."[5]

Miller had early demonstrated his great abilities, and hence he was widely regarded as the department's heir apparent as early as 1898. For a Canadian, he developed an extraordinarily high profile in the United States, and at home he became very influential in emerging chemical organizations. At Leipzig, he had started a lifelong friendship with an American fellow student, Wilder Bancroft; the two men earned PhDs under Ostwald in the same year. Bancroft founded the *Journal of Physical Chemistry* in 1896 and remained its editor until 1932, when he gave it to the American Chemical Society (ACS). At the outset he asked Miller to head its staff of reviewers, placing him in a focal position among physical chemists, certainly in North America, if not more widely.

A few years later Miller received a lengthy letter "earnestly ask[ing] of you to consider the advisability of becoming a member of the American Chemical Society, in which event you will have our united nomination and support for sub-editor [of the society's journal] dealing with Physical Chemistry." Miller served as an associate editor of the *Journal of the American Chemical Society* from 1913 to 1924 but had already been active in ACS affairs. For instance, he was secretary of the local committee for its thirty-sixth meeting, held in Toronto in 1907. He served for three years as a councillor-at-large and in 1909 was a member of the executive committee of its Division of Physical and Inorganic Chemistry. In 1926 the ACS elected him an honorary member — the fiftieth person and the first Canadian so named.

From its inception in 1902 he was very active in the American Electrochemical Society (AES), and he served as its president in 1912. In 1929, when the AES was meeting in Toronto, it made him an honorary member. He became vice-president of the American Association for the

Advancement of Science in 1921 and chaired its Chemistry Section. He also served as vice-president of the British Association for the Advancement of Science and belonged to the Washington (D.C.) Academy of Science and the Franklin Institute. Yale University named him one of the world's seven greatest chemists and asked him to speak in April 1923 at the opening of its new Sterling Chemical Laboratory.

At the turn of the century Canada had no organization where scientists could meet for discussions, except for certain sections of the Royal Society of Canada (RSC). That body, then as now, elected its members, or fellows (FRSCs). It elected Miller in 1900, and in 1935 he served as president. Miller brilliantly outlined the history of chemistry in Canada for an RSC volume of 1939.[6]

When a Canadian Section of Britain's Society of Chemical Industry (SCI) formed late in 1901, Miller became a charter member, and he later served as chairman. Miller became prominent too in the later-emerging Canadian Institute of Chemistry (now the Canadian Society for Chemistry) — becoming its president — and the Canadian Chemical Association. In all three bodies, he struggled for development of local sections.

Research: Thermodynamics, Electrochemistry, and "Bios"

Miller wrote or co-authored nearly 150 research papers — a phenomenal number for the era. He also collaborated with colleagues such as F.B. Kenrick, and he attracted splendid graduate students early in his career — for example, A.R. Gordon. He frequently omitted his own name on papers describing students' work that he supervised. Yet according to Jack Mitchell, who left Toronto for MIT,[7] Miller's PhD candidates might work "miserably year after year, sometimes up to 6 or 7 years, before being granted their degrees, or giving up in despair.... Many of us, as undergraduates, suspected that Miller, Kenrick *et al* were using the students as laboratory technicians who simply provided the data for more publications."

As we saw above, at Leipzig in 1892 Miller demonstrated that melting the metal does not alter the electromotive force of a metal electrode. He later used this result, predictable from Gibbs's thermodynamics, as a tool in directing and interpreting research. He thereby explained an observation by a fourth-year student (F.B. Kenrick) — namely, that salt increased the partial pressure of alcohol in the vapour of aqueous alcohol. This led to one of his classic papers, "The Second Differential Coefficient of Gibbs, Function ζ" (1897).[8] He also taught from Gibbs's monograph on thermodynamics and once allegedly bought up the residual stock to ensure supply for his students. Another of Miller's early classic papers with Kenrick — "On the Identification of Basic Salts"[9] — again invoked Gibbs's writings on the phase rule. From about 1902 to 1912 Miller published a long series of papers on rates of reactions, especially of the self-induced, or autocatalytic, type. This research was original in experiment design and generated very useful results.

Miller also did research on electrochemistry early in the century, working on transport numbers, overvoltage, diffusion, and high-current arcs. One major paper — with Professor T.R. Roseburgh of Electrical Engineering — was "Mathematical Treatment of the Changes of Concentration at the Electrode, Brought About by Diffusion and Chemical Reaction."[10] From other work on induced reactions and overvoltage, these two men later published the first tables of certain functions of e^{-n} required for the analysis of transport phenomena — a massive undertaking for the times.

From 1905 until the late 1940s, a sub-department of Electrochemistry performed research, using space that W.H. Ellis ceded to Miller in the Mining Building's basement, across King's College Road from the (Old) Chemistry Building. Projects included concentration gradients, polarization, and studies of electrolysis and its products. Papers in the 1920s could be very practical: "The Characterization of Electric Furnace Arcs," "Electroplating Baths," and "Multiple Electrode Systems and Throw in Electroplating Baths." One of Miller's collaborators was A.H. Heatley, later adjunct professor of chemical engineering at the University of Waterloo. And the electrochemical laboratory, without Miller, pursued commercial possibilities, improving storage batteries and (so the story goes) producing highly durable glass for almost-unbreakable beer bottles. J.T. Burt-Gerrans (PhD, Toronto, 1924) had become lecturer in 1913 and was key in these studies. Countless students

J.T. Burt-Gerrans.
Courtesy University of Toronto Archives.

remembered his mnemonic: "The cathode's next the window and the anode's next the door."

Much of Miller and his students' pre-1914 research related to the effect of various substances on simple living organisms such as bacteria or yeast. This work originated in the study of the partial vapour pressure of aqueous alcohol when one added salt. Miller applied similar reasoning to account for a German observation — that the toxicity of an aqueous solution of phenol increased with added salt. When he and his students started investigating other cases of such toxicity, they used anthrax and staphylococcus bacteria as substrates, but after some near-accidents they switched to yeast. Because of his yeast's irregular growth and death, Miller sought a synthetic medium for its culture, in order to create a reproducible substrate. It appears that Miller suspended this research during the First World War, since he had no publications from 1915 until 1920 — perhaps he was too busy directing the Chemistry Department in Lang's absence.

Miller eventually recognized that the medium required nutrients besides sugar and inorganic salts, and for nearly twenty years he looked for these substances. The term "Bios" came from a Belgian named Wildier, and the Toronto researchers, including Miller's former students in the Connaught Laboratory, showed that Bios must consist of several substances working harmoniously together. They identified two — optically inactive inositol (i-Inositol) and hydroxyaminobutyric acid. They sought, but could not identify, at least two others.

In pursuit of Bios, Miller had assembled a large research group and obtained help from other colleagues. A tremendous amount of work generated a flood of papers. Today the endeavour seems a misdirection of Miller's talents. Possibly today's means of separation and identification might have led to success.

About 1900, Miller and Kenrick were busy designing and making bulky equipment for lecture demonstrations to large classes. The "Universal Measuring Machine," still in use in 1937, was essentially a huge Ampere-Voltage-Ohms meter that one could wire into the circuit of any process being demonstrated.

Kenrick, Miller, and the "Universal Measuring Machine."
Courtesy Department of Chemistry, University of Toronto.

Teacher and Troublemaker

What was Miller like as a teacher and educator? Inscribing a booklet for Miller from the graduating class of 1929, someone quoted Sir

Leslie Stephen: "The only way in which one human being can properly attempt to influence another is by encouraging him to think for himself, instead of endeavouring to instill ready-made opinions into his head." Miller taught chemistry students physical chemistry in each of the three upper years. He did not lecture to them; instead, he asked them probing questions, bullied them, and cajoled them into finding answers inductively. It was Socratic teaching, with the chain-smoking professor sprawled on his back on the lecture table or sitting in the front row with his feet up against the table. He would send students to the blackboard to work out this or that idea and cut them to ribbons if they talked nonsense. "In the cases of a great many people it activated brain cells which would otherwise have lain dormant, and those people remained grateful to Miller for having shown them how to think."

He taught directly from Gibbs, retaining Gibbs's Greek symbols. Only μ survives. Students agree that they never had a teacher quite like him but otherwise differ widely on the subject. Fourth-year lectures in physical chemistry — supposedly an hour long — began at nine o'clock in the morning. Miller's classes seldom ended before eleven, but no one left at ten! Miller had studied organic chemistry, and he long insisted on lecturing on it to medical students, but he never ran overtime.

Jack Mitchell recalled, "1937 was the year that Lash Miller retired, fifty years after his own graduation in Chemistry, at the same university. I well remember attending the last lecture he gave. It seemed to me that he would probably make some mention of this turning point in his career, a little personal comment, perhaps. But no, not he. The bell rang, he closed his notebook, lit another cigarette (from a 'Flat 50' tin of W.D. and H.O. Wills' 'Gold Flake') and backed out of the room." Mitchell continued, "Peter McBryde describes Miller as an inspiring yet terrifying teacher.[11] When he glared over his half-moon glasses at me on one occasion and asked me a question, I was so terror-stricken that I could not speak. He just snapped, 'Too much beer before breakfast!' and moved on to the next victim." The department's portrait of him "is a very good likeness. He had a certain haughtiness of expression, made more human by a tobacco-stained handlebar moustache. As students we were deeply respectful of him. We knew that he ... had put the electrochemical industry on its feet" and was "the foremost exponent of the thermodynamics of Willard Gibbs."[12]

Undergraduates "saw him only at his lectures. He never dropped in at our laboratory work and, to us, was a distant, though imposing, figure. Post-graduate students working under his supervision were, rightly, more privileged than we." "On one occasion he seriously told us that a good chemist should be able to carry out chemical experiments in the laboratory, wearing a white tie and tails, without spattering his clothes." Yet Miller did have a sense of humour, observing once at the end of a lecture, "There now, I have earned my salary and not one of you has understood a word I have said!" Dr. Louise Elder (PhD, Toronto) has written about life in the department in the Miller years.[13]

During his long academic career, a number of issues distracted Miller from his teaching and research. First, when he became associate professor of physical chemistry in 1900, he understood that he would receive $2,000 per year, which would rise to $2,500 by annual $100 increments. When he received the formal contract from the province, it gave his annual salary as $1,800 and made no mention of increases. Miller responded with a series of letters, some to the minister.[14]

Second, later the same year Miller had a major disagreement with W.R. Lang. Miller had worked for several years in a research laboratory in the (Old) Chemistry Building, but Lang was taking it over. Miller suggested that they share the space, but Lang said no. Again, letters followed, this time to President James Loudon. In December, Loudon imposed a sharing arrangement, which W.H. Ellis at SPS was to monitor. That was the end of the problem.[15]

Third, in 1910 Professor A.B. Macallum of Physiology proposed — in the Faculty of Arts council and later in the senate — that Toronto forbid original undergraduate research, which Pike had introduced and Miller strongly supported. Macallum's motions lost, but bad relations persisted for years between the two men.[16]

Fourth, in 1931, Miller proposed to the Faculty of Applied Science council that his department should teach all chemistry courses, even to students from Applied Science. After a bitter exchange of letters and extensive debates, Applied Science rejected the proposal, thinking teachers from Chemical Engineering more suitable.[17]

Fifth, throughout Miller's long career, bad relations subsisted between Chemistry and Physics. In 1900, Miller accused physicist J.C. McLennan of improper selection of a successful candidate for an 1851 Exhibition Scholarship.[18]

Another dispute relates to Miller and Kenrick. A distinguished visitor, Irving Langmuir (later a Nobel laureate), was lecturing to the Physics Department about thin films on the surface of water and the effect of electric charges on them. Afterwards, Miller allegedly congratulated Langmuir and claimed to have experimental verification for his theory. Kenrick wheeled in a large tank of water with beer bottles floating in it, bottoms up. He rubbed the straws of a common straw broom on Miller's hair and then, with the broom, touched each bottle, which instantly flipped over, bottom down.

Water in the bottles made their vertical flotation slightly unstable with tops down but quite stable with bottoms down. The broom-in-air rubbing mimicked McLennan's habit in lecture demonstrations of charging an ebony rod by rubbing it in his luxurious growth of hair when he was displaying the mutual repulsion of electrically charged pith balls.

This performance may have delighted the audience but did nothing to enhance interdepartmental relations. Another version of this story has Rutherford as the visitor.

Yet another (unconfirmed) story relates to chemist Howard Martin's late 1920s studies on the scattering of light in solutions. He wondered if a shift in wavelength occurred and asked McLennan to lend him a spectrometer. McLennan refused, unless Martin did the experiments in the Physics Department. Many people inferred that McLennan didn't think Martin competent to use the equipment. So C.V. Raman discovered the Raman effect[19] and won the Nobel Prize.

These disputes show Miller as aggressive and controversial, a tower of strength to Chemistry and the university, but irritating on occasion and unpopular with many powerful people.

Chemistry at Toronto: A World Apart?

Miller's idiosyncratic chemical views helped shaped the department and its outreach, especially in the 1920s and 1930s, when Miller's influence was at its peak. As we saw above, Miller had passed two summers with

Wilhelm Ostwald, as did Frank Kenrick, Miller's long-time associate. The two Torontonians had been his students when Ostwald was creating physical chemistry — a "science without substances." This exposure shaped their young minds and continued to influence their chemistry, and hence Toronto's, even Ontario's, long after Ostwald in 1912 publicly accepted atoms and molecules. (In view of his extensive interaction with American chemistry, including his work refereeing papers with the American Chemical Society, one can wonder whether his views had significant impact in the United States.)

Thus the Toronto version of chemistry was devoid of a particulate theory to explain or even coordinate information. It interpreted and explained all chemical events in terms of laboratory observations or measurements. McBryde[20] stated in its defence, "It did encourage a manner of clear, critical thinking on the part of students, a recognition of the limitations inherent in scientific explanation, and a questioning attitude concerning the integrity of scientific evidence. It discouraged among graduates of the department a reliance on 'hand-waving' arguments in support of this or that idea."

From 1932 on, all first-year students took a course — using Kenrick's text, *An Introduction to Chemistry* (1932) — that tried to make them forget their high school chemistry. First, the book redefines any common chemical terms operationally: for instance, a "solution" becomes "an intermediate member of a continuous series of non-mixtures." Second, although Mendeleev's Table coordinates descriptive chemistry and provides a basis for assigning reacting (not atomic) weights, the text does not explain the periodic law. Third, the book explains the electrical-conducting properties of certain solutions, and the constitution of compounds, in terms of "fictive constituents," such as hydrogenion (one word). Also, a species such as CuO was a possible "fictive" constituent of bluestone ($CuSO_4.5H_2O$), a favourite substance in Kenrick's lectures.

Beyond first year, all students took four full courses in physical chemistry, three in organic chemistry, and a half-course in electrochemistry. As we saw above, Miller taught in sequence three of the physical chemistry courses, on classical thermodynamics; the fourth dealt in the autumn with interpretation of phase-equilibrium diagrams and in the spring with classical work on colligative properties, membrane equilibria, and a bit on colloids. Note the absence of many topics in physical chemistry.

The three years of organic chemistry dealt with the taxonomy of organic compounds and reactions, including careful review of some classic structure proofs, such as Emil Fischer's on sugars and uric acid. There was nothing about recent work by people such as Robert Robinson and C.K. Ingold to rationalize the maze of facts in organic chemistry. The department offered no inorganic chemistry or lecture work in analytical chemistry, but focused on practical analytical work, often in the Mining Building.

Also, fourth-year chemistry candidates studied the history of chemistry and took a college elective, each one hour per week, and had the rest of the time for research. (In physics and chemistry [P and C], there were physics classes and laboratory work, with somewhat less time in the chemistry laboratory.)

The impact of Miller's conservatism spread. Toronto was and is in effect the provincial university. Until the early 1960s, while the province administered matriculation examinations centrally, Toronto's faculty influenced Ontario's high schools. The examiners were professors, and the university originally set curricula, later giving way to committees that regularly included professors.

As early as 1905 Miller published, in the university's name, the chemistry course for high schools, and he, Kenrick, and Allan edited a chemistry text for Ontario high schools. These publications denigrated the atomic theory and various other hypotheses and enunciated the editors' approach to chemistry. The authorized chemistry text in middle school in 1934 was by Toronto colleague W.H. Martin, and it too plays down atomic theory and all its implications. Miller's chemistry was a fine intellectual discipline, but for most people it was out of touch with the world around them. The Chemistry Department had been growing since Miller joined it in 1890, and it would continue to expand in the 1920s and 1930s under his distinctive leadership. In 1921, it had eight teaching members, all Toronto graduates — a major increase from the three in 1890.[21] It had three professors, William Lash Miller (physical chemistry), F.B. Allan (organic chemistry), and F.B. Kenrick (chemistry); an associate professor, J.B. Ferguson; and two assistant professors, L.J. Rogers (analytical chemistry) and J.T. Burt-Gerrans (electrochemistry). Two lecturers completed the

Chemistry staff, 1932, beside the Old Chemistry Building.
Front row (left to right): Miss H.J. Bell, Dr. J.T. Burt-Gerrans, Dr. F.B. Allan, Dr. W. Lash Miller, Dr. F.B. Kenrick, Professor J.B. Ferguson, Miss M.A. McQuhae.
Second row: M. Freed, Miss L. Farrell, Dr. A.R. Gordon, Professor W.S. Funnell, Dr. W.H. Martin, Professor L.J. Rogers, Dr. E.V. Eastcott, O.H. Howden.
Third row: J.V. Young, H.A. Showwalter, Miss M.L. Elder, Dr. F.R. Lorriman, Dr. H. Stantial, F.E. Beamish, Miss B.M. Shannon, H.R. Timpson, J.G. Duncan.
Fourth row: D.S. Calder, F. Bremner, T.J. Wright, L. Hynes, G.E. Moore, E.J. Repath, W.O. Reevcly, G.W. Alles, A.C. Medcalf, A.C. Morris, E.E. Wood, J.C. Morgan.
Courtesy University of Toronto Archives.

staff: W.S. Funnell and W.H. Martin. The fourteen half-time assistants were graduate students.

Until 1934, four men taught virtually all the honours students: Miller and Kenrick, elementary and physical chemistry; Allan, organic chemistry; and Burt-Gerrans, electrochemistry. Allan, the department's (and Miller's) first PhD graduate, had done his thesis in physical chemistry. He lectured and directed graduate students in organic chemistry until, after he became dean of arts in 1934, terminal illness struck in 1935, and he died in 1936. Every PhD thesis that he supervised dealt

Francis B. Allan.
Courtesy University of Toronto Archives.

with some variation of the Friedel–Crafts reaction. Burt-Gerrans, whose first degree was in pharmacy, did a PhD under Miller and then managed the electrochemical laboratories that Miller had set up in the Mining Building. It was, and long remained, a closed shop, following Miller's chemistry for more than forty years.

Nonetheless, it was a highly developed research school and produced many successful graduates, some of whom did very well in the United States. Robert Kennedy Duncan, for example, became a famous industrial consultant and writer, first at the University of Kansas and later as a charter member of the Mellon Institute. The department's students club for a time called itself by his name. James McBain, a close friend of Miller's in Toronto, had later studied with Ostwald and settled at the University of Bristol; Miller tried in 1920 to coax him back, but Bristol offered him Britain's second-ever professorship in physical chemistry. Later he settled at Stanford in California.

L.V. Redman was a staff member in Toronto briefly; he, virtually simultaneously with Baekeland, invented the thermosetting plastic Bakelite. The two inventors joined forces, and Redman rose to chair the Bakelite Corporation. W.C. Bray took his PhD with Miller and then worked with Amos Noyes at Massachusetts Institute of Technology. Noyes and Bray's renowned textbook displaced Fresenius's as the bible of qualitative analysis. Later Bray moved to California and became a long-time associate of Wendell Latimer's. Saul Dushman was for several years the department's demonstrator in electrochemistry; then he went to the General Electric Company in Schenectady, New York, where he rose to director of research. He wrote a famous text on quantum mechanics, despite Miller! R.A. Gortner was one of the American graduate students who came to Toronto because of Miller's high profile, and he later became a well-known biochemist.

Conclusion: A Free Spirit

To conclude this account of Miller and his career, it is fitting to add a few general comments. There is abundant evidence that "Miller was brilliant, high-spirited, gregarious, yet very much an individualist, full of self-confidence and with a propensity on occasion to try to impress others. His best years scientifically were undoubtedly those prior to the Great War." After that until his retirement, he became enmeshed in his research on Bios, a not very significant topic, and one perhaps beyond his experimental means. "He had his own [intense and inflexible] vision of how chemistry should be taught and who should teach it." This resulted in a unique school of chemistry. "The University of Toronto and the chemistry profession are unquestionably the richer for his life and achievements, even though when examined long after, some of his shortcomings become evident."

In 1937, fifty years after his first degree at Toronto, Miller retired as professor emeritus, having inexplicably declined an honorary degree from his university. He had become Commander of the British Empire. He died on September 1, 1940, just before his seventy-fourth birthday. Several extensive articles[22, 23] and obituaries[24, 25, 26, 27] give many further details of the life and achievements of this seminal figure in the history of the department and the university.

Finally, Miller's student, colleague, friend, and successor, Frank Kenrick, captures something of this wild, exotic character: "In his life outside the laboratory Miller applied much the same principles as in his chemical researches. He ran rifle associations, blasted rocks, built boathouses, organized societies, grew irises, and collected books with the same energy, with the same logic and clear thinking, and with the same kindness and generosity that he showed in the laboratory, and the fact that he never threw anything away, never tidied up his room, and never knew who anybody was, only endeared him all the more to his friends."[28]

Chapter Five

Frank B. Kenrick and War Research
(1937–1944)

Frank B. Kenrick was a long-time friend and colleague of William Lash Miller, whom he succeeded as department head. Kenrick, born in 1874 in England as one of five brothers, arrived in Canada at an early age, graduated from Toronto's Upper Canada College, and obtained a BA and in 1894 an MA from the University of Toronto. Like Miller, he studied in Germany under Ostwald at Leipzig, where he obtained a PhD in physical chemistry in 1896. On returning to Toronto he became demonstrator in chemistry. When he rose to lecturer in 1900, his annual salary became $1,000.

Frank B. Kenrick.
Courtesy University of Toronto Archives.

During the First World War, Kenrick helped organize the Officers' Training Corps and later, with the rank of major, trained Polish soldiers at Niagara-on-the-Lake, for which the government in Warsaw gratefully awarded him the White Eagle of Poland in 1918. Kenrick advanced through the academic ranks over the years, becoming professor of chemistry about 1930. On Miller's retirement in 1937, he replaced him as head of the department.

The first section of this chapter examines Kenrick as meticulous researcher and as teacher; the second, the department's war research, especially the influential role of Professor George F Wright. A brief conclusion looks back at Kenrick's career.

Kenrick: Researcher and Teacher

Though a devotee, like Miller, of Gibbs's thermodynamics, Kenrick does not appear to have taught the subject (A.R. Gordon took up this role after Miller retired). However, he did continue the department's emphasis on physical chemistry and its negative attitudes towards molecules and atoms. He was moderately active in research. There is a published account of some of Kenrick's important experiments on the potential break between gases and liquids, and liquids with liquids.[1] Also, his investigations of adsorption on powder surfaces[2] and on light scattering in liquids[3] were valuable contributions. Some of his other publications, such as "Are We Teaching the Right Chemistry?,"[4] "Sour Taste of Acids,"[5] and "Superheating of Liquids,"[6] deal with more practical problems. Ron Fawcett, a Toronto graduate, observed, "By today's standards, Frank Kenrick was certainly not a prolific publisher of scientific research, but what he did turned out to be as important, if not more important, than the work of his contemporaries in the department."[7]

Kenrick's PhD research at Leipzig included the first experiment to measure the work function of a single ion in an electrolyte solution. His much-cited article appeared in 1896 in *Zeitschrift für Physikalische Chemie*.[8] English and Australian chemists later repeated Kenrick's work, which is important in solution chemistry. Few researchers today realize that such a measurement is possible.

Kenrick's "unusual dexterity of apparatus manipulation" and glass-blowing became legendary. He also assisted Miller in running the department. Don LeRoy has reported that Kenrick used to do the typing for Miller; supposedly "the Department lost all its files on one occasion when Kenrick sent his suit to the cleaners"![9]

For many years Kenrick taught the first-year course in chemistry. According to one first-year student in the early 1940s, a lecture in honours chemistry went something like this: Men entered the steeply sloping large lecture hall of the Old Chemistry Building from the top back, having entered the structure through the front door (north side). Women used a door at the bottom of the room. (Students later left by the same route.) At 10:00 a.m. Fred Twigg, a Dickensian character, rushed in and washed the blackboard — so that it would be dry when the "master" entered at precisely 10:10 — cleaned the chalk trough, and placed new chalk in it. Someone locked the doors promptly at ten past the hour. Students sat in assigned, numbered seats; at the start of the lecture somebody checked and recorded empty seats — one way to ensure attendance!

Kenrick lectured from the most recent edition of his own *Introduction to Chemistry*[10] (1932). There was no real discussion of atoms or molecules (except in bulk) and these he, like Miller, described as "fictive constituents." Lectures dealt mainly with the use of precise definitions to describe chemical behaviour and descriptions of bulk properties of chemicals. Early each academic year, Kenrick started the experiment that demonstrated the diffusion of copper sulphate in water using a large graduated cylinder. Throughout the year the water gradually became more uniformly blue. This experiment led to Kenrick's nickname — "Bluestone Kenrick."

The rather boring lecture material was unexciting and discouraging to students after high school instruction that had dealt with atomic and molecular theory and chemical equations. First-year chemistry with Kenrick and the exciting lectures of John Satterly in physics, with his classic on liquid air, may well have diverted many candidates to the mathematics, physics, or life sciences programs.

In the mid-1940s, Lecturer Dr. Edna Eastcott supervised the first-year chemistry laboratory, in which students analyzed bluestone ($CuSO_4 \cdot 5H_2O$) in various ways. The manual for this course was Kenrick's. There was a very limited supply of glassware in lockers (which other groups used), so all glassware needed cleaning after each session.

Students had to replace any breakage from a storeroom in the care of a severe Mr. Fortescue, always in a black jacket, who took careful notes of material that he supplied. Each student received a yearly breakage bill and had to pay it to the financial officer in Simcoe Hall in order to write final exams. It became apparent years later that Fortescue occupied an apartment on the second floor and may have also served as night watchman.

George F Wright and War Research

In 1934, F.B. Allan, the senior organic chemist, became dean of Arts, limiting his undergraduate teaching. The next year he suffered a stroke, and he died early in 1936. Candidates to replace him in Chemistry included Alexander Todd from Cambridge, future Nobel laureate and British peer, who turned down the offer of an assistant professorship.

The position eventually went to George F Wright in 1937.[11] Wright, born in Council Bluffs, Iowa, in 1904, attended the U.S. Naval Academy and (according to his account) ran liquor by car into the U.S. Midwest for the Chicago mobs. He later entered Iowa State College of Agriculture and Mechanic Arts in Ames, where he obtained both a BA and, in 1933, a PhD in organic chemistry with work on furan directed by the internationally known organometallic chemist Henry Gilman. At the time there were serious controversies as to whether furan was an "aromatic" compound, an issue on which even Wright and Gilman did not agree.[12] Wright did post-doctoral studies at Harvard and then (as a U.S. National Research Fellow in Chemistry) at the Institut für Medizinische Chemie in Vienna, where he developed expertise in microanalysis.

George F Wright.
Courtesy Department of Chemistry, University of Toronto.

In 1935 he became a lecturer at McGill University, where he began research on lignin. In 1937 he joined the Toronto department, becoming the first appointee since Lang in 1900 not to have a Toronto degree. Wright proceeded rapidly through the ranks, becoming professor in 1941.

The outbreak of war in 1939 transformed research at Toronto, and many faculty members took on war-related problems. Wright joined Canadian efforts to develop the new explosive RDX. It was much superior, particularly in explosive power, thermal stability, and low toxicity, to the trinitrotoluene (TNT) that found extensive use in the Great War. However, the compound was sensitive to spontaneous explosion, because of traces of impurities and the form and size of the crystals produced. These issues needed immediate attention, since the military had to prepare and purify RDX by the ton quickly and efficiently.

Wright assembled an active research group, most of its members graduate students with military service delayed for this project, working in the basement of the Old Chemistry Building. Wright earned the wartime reputation of being a slave driver, and he himself worked until midnight most days, including Sundays and holidays. His PhD graduate Doug Downing recalls, "Wright's usual practice with a newcomer was to fire off a succession of questions which left the student totally confused in the morass of his answers, cowering under a string of uncomplimentary remarks, and sure only of the fact that he had a lot to learn. Fairly typically I progressed through confusion, discouragement, bone-weariness for months on end, rage, a surprising occasional discussion on the near-equal level, and finally something more than a sneaking admiration."[13] Downing's experience may not have been typical: "Not all his students touched every stage." He reports as well, "I know for a fact that there were students who worked in the lab until midnight every night for six months, without a single evening off."

Yet the professor showed signs of profound humanity: "Wright's insistence on the students' names appearing before his as authors of joint publications; his odd reluctance to make critical remarks about individuals in their absence — quite the opposite of the salty enthusiasm with which he assailed them to their faces; his habitual courtesy to non-professionals working in the department." Also, Wright seemed to respect individuals who stood up to him, while the more timid received more than their share of verbal abuse. Many students left without degrees and hating him, and the department developed a bad reputation countrywide for the way he treated graduate students. Other published descriptions reveal a variety of opinions.[14]

Several other Canadian universities did RDX research, particularly McGill, where J.H. Ross and his student R. Schiessler developed a new route to the explosive. Other individuals, including R.V.V. Nichols and Raymond Boyer, joined in later. In early 1941, Werner Bachmann at the University of Michigan at Ann Arbor developed an even better process, combining the earlier methods.

Eventually Wright personally solved some of the manufacturing problems and ended up heading Canada's RDX program, chairing the National Research Council's Committee on Explosives from 1941 to 1944. The project required delicate liaison and collaboration with the Americans and the British, and Wright created some friction, to the evident consternation of C.J. MacKenzie, then head of the Canadian war research effort. Physical chemist A.R. Gordon, a former student of Miller's and soon to be head of the department, also participated.[15]

Wright was running virtually a small explosives factory in the chemistry building. One day in 1944, Professor F.E.W. (Frank) Wetmore was lecturing on physical chemistry to second-year chemistry and physics and chemistry (P and C) students in the large lecture theatre of the Old Chemistry Building. His logic and clarity, coupled with his interest in students' problems, made him very popular. He had studied at the University of New Brunswick and done graduate work in Toronto, becoming A.R. Gordon's first PhD.

That day, the class heard running and some excitement in the corridor outside and then saw black smoke suddenly emerge from under the door at the front of the room. Wetmore immediately called for a rapid and orderly exit through the upper back doors. As students emerged, they observed a white-haired individual dashing by through the upper laboratory towards the south side of the building. They learned later that, in an abandoned elevator shaft adjacent to the lecture room, Wright had installed a machine that was milling RDX with other compounds to make a "plastic explosive." This mixture had evidently overheated and ignited. The building contained a large quantity of explosives, and the white-haired Wright had dashed to address the crisis. The department cancelled lectures for several days until it had cleaned up the soot throughout the building.

While ultimately the American synthetic route to RDX dominated manufacture, Wright and his students made valuable contributions, for which he received the rank of officer of the Order of the British Empire in 1943 and the United States Medal of Freedom in 1944. Wright reappears below in later chapters.

Other faculty members also took on war work, much of it secret. One example about which we know: Fred Beamish, a distinguished analytical chemist, was an expert on the separation and chemistry of the platinum group elements. He helped develop detectors for poison gases and an electrochemical device to detect submarines. Later he participated in the atomic Manhattan Project, the Montreal Project (Canada's work on the atomic bomb), and later the Chalk River nuclear project. Wright's students would sometimes kidnap a Beamish student from next door to test a possible new sternutator (another war project, seeking compounds that make people sneeze). Beamish lectured to the chemists on analytical methods.

In the early 1940s the campus was alive with uniforms. Some enlisted men lived in college residences while they took courses such as navigation in the university. Almost all the men on campus were in the Canadian Officers' Training Corps, the Royal Canadian Air Force Reserve, or the University Naval Training Division (UNTD). They paraded at least once a week on campus in uniform, as well as at their armories on Saturdays.

The UNTD, after "falling in" at 4:00 p.m. on the Front Campus for inspection and attendance rolls, marched to the Old Chemistry Building for lectures by experienced sailors, many unused to lecturing and uncomfortable dealing with noisy university students. Uniforms were not ideal clothing for a chemical laboratory, particularly one involving strong acids. While army and air force men could remove their jackets relatively easily and don protective lab coats, navy men had to tug the lab coats on over their tight-fitting jackets and collars. By the end of 1945, military service was over, and many returning servicemen entered the classroom, necessitating university expansion.

KENRICK: END OF A LONG CAREER

In 1944, Frank Kenrick reached seventy and retired. His fascinating "daybook" records his daily activities as head.[16] He had seen the department's faculty grow from three in 1900 to fourteen (including two cross-appointees). A former student, Laurence Cragg, wrote, "Neither he nor his book, *An Introduction to Chemistry*, was exciting, but both were thorough and thought-provoking. In my later career I taught first-year chemistry ... and was increasingly aware of how much we students had learned from him, not only about the fundamentals of chemistry but also about clarity and precision in thought, in speech, and in writing." But he had other facets: "He was a talented painter in oils; he was a lover of books and read widely; he was an experienced and resourceful naturalist and woodsman; he was a skilled and ingenious carpenter — the cottage he built on Georgian Bay was a marvelous creation — and like Water Rat (in *The Wind in the Willows*), he enjoyed 'messing about in boats' though with much greater competence."[17]

A.R. Gordon, in an obituary, wrote of Kenrick, "The kindliest of men, his shyness sometimes made him seem gruff and aloof to those who did not know him well, but he possessed to a marked degree the prime requisite for any research worker — a lively intellectual curiosity. His attitude toward science can perhaps best be expressed in his own words: 'There is no such thing as a wrong result. What you found was the correct answer for the experiment as you performed it. Ask what the chemicals are trying to tell you; the chemicals always talk sense even if the chemist does not.'"[18]

A.R. Gordon and Postwar Expansion (1944–1960)

When Frank Kenrick retired in 1944, Andrew (Andy) R. Gordon became head of the Chemistry Department, a position that he held until 1960. Following army service and a serious injury during the First World War, Gordon had obtained his BA at Toronto in 1922, and his PhD under William Lash Miller in 1925. He then joined the department as a lecturer and became assistant professor in 1928 and full professor in 1938. This chapter looks in turn at Gordon's career, including his years as head (1944–60); at the department in the mid-1940s; and at the postwar period, which saw construction of the Wallberg Memorial Building, rapid growth in faculty and graduate work, and Gordon's retirement as the last head in 1960.

Gordon: Teacher, Researcher, Administrator

While pursuing his theoretical research, Gordon gradually took over the teaching of classical thermodynamics from Miller. Retaining a Gibbsian approach, he stressed the practical evaluation and use of thermodynamic data. His lectures were masterpieces of clarity and logic. In the early 1940s he lectured on thermodynamics to the second- and third-year students in honours chemistry and honours physics and chemistry.

Gordon always looked dapper in his dark blue suit, sitting on the corner of the lecture bench of the small second-floor lecture room in the Old Chemistry Building, with a lit cigarette dangling from his fingers. He generally carried a "flat 50" of cigarettes into the lecture room (as had Miller) and an ashtray. He never appeared to use notes, never recommended a textbook (their non-Toronto sign conventions would have confused many students), and occasionally used Miller's technique of suddenly asking a student a question. Gordon's students, like Miller's, found such grilling quite terrifying. On occasion, feigning disgust at students' ignorance, Gordon would storm out in mid-lecture, leaving almost everyone apprehensive. Gordon was a blusterer: he used this technique to intimidate people — staff members and students alike — who generally preferred to avoid a confrontation. His colleague George Wright was also a blusterer, and it was never clear which one would win an argument.

Andrew R. Gordon.
Courtesy University of Toronto Archives.

Gordon's experimental work, which began under Miller, continued to involve problems in electrochemistry. However, Gordon was early to appreciate the chemical significance of the new quantum theory; he made himself conversant with it and pioneered the application of wave and statistical mechanics to chemical problems. He devised mathematical methods of dealing with the complex computations, albeit laboriously, on a desk calculator. Gordon had written such a paper with Miller in 1931 — "Numerical Evaluation of Infinite Series and Integrals Which Arise in Certain Problems of Linear Heat Flow, Electrochemical Diffusion Etc."[1]

In 1933 he published the first calculations of the thermodynamic properties of a triatomic molecule using spectroscopic data,[2] and during the period 1932–38 he published, often with Professor Colin Barnes of Physics, fifteen papers on quantum statistical mechanics that helped shape the field of statistical thermodynamics.

In the basement laboratories in the Mining Building, Gordon's students investigated the physical chemistry of solutions of electrolytes. They worked initially on aqueous solutions but about 1945 began studies in methanol or 50 percent water-methanol mixtures. Skeptical of applying dilute-solution theories to concentrated ones, Gordon saw the need for more precise evaluation of thermodynamic and transport properties. Nothing has ever superseded the accurate data from his laboratory on diffusion coefficients, electrical conductivities, electromotive forces, transference numbers, and vapour pressures.

Gordon usually assigned new fourth-year students to work with graduate students to acquire high-precision expertise. Though busy, he would drop in at least twice a week, usually around 2:00 p.m., after pacing audibly next door, which appeared to stimulate his best thinking. He let them follow their own ideas and would always fund equipment for them. Some found him intimidating but eventually relaxed. He prided himself on choosing "good students," and "once you had been selected, he gave you his full support." His fourteen PhD graduates included John Butler, John Davies, Robert Jervis, Harry Macleod, and Harold Schiff. Jervis became a professor in chemical engineering at Toronto, where he did work on nuclear and analytical chemistry (see Chapter 8 below).

Byron Lane, a former undergraduate student in biochemistry, unusually chose Gordon's thermodynamics course as a minor for his PhD. He did brilliantly in the course and later became a professor of biochemistry at Toronto. In his excellent memoir of Gordon,[3] Lane quotes Claude Bissell,[4] former president of the University of Toronto, on Gordon: "He was a short, slight man, whose rapid walk and energetic gestures seemed to be an overflow of intense intellectual energy. I [Bissell] am told by a favourite graduate student of Gordon's that his best ideas would emerge as he paced up and down interminably in his office." Bissell thought of him as "an explosive Tory in his attitude; respectful of top authority and intensely loyal to the person who embodied it; contemptuous of the encroaching liberal gospel with its emphasis on egalitarianism and democratic procedures; in essence, an elitist who valued intellectual distinction above all else. In defence of his ideas he was often, by academic measurement, violent and abusive; and his quick, intense, concentrated outbursts in the Senate were one of the more attractive features of that solemn body."

Gordon built an international reputation, and, when Kenrick retired in 1944, he became the first Canadian to be official head of the department.[5] He downplayed his research as simply making "fudge factors" for chemists. He always praised Gibbs and his chemical thermodynamics.

Gordon was an administrator in both the university and science. He sat on the executive of the National Research Council from 1945 to 1951. He became chairman of the Science Division of Toronto's Graduate School in 1947 and dean in 1953, succeeding the great historian Harold Innis. In a convocation address in 1959, he warned of the dangers that "contract research" held for curiosity-oriented "basic research." His concern is not less relevant today.

Yet he certainly valued applied research, advising the Chemical Warfare Branch of the Department of National Defence during the war and becoming an officer of the Order of the British Empire when peace came. Gordon sat on the Defence Research Board from 1951 to 1955 and on its Harkness Committee on biological warfare, which urged Canada to develop "the requisite knowledge to counteract the effects of biological warfare on the Armed Services and the civilian population" — still timely advice. On the board (1952–66) at Atomic Energy of Canada, Ltd., he helped make decisions to continue developing the heavy-water CANDU reactor and de-emphasize organic coolants such as terphenyl — "flame-throwers," he called them. Byron Lane concluded: "Vehement as his advocacy could be," Gordon displayed "a sober, cautious prudence and an ever-present wariness of possible private and/or U.S. manipulation of Canadian research development."

As for Gordon's administrative work, Lane observes that people called him "'brilliant', 'dynamic' and 'explosive'. These were all ingredients that helped to position the chemistry department in the vanguard of structural modernization at the U of T in the 1960s." Claude Bissell once said of him, "To the best of my knowledge, this is the only university with a built-in H-bomb."

Most people in the university understood and expected that university administrators would "fight for their people" — a far cry from the later emphasis on the "forging of consensus." Departmental correspondence reveals Gordon's constant loyalty to his staff — for example, his defence of George Wright, whom other faculties constantly criticized for making his exams too difficult for their students!

The Department in the Mid-1940s

What about professors, courses, and students as the war wound down and peacetime routines re-emerged? Five professors — Gordon, Kenrick, Lorriman, Wetmore, and Wright — taught most of the chemistry courses to students in chemistry and in P and C. In the Chemistry Department in the 1940s, the honours undergraduate programs included second-year thermodynamics from Gordon, and introductory organic chemistry, based on the common functional groups of organic chemistry, taught by Fred Lorriman to students in chemistry, P and C, and household economics in the large lecture room of the Old Chemistry Building. He had obtained his PhD at Toronto under F.B. Allan in 1924. He was an excellent lecturer, much liked by students. In his organic lectures he recommended several books — most unusual, as we saw above, for Toronto chemistry lecturers.

George Wright lectured in organic chemistry to third-year chemistry and P and C students and a few graduates taking his course as a PhD minor. He never recommended texts, and his unique course — containing parts from the current literature — would not have appeared in any single book. He was a stimulating, expressive speaker who kept his lecture notes in a lab book. He periodically gave problems — unconventional, challenging, and difficult — for students to hand in about a week later for term marks. Classes learned how to prepare (on paper) simple organic starting materials, and then complex, multi-carbon compounds starting only with elemental carbon and inorganic materials.

Gordon, in addition to the lectures in thermodynamics, also conducted an "arithmetic class" in a laboratory in the former McMaster Building on Saturday mornings, presenting data for attendees to plot in special ways by drawing graphs of various thermodynamic relationships. Don LeRoy, an undergraduate in the early 1930s,[6] recalled that Gordon offered the arithmetic classes "to counter-balance ... three years of classical thermodynamics à la Gibbs." "In these we learned more about partial differentiation than we did in our mathematics courses. We also learned some things about numerical methods," but these sessions in effect translated "Miller's terminology and method of calculation into the [dominant thermodynamic] language of Lewis and Randall."

LeRoy also noted "a distinct prejudice in the department against chemical kinetics," apart from "a lecture or two on 'rates of reaction' in second year from Kenrick. No mention was made of mechanisms, and it was simply a question of 'first order' and 'second order' arithmetic." This was at a time when "[E.W.R.] Steacie, at McGill, was acquiring an international reputation for kinetics and photochemistry." Things changed at Toronto only in the mid-1940s, when LeRoy himself gave the fourth-year physical chemistry lectures.

Third-year chemistry students also took a half-course in inorganic chemistry, and Frank Wetmore taught both them and P and C students a half-course in electrochemistry (which Burt-Gerrans had previously given) in the Mining Building. Wetmore later became associate dean of Arts and Science and still later principal of New College, which named a residence in his memory after his sudden death.

The first term of the third-year laboratory courses (with Wright) gave students their first exposure to experimental organic chemistry. Those in P and C had two lab periods per week, and chemists, more. Students in physiology and biochemistry (P and B) took their labs with the chemists. From 1910 to 1949, such sessions took place on the second floor of the McMaster Building.

Wright's manual was unique in its sophistication. Participants had to identify unknown substances, using qualitative elemental analysis, functional-group detection, and physical properties, and to prepare at least

The McMaster Building housed undergraduate organic laboratories.
Courtesy University of Toronto Archives.

two derivatives, while doing other experiments on a more rigid schedule. If students ran out of their small test-tube supply of the material and needed more, they lost marks. Synthetic experiments included the generation and separation of geometric isomers and the preparation of TNT.

George Wright roamed the laboratory almost every afternoon and sat down at the bench to grill students and to mark their notebooks. He got to know the students, but his marking could be an unnerving experience. If someone had a bad day, Wright became louder and louder, and everyone learned of his disapproval. Having a demonstrator mark one's book was much easier.

Storekeeper Bert Chadwick had his little empire on the third floor, where he also sold apples and the occasional chocolate bar.

In the second term, the laboratory, which took place several afternoons each week, switched to physical chemistry under Wetmore in the basement of the Mining Building and involved many electrochemistry experiments. One major experiment, which Kenrick probably originated many years earlier, involved glassblowing using soft glass (i.e., not Pyrex) to make bulbs, joints, ring seals, and a trap. Annealing the glassware properly was tricky, demanding, and time-consuming; the demonstrator would drop the glassware gently on the bench to test the student's annealing ability. If it broke, start again!

The Mining (and Chemistry) Building.
Courtesy University of Toronto Archives.

In fourth year, Wright presented further organic chemistry, and Don LeRoy, former student of Gordon's, taught kinetics and statistical mechanics. Also, Stanley Funnell presented a short course to chemists on the history of chemistry, in which the students gave brief talks on famous chemists or discoveries.

Most of the time in fourth year involved research with a professor and his group. Several students worked for Wright in a big laboratory (Room 2) in the basement of the Old Chemistry Building, which held five or six persons, mostly graduate students. A side room held the department's organic chemical stores and a machine for testing the shock sensitivity and power of Wright's explosives. Some students worked at the other side of the building. Beamish's students also worked in the Old Chemistry Building. Gordon and Wetmore carried out their research in the basement of the Mining Building. In the mid-1940s and later, Gordon's students purified methanol for conductivity studies by distilling it in a tall still in the abandoned elevator shaft of the Old Chemistry Building. Also, there was a relatively fireproof room for purifying solvents in twelve-litre amounts. Wright's students took turns preparing these solvents, which they needed for their organic research.

Professor Jim J. Rae also had his office in the basement: he gave organic lectures to students from faculties such as Dentistry and Nursing. Rae opposed fluoridation and was much quoted when Toronto was considering fluoridating its water supply in the 1960s.

Opposite Wright's lab, the chemical solutions room stored all the department's inorganic chemicals. Running it was Bill Banton, a friendly, portly fellow with a large moustache and a roll-your-own cigarette usually behind his ear or in the corner of his mouth. He spent much of his time in two-finger typing of student papers and theses (for a fee) on his ancient Royal typewriter, while his assistant, Ronald Porter, who started work at age seventeen in 1944, dealt with chemicals. Porter became a distinguished scoutmaster; he retired from the department in 1993 after forty-nine years of service!

The basement of the Old Chemistry Building had brick walls and a raw, uncovered, asphalt floor. Down each of the main corridors ran troughs, covered by long steel plates, to handle accidental floods. This was a favourable environment for students to engage in inter-lab water fights in the evenings to relieve tension. A favourite weapon was a three- to four-foot length of three-eighths-inch rubber tubing, with a knot at one end and a spring clamp at the other. Filled with water under pressure, the tubing swelled to one inch or more in diameter (if too much water was forced into the tube, it burst, soaking the user). Students draped these weapons round their necks and under their lab coats and, after sidling up to an unsuspecting person, released the spring clamp, which expelled a stream of water at the innocent victim, who usually responded similarly in the next few hours. All this water would drain into the troughs and disappear.

Gordon's group initiated new graduate students in an exploration of the underground tunnels that conveyed steam for heating university buildings. Journeys went as far as Whitney Hall and the Royal Ontario Museum!

Postwar Expansion: Wallberg and Growth

Shortly after Gordon became head of the department in 1944, the war ended, and the university made plans to accommodate the influx of returning servicemen. Gordon proposed a program for research in his crowded, widely dispersed department,[7] which occupied the Old Chemistry Building and parts of Mining and McMaster. Because of lack of space, and even though the department had awarded PhDs to numerous women (e.g., Clara Benson in 1903 and Louise Elder in 1937), Gordon ended that practice: "He was not prepared to give up space to a person who was not expected to make use of the training received after graduation." Don LeRoy's student Daphne Schiff (neé Line) had to leave the university with her MA but became a professor of natural sciences at Glendon College of York University and a famous flyer, conveying relief supplies into parts of Africa and piloting a light airplane around the world.

The university decided to construct a new building on the north side of College Street between King's College Road and St. George Street. The Wallberg Memorial Building (in honour of engineer Emil Wallberg, a major donor to the university) was to house Chemistry in the eastern half and Chemical Engineering in the western half. Gordon charged Don LeRoy, then a new assistant professor, to design the interior of Chemistry — offices, laboratories, and lecture rooms. Premier

George Drew laid the cornerstone in the spring of 1947, with academics and guests standing on the sidewalk and graduate students watching from the structure's unwalled skeleton. The new home opened in the spring of 1949 with lectures by Dr. Henry Gilman of Iowa State College (Wright's PhD supervisor) as the organic lecturer and Dr. Fred Dainton on physical chemistry, as well as Drs. G.G. Brown, Louis G. Longsworth, A.P. Sherwood, and T.K. Sherwood.

Partial occupancy began in the summer of 1949, and rising numbers of undergraduates, graduate students, and members of faculty soon filled the edifice. The undergraduate laboratories, the storerooms, and Fred Lorriman's office moved there from the McMaster Building. Eleanor Baker presided over the new, much larger library, now open to undergraduates. Each floor had glassware and equipment storerooms: Bert Chadwick ran the third floor (organic stores), George Austin the second, and Mr. Fortescue the first. Being under a partial vacuum, all

The storekeepers and Professor Beamish. Front row: Heriton Thom, R. Fortescue. Back row: George Austin, Herb Parish, Fred Twigg, Beamish, Ron Porter. Missing: Bert Chadwick.
Courtesy University of Toronto Archives.

the dust and dirt from College Street was sucked into the building, making it gritty most of the time.

Wright's large, main student laboratory on the third floor featured a room-length trough with a stainless-steel "rack" above, on which to run most reactions (there were no fume-extraction facilities above). The room had a wall of fume cupboards, with one dedicated to a cleaning bath — an enamelled dish-washing pan filled with a mixture of concentrated sulphuric and nitric acids, heated by a gas burner. It was essential to wear goggles and rubber gloves when immersing and removing glassware from the pan, and clothes frequently developed holes.

Growth continued apace. In 1948 and 1949, Chemistry appointed four new assistant and associate professors — three of them in 1948 — to deal with extra classes. Maurice Lister (PhD, Oxford) had worked at Chalk River during the war: he became the department's first inorganic chemist. W.A.E. (Peter) McBryde (PhD, Virginia), an MA from Fred Beamish's laboratory, joined the analytical staff. R.L. (Bob) McIntosh, a physical chemist from McGill, arrived as an associate professor. G.E. McCasland became assistant professor of organic chemistry in 1949.

The Wallberg Building. Chemistry occupied the near third.
Courtesy University of Toronto Archives.

By December 1949 the department had thirteen members:

- four full professors: F.E. Beamish, A.R. Gordon, L.J. Rogers, and G.F Wright;
- four associates: D.J. LeRoy, F.R. Lorriman, R.L. McIntosh, and F.E.W. Wetmore;
- four assistants: M.W. Lister, W.A.E. McBryde, G.E. McCasland, and J.J. Rae; and
- one lecturer: Edna V. Eastcott.

Fortunately the National Research Council of Canada (NRC), under E.W.R. Steacie, a distinguished physical chemist, was regularly funding faculty applicants to help support graduate students and pay for research supplies and equipment. Recognizing the economic value of active research, the government encouraged university research, in the mid-1950s even paying faculty for approved research projects during the summer (most chemists would have stayed anyway!). Universities now expected active research by all faculty members.

In the early 1950s the Chemistry Department began making almost annual junior appointments. Adrian Brook (PhD, Toronto, 1950) had studied under George Wright, taught at the University of Saskatchewan, and then been a post-doctoral fellow for two years; in 1953 he became a lecturer. He took over LeRoy's first-floor laboratory

Organic Laboratory in the Wallberg Building.
Courtesy University of Toronto Archives.

in the Old Chemistry Building, while George Wright, always looking for more space, moved into the second-floor library. In 1954 John Page (PhD, McMaster), an analytical chemist, joined as a lecturer, and in 1956 John Polanyi (PhD, Manchester) did likewise; he had worked in Ottawa at the NRC and then at Princeton. They both moved into the Wallberg.

Robin Thomson had been A.R. Gordon's secretary since the war years and remained on staff into the 1960s. She was a delight — a wise and helpful counsellor and advisor to many people — and she helped manage the still-spread-out department.

After a few years in the Old Chemistry Building, Brook graduated to the third floor of the Wallberg. Dick Hiatt, an organic chemist, occupied the adjacent office until he left for the new Brock University in St. Catharines, and down the corridor was Fred Lorriman, much visited by his undergraduate students in Pharmacy and Medicine — most of whom thought him their best teacher ever. Also in that area, renowned forensic chemist Jocelyn Rogers, who had earlier taught analytical chemistry to undergraduates, was often examining bits of deceased persons. Apparently he had no refrigerator, and in the hot summers he stored human remains on his window ledge. On at least one occasion the wind swept them off, and they landed beside A.R. Gordon's new car, causing a horrific odour!

The department had little social life in the early 1950s. Junior faculty members met socially from time to time, and a few senior members and their wives sometimes dined as a group. In 1953, just before Christmas, faculty and staff had their first party together in one of the Wallberg laboratories.

The Chemistry Club Banquet was a long-standing annual event. Following a dinner in, for example, a meeting room in the YMCA building on College Street near Yonge (in earlier years) or a banquet room in the King Edward Hotel (in the 1970s), students from second year up to and including graduates put on skits, usually takeoffs on their professors. George Wright and A.R. Gordon were particular favourites. Maurice Lister was the champion of the after-dinner speakers, giving one of the event's funniest talks ever.

Historical Distillates

As the faculty increased, so did graduate student numbers and research money. An NRC fellowship program took Canadian and overseas PhDs to the NRC's Ottawa laboratories as post-doctoral fellows, and many later taught at Toronto (including Harrison, McLean, Polanyi, and

Department of Chemistry Christmas Party, December 1953, Undergraduate Inorganic Laboratory, Wallberg Building. Personnel (clockwise from upper left): unknown post-doc (with A.R. Gordon), Alison Simpkins (post-doc with G.F Wright), George Austin (stores), Bob Simpkins (post-doc with G.F Wright), Reg Carter (machine shop), Herb Parrish (stores), Heriton Thom (stores), Professor James Rae, Ron Porter (stores), Bert Chadwick (stores), R.L. (Bob) McIntosh, Bill Banton (chemical stores), R. Fortescue (head of stores), unknown post-doc (with F.E. Beamish), Fred Beamish, G.E. McCasland, W.A.E. (Pete) McBryde, M.W. Lister, Eleanor Baker (librarian), A.G. Brook, F.E. Wetmore, Fred Twigg (caretaker), A.R. Gordon (head), Mrs. Robin Thomson (department secretary), G.F Wright.
Courtesy W.A.E. McBryde.

Bill Brown, George Wright, Don LeRoy, Andy Gordon, and a student in a skit.
Courtesy University of Toronto Archives.

Valleau) and elsewhere. Greater funding also supported numerous post-doctoral fellows within the department, which greatly enriched the academic environment. Support came mainly from the NRC, since Gordon did not approve of approaching industry for funds.

Toronto was redefining graduate studies in all disciplines. Requirements of research and two minor subjects (the chemistry minor involving an oral exam) gave way to an emphasis on the new graduate courses. Eventually the university required candidates to pass such courses to obtain an MSc or a PhD. Rapidly expanding knowledge — especially, for example, in the mechanistic and theoretical areas of chemistry — motivated this profound shift.

York University came into being in 1960 as part of the University of Toronto and started in a mansion on the Glendon campus in the city's northeast. Toronto's Chemistry Department gave York's first chemist, Bill Lundell, a room and made him feel comfortable. He moved later to the Glendon campus and eventually into York's new facilities in northwest Toronto.

About 1960 Dr. George Olah, director of research for the Dow Chemical Company, Canada, gave a series of splendid lectures at Toronto. He spoke on his research, which dealt with very strong "magic" acids; he postulated the formation of relatively stable carbonium ions — a remarkable proposal in those early days of mechanistic organic chemistry. Olah was in fact "preaching for a call" to the department, which it never issued. When he revisited Toronto after he had won the Nobel Prize in 1994, he commented on the department's oversight in the 1960s.

Gordon retired as head of Chemistry in 1960 but stayed on as dean of the Graduate School until 1964. He was the last "head" of the department; the university's new Haist Rules renamed the post "chairman" or "chair."

Part Three
LASH MILLER'S LEGACY
(1960–2005)

Chapter Seven

EXPANSION AND RETRENCHMENT
(1960–1974)

The Chemistry Department, as we saw previously, had six heads between 1843 and 1960: Part I covered the seventy-seven years (1843–1920) of gentleman British professors Croft, Pike, and Lang; Part II examined the forty years (1920–60) with the early Canadian builders, Miller, Kenrick, and Gordon. Part III surveys the department's history under the eight chairmen since 1960 — this chapter, Don LeRoy (1960–69) and Adrian Brook (1969–74); Chapter 8, Keith Yates (1974–85), Stuart Whittington (1985–88), and Michael Dignam (1988–93); and Chapter 11, Martin Moskovits (1993–99), David Farrar (1999–2003), and Scott Mabury (2003–present).

In 1963 the entire long-scattered department moved into the new Lash Miller Chemical Laboratories on St. George Street, at the southwest corner with Willcocks Street. Shortly later the new suburban campuses at Scarborough and Erindale came into being (see Chapter 9). The Lash Miller Building became a home for many increasingly sophisticated research tools and for the talented personnel who use and/or service them (Chapter 10). The recent transformation of the building, thanks to the generosity of one remarkable family, forms a major theme of Chapter 11.

Donald J. LeRoy.
Courtesy Department of Chemistry, University of Toronto.

This chapter's four sections examine Don LeRoy's early career; his 1960s role in the department's restructuring, expansion, and new home; the university's expansion and tumultuous academic change in that era and their impact on his department; and Adrian Brook's tenure in the very different and difficult early 1970s.

Don LeRoy, to 1960: Precision and Involvement

Long before becoming its first chairman in 1960, Don LeRoy had helped develop the Chemistry Department through the quality and imagination of his research and his planning and management work under A.R. Gordon, his predecessor.

Donald J. LeRoy was born in Detroit, Michigan, to Canadian parents, and the family later returned to Canada. A heart attack in his second year of high school cost him a year of education, and he spent months in bed. In his autobiography he observed, "It was this event that undoubtedly led me to become a chemist. To keep me occupied my mother used to go to the library to pick up various kinds of books to see if they would keep me interested. These included books on chemistry. I became so interested in the subject that I knew what I wanted to do from then on. It is interesting that when I went back to school after my year off my grades improved tremendously, because I had clear objectives in mind. I graduated from high school in 1931 and was valedictorian for that year."[1] However, heart problems became a lifelong concern.

At Toronto LeRoy received his BA in physics and chemistry in 1935, an MA in 1936, and a PhD in physical chemistry in 1939. In his doctoral research he worked with Gordon on use of the moving-boundary method to determine transference numbers, transforming method and accuracy. After graduation he studied adhesives for a year at the Ontario Research Foundation and then joined the NRC in Ottawa, where he worked until 1944 with E.W.R. Steacie, in part on chemical kinetics and photochemistry. Initially he was Steacie's only scientific colleague in the field: he showed that the triplet excited state was the active intermediate species involved in the mercury-sensitized photolysis of ethylene.

In 1944 he returned as an assistant professor to Toronto, where his research was to involve chemical reaction kinetics, electrochemistry, and photochemistry. "The nearly three dozen people who took their PhD under him constitute almost a who's who in Canadian chemistry. He was a Fellow of the Royal Society of Canada and received a Canadian Centennial Medal in 1967, the C.I.C. Medal of the Chemical Institute of Canada in 1970 and six honorary degrees."[2]

LeRoy soon took on a variety of responsibilities in the department. For example, in 1945 Gordon asked him to develop designs for the interior of the Chemistry part of the new Wallberg Building, including the laboratories, offices, and lecture rooms. He often had to reconcile and even reject the proposals of his academic superiors, which he did with considerable diplomacy and success. When Gordon joined the administration of the Graduate School in 1953, LeRoy became his lieutenant in Chemistry. Gordon had till then done little to expand the department, which in 1949 had thirteen faculty members.[3] LeRoy encouraged

Gas-phase kinetics apparatus, probably belonging to LeRoy's group, and Dean Gordon.
Courtesy University of Toronto Archives.

growth, leading to the hiring of three lecturers in the mid-1950s: A.G. Brook, J.A. Page, and J.C. Polanyi. During LeRoy's years as chairman (1960–69), faculty and staff numbers grew markedly.

As we saw above, heart problems were to bother LeRoy throughout his career. Bouts with angina pectoris, in 1955 and periodically over the next twenty years, reminded him not to stretch himself too hard. He learned how to relax, how to sleep properly, and how to avoid worry. He says, "as a result I learned to work more efficiently and so was able to take on even more responsibility" — including the department's top job for a decade.

The LeRoy Years (1960–69): Restructuring, Expansion, and a New Home

John C. Polanyi.
Courtesy J.C. Polyani.

In 1960 LeRoy became the department's first chairman. The university's new Haist Rules introduced the term and replaced unlimited terms of office with one of five years, renewable once. (The university waived the latter condition for LeRoy.) These short, fixed terms for chairmen tended to reduce long-range planning and continuity in the direction of departments.

LeRoy was a very approachable man with a vision of the future towards which he constantly worked. His low-key, relaxed demeanour allowed him to be the adviser and confidant of the faculty, eager to help in solving problems. He made a number of key appointments and laid the foundations for continued growth in numbers, breadth of coverage, and stature. He was very helpful in establishing new colleagues in their research.

Nobel laureate John Polanyi, one of LeRoy's most successful appointees (1956), recalled him as "hugely generous in fostering my early career. On my arrival he persuaded his MSc student Ken Cashion to do his PhD with me, rather than with him. Ken bravely did so ... he worked on infrared chemiluminescene.... He already knew, from his time with Don, how to operate the sole departmental infrared spectrometer.[4] It was Don LeRoy who encouraged us to annex it." And LeRoy continued his support: "It was Don, subsequently, who saw to it that we got a new $1,000 prism, more suited to our experiment, and it was he too who said to me (shyly): 'Your results are pretty nice, don't you think it would be a good idea to publish them soon?' I took the hint, and sent a letter to *J. Chem. Phys.* It acknowledged Don's encouragement." LeRoy later "wrote a carefully crafted letter to Dean Vincent Bladen (Arts and Science) suggesting that the university risk the substantial sum of $10,000 to buy me my own infrared spectrometer. 'I planted a seed,' Don told me, as he awaited a response from the Dean to that request. When the money was eventually promised, I offered to pay it back from future research grants. 'I wouldn't,' Don advised me. So I didn't."

Beginning about 1960, LeRoy and his wife, Lillice, assisted by their four sons, gave regular dinners in their home on Oriole Parkway for the whole faculty and their spouses. In the early years these sumptuous banquets would take place at their enormous dining room table. In later years the boys would set up numerous card tables for an expanding faculty. Faculty members got to know one another, increasing the sense of community.

J. Bryan Jones, who in 1963 became assistant professor in biological chemistry (Canada's first), recalls lively events: "Within the first term, my wife Diane and I had been invited to dinners/parties at many homes, involving faculty across all disciplines — organic, physical and inorganic. An early July party at George Wright's was the first and perhaps the most memorable, since it contrasted so dramatically with the formal staid gatherings at Oxford ... when we arrived, D.J. [LeRoy] was standing on his head at the wall to demonstrate that he had fully recovered from his recent heart attack. And his wife Lillice, when she saw us come in, hitched up her skirt to her waist and clambered over the back of a chesterfield to give us both a welcoming hug. [She] was smoking her pipe."

Soon after becoming chairman in 1960, LeRoy helped establish the mathematics and chemistry (M and C) course. Two students finishing the first year of the new mathematics, physics, and chemistry program (MPC) — a combination of M and P and chemistry from the honours science stream — had regretted that they could not continue in chemistry while taking advanced math. LeRoy realized that such a route could generate first-class theoretical chemists, one of his interests.

He contacted Dan Delury, chairman of Mathematics, and they devised a second-year M and C course. By this time, two other students had asked to join. Fortunately, all four graduated with first-class honours, and Delury and LeRoy decided to require first-class honours out of MPC for admission to the very challenging new course. They developed the third and then the fourth years; in the fourth, students could major in either mathematics or chemistry. LeRoy and Delury did not expect or indeed want many students in this course. An early graduate — Robert J. LeRoy, one of the chairman's sons — became a theoretical chemist, a professor at the University of Waterloo, and director of the Guelph–Waterloo Centre for Graduate Work in Chemistry.

The Chemistry Department set up a Graduate Studies Committee (GSC) to replace the university's School of Graduate Studies (SGS) as selector of candidates for graduate studies in chemistry. The GSC made recommendations to LeRoy, and thence to SGS. With its own secretary, Rollie Sharples, and later Madeline Corry, it also oversaw student programs, arranged for defence of theses, and so on. This arrangement helped the program operate smoothly and removed the selection process from the non-chemists in SGS. The department contemplated eventually having up to 250 graduate and post-doctoral students!

When LeRoy became chairman, Gordon advised him "to keep organic chemistry under control" — for twenty years "George Wright had run roughshod over the Department to the extent that he had acquired most of the available research space and gave all of the honour student lectures in organic chemistry." He could be difficult to work with and a hard taskmaster. As a result, "the department was no longer attracting competent graduate students in organic chemistry. In the autumn of 1959 the department admitted only one graduate student in organic chemistry, "and even that one should have been refused admission."[5] LeRoy prohibited Wright from directing any further graduate students. In later years Wright hired post-doctoral fellows and technicians to carry out his research in such diverse areas as carcinogens in tobacco smoke and precise dipole-moment measurements of organic compounds. He also founded a small company on King Street West, where he manufactured generic pharmaceuticals, one of the first such ventures in Canada.

Despite Gordon's advice, LeRoy began to look for a senior organic chemist. In 1960 he appointed Peter Yates from Harvard as full professor. He selected Stewart McLean, also an organic chemist (a post-doctoral fellow at the NRC) as assistant professor. LeRoy wrote, "Yates' appointment was very important, since thereafter there was no trouble attracting top-notch students and postdoctoral fellows in organic chemistry." He created a large and productive research group.

According to Stewart McLean, "Peter's research took advantage of the flood of new instruments and instrumental techniques that were

Peter Yates.
Courtesy of Department of Chemistry, University of Toronto.

being developed and made commercial in that era. Photochemistry and its application to organic chemistry was one of his central interests. Ultraviolet spectroscopy had been used for about 30 years by organic chemists as a tool to investigate structure, and infrared spectroscopy was also an established tool by 1960. Peter had become a master at both, and he contributed to further development in their use." He also mastered the new nuclear magnetic resonance (NMR) spectroscopy.

As well, "Peter was an enthusiastic supporter of the organic cumulative examinations for graduate students and of the Monday night organic chemistry seminars, where he could almost always be trusted to stimulate vigorous discussion of the material presented, usually by a graduate student. Following the seminar he then led a session devoted to solving problems.... Students (and sometimes professors) took pride and pleasure in being the first to be able to go to the board and show the solution to the current problem."

As for the departmental library: "From the beginning he took an active role in building up its holdings, and he said that he wanted to be able to find in the department library any journal that used any variant of 'chemistry' in its title. The literature was expanding exponentially.... Invariably he had to battle for funds and against the centralizing forces of the main library.... Peter Yates can still be thanked for setting up our Departmental Library [now known as the A.D. Allen Library] on a firm foundation." Yates was also an excellent lecturer and launched a colloquium series with a wide variety of distinguished speakers.

Stewart McLean comments on Don LeRoy's period as chairman: "LeRoy had grown up in the days when the department was run autocratically and was dominated by classical physical chemists. His style reflected his background but he had a vision of the department that made his approach smoother. He saw the department moving into a new era with strengths in all sub-disciplines of chemistry." He usually assessed people and projects accurately. His manner of decision-making was informal: "When he wanted to discuss or implement one of his ideas, he made minimal use of formal committees. He was a master at cornering the people he wanted to talk to, sometimes in the hall, sometimes at a social event, but rarely by a summons to his office. He knew whose opinions mattered for each of his proposals, and he did his homework, so when he announced a decision he was rarely challenged by his colleagues: he had a personality that generated loyalty and affection." In sum, "He was the chief architect of the department that burgeoned in the second half of the century, and his legacy is what we have today."

McLean concluded, "I see Don LeRoy and Peter Yates as key architects of the Department we now know. Don was responsible for the overall design, and Peter set his print on the organic chemistry component."

In the 1960s, under LeRoy, the department grew substantially. According to the university's *Arts and Science Calendar* for 1960–61, the department had six professors, four associate professors, six assistant professors, and one lecturer (a tenure-track position), for a total staff of seventeen. The calendar for 1969–70 shows twelve professors, thirteen associates, thirteen assistants, fifteen part-time lecturers (all with PhDs), two (non-tenure-track) lecturers who supervised laboratories, three instructors, and one laboratory supervisor/administrative assistant, for a total of fifty-nine. The non-academic staff, who helped run the department and the faculty's research, also expanded.

Beginning in 1958, just before he became chairman, LeRoy arranged the appointments of Michael Dignam (later chairman), A.D. (Bert) Allen (later dean), and Alex Harrison (later associate chairman). Harrison has suggested that LeRoy hired him to use the mass spectrometer that he had acquired for his own research and no longer needed.

Appointments blossomed in the 1960s under LeRoy:

- in 1961, Stephen Danyluk, Jacques Deckers, E.A. (Peter) Robinson, John Valleau, and Keith Yates;
- in 1962, Malcolm Bersohn, George Burns, John Dove, and James (Jim) Guillet;
- in 1963, J. Bryan Jones and George Schmid;
- in 1964, Imre Csizmadia, Chris Cook and Ron Harris (Scarborough) (both former PhD students with Bert Allen), and Stanley Nyburg;
- in 1965, Bill Reynolds, Ian Still (Erindale), and Alan Walker (Scarborough);
- in 1967, Otto Meresz and Jim Thompson; and
- in 1968, John Bunting, Tom Lynch (Scarborough), and John Powell.

Jacques Deckers (at front) and his molecular beam apparatus.
Courtesy University of Toronto Archives.

LeRoy recognized the potential importance of molecular beam experiments for studying reaction dynamics; hence the addition of Jacques Deckers, who had been studying flames with van Tiggelen at Louvain, Belgium, before working with John Fenn (Nobel laureate, 2002) at Yale on supersonic molecular beams. The department planned space in the new (Lash Miller) building for massive vacuum pumps to evacuate the large steel chamber for reactions. Sadly, few meaningful results emerged.

The appointment of Jim Guillet (BA, Toronto; PhD, Cambridge) — the department's first "industrialist" — in 1962 recognized the importance of polymer chemistry. His research led to a number of patents, including one covering photodegradable plastics (of great benefit to the environment). Similarly, biological chemist J. Bryan Jones (PhD, Oxford) was a splendid acquisition (1963) in an area of growing importance. He used naturally available enzymes to effect chemical transformations with high stereoselectivity, often having industrial applications.

Imre Csizmadia (PhD, British Columbia), a physical organic chemist (arrived 1964), used computer facilities extensively to calculate structures of a wide variety of molecules. Stanley Nyburg, also a 1964 addition, was an experienced crystallographer who used X-ray diffraction — a valuable tool for organic and inorganic chemists in particular — to determine the structures of molecules (see Chapter 10, below). Nyburg recalled his chance arrival: "In the spring of 1963, my wife and I visited friends in Toronto.... John Green (Professor in Politics and Economics) had to go to the U of T Library. He insisted on taking me by car to the campus and, in pouring rain, unceremoniously dumped me outside the Wallberg Building on College St., recommending I go 'and smell it.'" Nyburg happened to meet D.J. LeRoy's secretary, Myrna Gregson, who arranged to show him around. While he was having coffee, she returned and said "that Professor LeRoy would like to see me immediately. I knew there must be same mistake but of course I had to go along. LeRoy was welcoming and came to the point, 'Just read your book.[6] Are you looking for a job?' I ungraciously said I wasn't, but he invited me to spend a week at the U. of T. in May to give three (!) seminars. As a result of this I was offered the crystallography post which, because of Fulbright [Exchange Fellowship] rules, I could not take up until 1964."

In 1962 the department added Ann Odell, a recent graduate in physics and chemistry, as lecturer on a one-year contract to run some of the sizeable laboratories in first-year chemistry. First-year students in the new MPC program had lectures and weekly labs in chemistry. Frank Wetmore supervised both, and John Dove helped with the four laboratory sections and did some lecturing. Odell planned, wrote experiments, administered demonstrators, and worked with students. After Wetmore died suddenly in January 1963, Bert Allen replaced him, and it became clear how useful this new position was.

Odell left in 1964, and the department hired two women instructors for first-year labs. Mary Thompson Brereton, a P and C graduate, was working on her MSc in chemistry; Julie Gulens, a chemistry graduate, was finishing her master's thesis. Brereton had some 400 students in first-year MPC chemistry and honours science laboratories. Gulens handled laboratories for about 120 first-year students in pharmacy and pre-medicine. In 1966 both women became lecturers. Later Sally Lavery handled first-year general science laboratories, while Maurice Lister did the lecturing.

Pauline Plooard joined the department in 1967 and served over the years as part- or full-time lab instructor, lecturer, tutor, and senior tutor. She worked — with Professors Guillet, Harrison, Lister, Reynolds, and Thompson — in the service courses for pharmacy and pre-medicine, in chemistry for non-science students, and in non-specialist first-year chemistry.

When the department installed television, the lecturer or senior laboratory instructor prepared videotapes for the sessions. The senior tutor coordinated the activities of the tutors (mainly graduate students) and prepared material so that they could assist students in first-year chemistry. Under the "New Program" (1969), students joined tutorial sections and received one-on-one assistance in a study room.

Space for Chemistry had always been a problem, and the 1960s brought relief.[7,8] By the mid-1950s the Wallberg Building was clearly inadequate for further growth in Chemistry and Chemical Engineering. Already some Chemistry faculty members were occupying basement rooms on the Engineering side of the building, and many still had offices in the basement of the Mining Building.

LeRoy had expansion plans. The department set up a building committee late in the 1950s to prepare for the Lash Miller Chemical Laboratories to be built on the west side of St. George Street, on the "New Campus." Committee members were Adrian Brook (organic representative), Peter McBryde (inorganic), and Bob McIntosh (physical) as chairman. Tony Richards, a young architect (former Royal Navy) turned university administrator, assisted the trio — a very friendly and compatible group. Everyone smoked, except Peter McBryde; Michael Dignam, who joined later, found the smoke so bad that he gave up the habit! The Wednesday meetings ran from two o'clock until five or six or even seven, so members' wives soon learned to expect their husbands home late.

Ultimately the group presented Allward and Gouinlock Architects Inc. with detailed room plans. The architects then arranged these pieces to suit Chemistry's needs and the buildings'. Undergraduate laboratories were to be in one wing, the administration and research laboratories in another, and lecture rooms (most steeply sloped) in between the two, and near their juncture. This plan minimized student traffic through the research areas. The two orthogonal main corridors on the ground floor often served as covered walkways to avoid the outside elements.

No building in the university yet had air conditioning, and the board of governors regarded it as unnecessary and frivolous. However, LeRoy and the committee argued successfully that "temperature and humidity control" was necessary to protect some of the expensive instruments. Administrative offices and the library — near the research laboratories — benefited too. Years later, large summer courses necessitated air conditioning for the undergraduate laboratories.

The department wanted a good library, with a reading room and stacks. LeRoy discovered that William Lash Miller had donated many journals and books to the department and had so informed the university's chief librarian. Robert Blackburn, the current chief librarian, informed LeRoy that the new structure was to have only a reading room. (LeRoy found out later that some humanities departments had lost all right to decide on which books they needed for research, a task the university librarian had usurped![9])

LeRoy asked Peter Yates to itemize library holdings in the Chemistry Department at Harvard, which even Blackburn regarded highly. That facility had far more items than Chemistry had planned. LeRoy then

The Lash Miller Chemical Laboratories (1970s).
Courtesy University of Toronto Archives.

raised so much fuss that the president chaired a meeting where LeRoy put his case. Ultimately he obtained practically everything he wanted.

The laying of the cornerstone in October 1963 followed occupation of most of the building. In a small ceremony, gowned faculty members and administrators paraded down St. George Street to the new edifice. Five distinguished speakers gave the inaugural lectures: W.A. Noyes, Jr. (electrochemistry), R.G.W. Norrish (physical chemistry), H. Taube (inorganic chemistry), H.G. Thode (mass spectrometry), and R.B. Woodward (organic chemistry).

With the move, the department appointed a business manager to cope with the increasing responsibilities of non-academic staff, accounting for research grants, and countless other administrative issues. Faculty had traditionally had master keys to the storerooms so that they could sign out chemicals or glassware over the weekend. Some made the keys readily available at all times to their graduate students, who did not always sign out the materials. Business manager Jack Robertson decided to deny master keys to faculty, implying that he could not trust them. Shortly thereafter Kaj Bondrup-Nielsen, newly arrived from Denmark, replaced him. Nielsen retired many years later, giving way to David Priddle, then Adrienne de Francesco, and later others.

The Turbulent 1960s: New Campuses, "New Program"

The 1960s transformed the University of Toronto, bringing two new campuses and a revolutionary undergraduate New Program. Both developments had profound implications for the Chemistry Department under Don LeRoy. The early years of the decade saw rising demand for post-secondary education in Ontario. In response, the province's Conservative government created new universities (Brock, Lakehead, Laurentian, Trent, Waterloo, and York). The University of Toronto responded by creating two arts and science colleges, New and Innis, on the St. George campus. Also, in 1965 it opened Scarborough College in the eastern suburbs (now the University of Toronto at Scarborough, or UTSC) and, in 1967, Erindale College to the west (now the University of Toronto at Mississauga, or UTM). Each of these institutions required academic staff and wanted instant graduate programs, graduate students, and research equipment.

This rapid expansion necessitated more instructors and money for all departments, particularly for research — by then a crucial activity. Any increase in provincial funding now went to many more institutions. This situation seriously stretched the resources of the NRC and its successor, the Natural Science and Engineering Research Council of Canada (NSERC), the major supporters of scientific research at universities in Canada.

Universities also wanted more professors and graduate students to teach and conduct research, and science departments needed both graduate students and funding to succeed. Highly qualified personnel, particularly Canadians, were in short supply, and many foreign recruits were hired. At Toronto these newcomers not only taught but also had to be productive in research.

Scarborough and later Erindale were typical. First, they needed graduate students to act as demonstrators in undergraduate laboratories as well as to constitute research groups. But they had limited equipment and few senior professors. New graduate students tended to choose the better-equipped, more prestigious downtown campus.

Five years later the question of tenure emerged. The university and the Chemistry Department had decided on essentially identical graduate standards in all three locations — i.e., one graduate department of chemistry. Suburban instructors found it very difficult to obtain tenure, and several were turned down during the late 1960s and early 1970s, which hurt suburban morale.

Working or studying at Erindale or Scarborough usually involved extra travel. All graduate-level courses took place downtown, yet suburban graduate students taught or demonstrated at their home campuses. Some of the best suburbanite instructors obtained research space and offices in Lash Miller, to the detriment of their home bases.

A.D. (Bert) Allen.
Courtesy Scarborough College.

The 1960s and early 1970s brought student riots in the United States and later in Canada. Among demands at the University of Toronto were significant (even proportional) representation on the board of governors, the senate, and departmental committees (particularly for tenure and promotion). Many departments (including Chemistry) and a number of professors vigorously opposed these measures. This became a major issue in debates on the university's constitution both on campus (in the Committee on University Government, or CUG) and in the provincial legislature. Professors, students, and administrators spent thousands of hours in often very vigorous discussions.

During this tumultuous period, Albert (Bert) Allen became dean of Arts and Science (finally part of the faculty's title!). In that position, he led implementation of the New Program, which transformed undergraduate education at Toronto. After studying and teaching at University College, London, and working for Falconbridge Mines in Sudbury, he had joined Toronto's Chemistry Department in 1959. He and his student Caesar Senoff had just discovered that, in Nitrogen-Rutheniumpentammine complexes,[10] the nitrogen molecule was end-bonded to the ruthenium atom — a finding that many inorganic chemists and journal editors initially rejected. Senoff has reported the serendipitous circumstances under which he isolated the compound.[11]

Allen wrote to LeRoy requesting temporary relief from demonstrating tasks for Frank Bottomley, also in Allen's research group, so that he could work full time on the X-ray diffractometer to solve the crystal structure. LeRoy acquiesced, and the crystal structure emerged, confirming Allen and Senoff's interpretation. Their discovery became one of the "hundred milestones in Canadian chemistry" named at the Canadian Society for Chemistry meeting in 2000.

Ron Harris, one of Allen's PhD graduates and later a professor at Scarborough, wrote that Allen "was a quiet-spoken thoughtful man with a ready laugh, totally devoted to his family. Yet, in a time of clean-shaven men he sported a beard. This first appeared when he returned to the Department after a family camping holiday in the Maritimes. Bert had coffee with his students every afternoon but in the mornings he had coffee with the faculty. When Jim Rae came along to pick him up that first morning his first words on seeing Bert were, 'Jesus Christ!' 'That's a bit strong,' said Bert. 'No,' said Jim, 'That's who you look like.' So the beard stayed."[12]

Harris recalled, "It was difficult for Allen to set up his research work in the department. There was no equipment and certainly no chemicals. Don LeRoy's ambitions to build a widely representative department easily outstripped his ability to house them and his [Allen's] first laboratory was in the Old Chemistry Building.... Don had also hired Steve Danyluk as the first professor in the new science of Nuclear Magnetic Resonance. Because of the vibrations in the Wallberg Building, he could only run the machine late at night when the streetcars were not running on nearby College Street."

Allen "was passionately interested in the teaching of first-year chemistry. In collaboration with John Dove and latterly, I think, with George Burns he started a program of inviting all first year students in small groups to his home. Given the numbers involved it must have been a labour of love for his wife Lexa. His research group was involved as well if only to assure the somewhat nervous students that it was possible to survive first-year chemistry." When he became dean, "the faculty had someone who had the ability and beliefs to persuade all the various departments that fundamental changes in the undergraduate numbers and programs were essential to the future of the university."

As dean, Allen participated in many deliberations in the late 1960s concerning the university's future. Among other major proposals for change was one to alter the course structure in the Faculty of Arts and Science.[13] The faculty was to abandon its treasured honours undergraduate programs, which prescribed courses in each of four years. Pressure from undergraduates spurred the change, along with the views of some professors that general-course students were receiving a poor deal. The faculty surrendered the alleged elitism of the honours programs in favour of the New Program.

Starting in 1969–70, all courses were to be "equally demanding" and of equal credit value. Students required fifteen courses for a three-year degree and twenty for a four-year degree. They could concentrate in a subject or subjects — a specialist program — provided that they met certain prescribed standards. They could take courses in any year. As extreme examples, they could take fourth-year courses in first year — or first-year courses in fourth!

The designers forgot that maturity and the acquisition of basic information were necessary for upper-level courses. For example, allowing first-year students to take third- and fourth-year courses was a recipe for disaster for both the students and the quality of the courses, particularly in the humanities and some social sciences.

The science programs fared better, since the departments had recognized some of the potential problems and therefore demanded prerequisites for all advanced, specialist courses. For example, to enter a third-year specialist course in physical chemistry, candidates had to have an appropriate second-year course in physical chemistry, as well as prerequisites in mathematics and physics and possibly a co-requisite (taken simultaneously) of another third-year course in physical chemistry.

The faculty and departments spent an incredible amount of time devising new curricula, courses, and sequences for the new system and working out specialist programs that approximated the former honours programs.

Dean Allen agonized over barbed comments from some professors about his alleged destruction of the faculty, but he worked very hard to ease his colleagues though this turbulent period. He spent countless hours at meetings, both of small groups and with the faculty as a whole, persuading them.

The Chemistry Department tried out several "new" ideas. It decided to offer only one first-year chemistry course, which all students had to take, and to implement different levels of difficulty and specialization through weekly tutorials, where specialists would receive enriched coverage, and poorer students, help sessions. Some graduate students needed as tutors lacked the background, dedication, time, and/or English-language skills to prepare and present the different levels of tutorials; some of their supervisors weren't too enthusiastic, either. The better and more experienced graduate students became demonstrators (teaching assistants) for the advanced laboratory courses. In the light of the resulting problems, the department soon abandoned this approach.

It also planned to integrate the introductory organic and inorganic chemistry courses in second year into a full course taught by two faculty members, one from each discipline. This strategy worked well when two dedicated and enthusiastic professors taught a single section. Unfortunately, the large size of the introductory program in organic chemistry (with courses also available for other faculties such as Medicine and Pharmacy) would have necessitated too many sections and instructors. Some other faculties saw no need for inorganic chemistry for their students. After a few years the department abandoned the integrated course in favour of two separate half-courses for chemistry specialists and a full organic course for other students.

Opinions differ on the quality of the chemistry specialist programs. Adrian Brook believes that they generally retained appropriate standards for lecture material. However, reduced laboratory experimental time for students — the faculty's narrow definition of a course limited laboratory time — was a major problem. After all, chemistry is primarily an experimental subject!

Also, under the old honours program, if students did poorly in a couple of prescribed courses and failed the year, they had to repeat the entire year's program. Because of the severe penalty, examiners' meetings often passed a student despite a poor mark in a core area (for example, physical chemistry). This supposed kindness could result in a student's simply piling weakness on weakness. With the New Program, students repeated only failed courses, and, if they took the now more readily available summer courses, they could maintain normal progress towards a degree.

Adrian Brook and Tough Times (1969–74)

Shortly after returning from a sabbatical leave at Princeton University in 1967, Adrian Brook received an invitation from the University of Guelph to take over its Chemistry Department. When Don LeRoy heard of this offer, he asked Brook to become his associate chairman, which offer he accepted.

LeRoy asked him to take on undergraduate affairs, and they worked together on numerous tasks, such as the budget. Brook had barely started when LeRoy received an invitation in 1969 to become vice-president (scientific) at the National Research Council in Ottawa. This was a major honour, which LeRoy accepted, and he took a leave of absence from Toronto. Dean Allen appointed Brook acting chairman

— the first organic chemist to lead the department! Brook had to learn the ropes quickly, in contrast to LeRoy's years of experience as Gordon's alter ego. Mike Dignam, a physical chemist, served as associate chairman for undergraduate affairs for two years. After two years, Allen asked LeRoy whether he would return to Toronto, and, when he said no, Brook became chairman, in 1971. LeRoy maintained his research group in Toronto and returned periodically, mostly on weekends, right through 1974.

Many new PhDs had trouble finding work, and some, including chemists, allegedly drove taxis — much publicized by the media! Some people started to ask whether universities were producing too many PhDs — and even whether Canadian graduate schools were admitting too many foreign students of questionable ability. Chemistry departments were receiving many applications from India and the Far East, Hong Kong in particular, and applicants' quality was often difficult to assess. Graduate programs needed active research programs to survive, and some of Ontario's smaller chemistry departments consisted largely of foreign graduate students — the only available research personnel.

The provincial government established a program to assess all university departments — the Advisory Committee on Academic Planning. That body in 1971–73 examined Toronto's Chemistry Department, which spent incredible amounts of time compiling data — on faculty members, support staff, courses taught, employment success of recent graduates, budgets, and equipment. The department also had to describe its intentions, its strengths, and so on. Associate Chairman Alex Harrison, on a three-year appointment, greatly helped the chairman and staff prepare the required documentation.

Four professors assessed the department: chemists Raymond Lemieux of Alberta (chairman) and Americans Fred Basolo and W.A. Noyes, Jr., and physicist George M. Volkoff of the University of British Columbia. They gave Toronto an excellent report. They recommended that some chemistry departments, including Toronto's, could offer PhD programs in all areas; some, just in certain areas; and others, only MSc programs. These recommendations ultimately became practice.

For the first time in decades, the annual budget for Chemistry began to decrease. While the department could handle small reductions for a year or two by cutting fat, the problem became serious and chronic. The department had to let technical personnel go, impose charges against research grants for material and services, and ultimately require faculty members to pay part of the support stipend for graduate students.

Professors were becoming keen to know what was going on administratively. Monthly faculty meetings, to share information and debate changes, replaced annual or semi-annual gatherings. While attendance was good for a while, interest and concerns soon waned, and meetings became less frequent.

In the period 1969–74, some new appointments occurred, despite budget problems. On the St. George campus, the inorganic chemist Brice Bosnich (PhD, Australian National University) became associate professor; he had been at University College, London, and a disciple of Sir Ronald Nyholm's. Other additions included Ronald Kluger (bio-organic), Ray Kapral and Stuart Whittington (theoretical), Michael Menzinger (physical), and Jon Van Loon (analytical, cross-appointed from Geology). Helen Ohorodnyk and Jackie Yuen became lecturers in charge of undergraduate labs. The suburban cohorts gained personnel. Scarborough acquired Bob Caton (physical) and organic chemists Jerry Kresge, Bob McClelland, and Tom Tidwell. At Erindale, Anthony Poë (PhD, London), an inorganic kineticist who had taught at the Imperial College of Science and Technology, London, joined the department as a full professor (inorganic). Geoffrey Ozin, another inorganic chemist, who was to focus on nanomaterials (nanochemistry), started out at Erindale. Also new there were Mitchell Winnik (organic — polymers) and Martin Moskovits (physical — inorganic). They and Ozin later moved their research groups downtown.

The department also lost some members of faculty. In 1972, Chris Cook, an associate professor in inorganic chemistry, resigned to join Englehart Industries in the United States. Tragically, he soon learned that he had a brain tumour, which ended his scientific career.

A.R. Gordon, the last head of Chemistry, died in 1967. With the help of his widow and his estate, the department's A.R. Gordon Distinguished Lecture Series began in 1971–72. Each year it brought in a renowned chemist — alternating annually among physical, organic, and inorganic-analytical fields — for most of a week to meet informally with professors and students and to present three lectures, one somewhat general and two more specialized. The first three lecturers — Dudley R. Herschbach (physical chemist, Harvard), Ronald C.D. Breslow (organic, Columbia), and Harry B. Gray (inorganic, California)

— are representative of the high quality over the years. Other lecture series have followed: Apotex, Boehringer Ingelheim (Canada) Ltd., Merck Frosst, and the Peter Yates Memorial.

Departmental secretary Myrna Gregson had replaced Robin Thomson during LeRoy's time as chair. She knew all about the department and had significant authority. Shortly after LeRoy went to Ottawa Gregson regrettably chose to leave for the West Indies, where she did well in business. Bridget Haylock came next and was a great success; she left in 1973 to raise a family. Keith Yates's part-time secretary, Sue McClelland, replaced her. After many years of outstanding work, she became the department's senior development officer, retiring in 2005 after thirty-eight years of superlative service. Don LeRoy had also hired technician Frank Safian, who could very ably repair equipment, use machine tools, draw diagrams for journal articles, and draw and make slides for lectures.

Ron Harris has stated about Brook's tenure as chair, "Falling budgets, falling graduate numbers, unruly students, and unrelenting change in undergraduate programs — these are telling examples of how the chair of chemistry had changed."[14]

Chapter Eight

BROADENING THE BASE
(1974–1993)

This chapter considers twenty years of departmental diversification under three leaders — Keith Yates (1974–85), Stuart Whittington (1985–88), and Michael Dignam (1988–93). Three sections deal in turn with each chairman; the other three look at personnel more generally: emergent academic groupings, the crucial role of support personnel, and massive changes in the late 1980s as faculty appointees of the 1960s retired.

A House with Many Mansions

In the 1960s, as a harbinger of important changes, the Chemistry Department offered — in addition to weekly colloquia by outside experts — *divisional* seminars by graduate students, often in the evening. By the 1970s there were four strong divisions in the department — organic, physical, inorganic, and analytical chemistry.

The *organic* chemists, inspired by Peter Yates, were keen on these get-togethers. However, as participation increased, seminars that attracted synthetic and structural organic chemists became less appealing to physical organic chemists, who frequently did not attend, and vice versa. Slowly the organic chemists split into two groups — synthetic and structural, championed by Peter Yates, Adrian Brook, and Stewart McLean, and later by Rob Batey and Mark Lautens, and physical organic, including John Bunting, Jerry Kresge, Bob McClelland, Tom Tidwell, and Keith Yates, which focused on mechanisms and rates of reaction. Later, a third group specialized in biological phenomena and biologically active molecules and in their modes of reaction. Faculty members such as Bryan Jones and Ronald Kluger were departmental pioneers in this area, and Juta Reed and Andrew (Drew)

Woolley added to its strength. Not surprisingly, many professors were active in more than one group.

Physical chemistry — strong at Toronto since the days of William Lash Miller — spawned four groups. Experimental reaction dynamics absorbed many researchers, including George Burns, Jacques Deckers, John Dove, Michael Menzinger, Martin Moskovits, John Polanyi, and (until the late 1960s) Don LeRoy. Chemical physics theorists included Ray Kapral, John Valleau, Stuart Whittington, and later Paul Brumer and Simon Fraser. Specialists in spectroscopy — both instrumentation and its application to analytical problems — included Alex Harrison (mass spectrometry), Bill Reynolds and Peter Macdonald (NMR spectroscopy), and later Cynthia Goh (atomic force microscopy). Work in polymers and materials started with the arrival of Jim Guillet from the Tennessee Eastman Company; Ian Manners, Geoffrey Ozin, and Mitchell Winnik joined him, followed still later by Molly Shoichet. Research topics ranged from organic- and inorganic-based polymers to tissue engineering.

Inorganic chemistry, represented for years solely by Maurice Lister and later by Bert Allen and some short-lived appointments, including Ross O'Brien, grew stronger in the 1970s with the addition of Brice Bosnich, from University College, London, and later included Stanley Wreford (for a short time), David Farrar, Ian Manners, Robert Morris, Geoffrey Ozin, Tony Poë, and John Powell.

Analytical chemistry has attracted faculty members since the department's founding. Henry Croft (see Chapter 1) did extensive research in forensic chemistry, particularly on deaths from poisoning. His acolyte William Ellis (at SPS) continued that tradition. Ellis's student L. Jocelyn (Josh) Rogers became professor of analytical chemistry at Toronto and taught many undergraduates. Rogers did forensic work from 1911 on, particularly for the province, and was often an expert witness in court. He retired in 1954 but worked with the Ontario Centre for Forensic Science until he was eighty. Forensic chemistry continued with Robert (Bob) Jervis, a PhD graduate of A.R. Gordon's, who became a professor in Chemical Engineering at Toronto. He started applying nuclear analytical chemistry to criminal cases in 1955. Dr. S. Krishnan, also of Chemical Engineering, succeeded him.

Fred Beamish, a distinguished analytical chemist and a McMaster graduate, became professor of chemistry at Toronto in

1946 and specialized in the platinum group of elements. His colleagues Peter McBryde and later John Page eventually left (for Waterloo and Queen's, respectively). After Beamish's retirement, the department cross-appointed Jon Van Loon from Geology, and Alex Harrison also handled some undergraduate courses. More recently Michael Thompson (DSc, Wales) and later Ulli Krull (PhD, Toronto) energized the area with research on biosensors and molecular recognition. In addition, analytical applications have emerged from much of Alex Harrison's research using mass spectrometry, and from the research of Bill Reynolds and others in NMR spectroscopy.

∞ Keith Yates (Chairman, 1974–85) ∞

Born in England, Keith Yates attended public school there and on graduation worked as a laboratory technician and then served two years in the Royal Navy. He immigrated to Canada and worked five years for the Dominion Bridge Company in Vancouver as a template maker and layout man. He next obtained a BA at the University of British Columbia and a PhD there under Ross Stewart, a well-known physical organic chemist.

After two years of post-doctoral work at Oxford, Yates moved to Toronto. "One thing I will never forget was arriving in the department in 1961, then located in the Wallberg building, and being exiled to the depths of the Mining Building along with several other staff members, because of lack of laboratory space in the Wallberg. The other exiles were John Valleau (theoretical chemistry), Mike Dignam (surface chemistry), Remi Barradas and Frank Wetmore (electrochemistry),

Keith Yates.
Courtesy Department of Chemistry, University of Toronto.

and Steve Danyluk (NMR spectroscopy)." In hot summers, "we seemed to spend an inordinate amount of time in the Elm Grill on College Street trying to stay cool. When we moved to the 'new' [air-conditioned, Lash Miller] building in 1963, it seemed like paradise."

Sometime after the move, Yates reports, "I found a wooden box outside my office door, which was across the hall from the Cold Room. The box was labeled 'Danger — Explosives'. It did not take long to deduce that this box had some connection with George Wright, of RDX fame. I asked George Wright what on earth this box was doing outside my office. He pointed out that he had just put some valuable samples in the Cold Room, and didn't want to take a chance on them being destroyed." Even though junior faculty members "were not high on George's priority list, [I] felt compelled to ask him to move the box to his office that was at the far end of the sixth floor. Very obligingly he did so, and our budding friendship continued to bud."

Yates became professor in 1968 and served from 1967 to 1970 as assistant dean of graduate studies and from 1974 to 1985 as chairman of Chemistry — despite being neither a physical chemist nor a Toronto graduate!

The expansion and excitement of the 1960s and the challenges of the early 1970s had passed but left their mark. The university's new unicameral governing council contained government appointees, administrators, faculty members, undergraduate and graduate students, and representatives of non-academic staff. However, funding remained a very serious problem.

Yates clearly enjoyed his role during his first five years as chairman. He then took a year's sabbatical leave (1979–80) while Jim Thompson acted in his place. Yates's next term was more difficult and less rewarding. Funding problems were affecting the entire university and provoked a rash of planning exercises and reports. The Faculty of Arts and Science's "Planning Statement" of May 1982[1] dealt with many issues and noted a 10 percent loss in tenure/tenure-stream faculty positions on the St. George campus in the 1970s, despite significant growth in full- and part-time undergraduate enrolment. The university had suggested that Arts and Science quickly drop from 11,400 full-time students to 10,200; the faculty did not agree.

The worried chairmen of the science departments in the Faculty of Arts and Science prepared a white paper in 1983.[2] Topics included

"Budgets and Funding in the Pure Sciences compared with the Faculty of Applied Science and Engineering," "Equipment Funding in Comparison to Library Acquision Costs," "Impact of Inflation on Scientific Costs," and "Technical Staff versus Library Staff." Humanities departments' budgets were mostly used for salaries of tenured faculty members, and cuts there would reduce numbers. Science departments spent heavily on supplies, equipment, and technical staff — perhaps less hurtful targets. In reality, even limited cuts could cause great damage. With Yates's active encouragement, the paper requested formal consideration "of establishing *a separate Faculty of Science*" — which might receive more insightful budgeting and more money. In the end, nothing came of the proposal.

Other problems beset Yates. Physical chemistry was never terribly popular, being both difficult and at times abstract. A number of professors thought some upper-level material better suitable for graduate students. The chemistry specialist program required full courses in analytical, inorganic, organic, and physical chemistry in the third year, whereas specialists in biochemistry and chemistry (B and C) could replace physical chemistry with biochemistry. At the time there were very few specialists in chemistry and many students in B and C — some perhaps potential chemists. In fourth year, both groups had almost the same range of courses available, and many students were taking B and C perhaps to avoid physical chemistry. The Chemistry Department was probably losing would-be students — and the concomitant provincial per-capita grants.

How to address this problem? Ideas abounded. Perhaps the department should reschedule the material and make it more descriptive and less abstract. The Undergraduate Curriculum Committee involved itself, and Yates proposed having third-year chemistry specialists take only three third-year courses in chemistry and one in another science. This infuriated the physical chemists and Yates retracted the proposal, but bad feelings remained.

Why was course content so troubling? Physical chemists considered their material as essential as that in any other core area of chemistry. In addition, just as a university's provincial funding depended on its enrolment and types of program, a department's related to its numbers of students and their programs. If significant numbers switched from Chemistry to Biochemistry, the university might further reduce Chemistry's budget.

~ Department Backbone ~

The department's smooth and successful teaching over the years depended heavily on demonstrators, lecturers, and tutors, who helped organize and run laboratories, tutorials, and even lectures. Many assisted the course's professor in charge, and some, the associate chair for undergraduate affairs; a few headed a course. During Yates's decade as chairman, Mrs. Alma Sleep, a long-time instructor in the undergraduate laboratories, retired. She had obtained an MA at Toronto in organic chemistry in 1930 following BA and MA degrees from Acadia University. She continued as an assistant and then demonstrator in the early 1930s until she lost her job because she married! This was the Depression, and the federal government had ruled wives out of the workplace. Sleep's husband had no work, and they lived very frugally for years.[3]

In 1951 Fred Lorriman persuaded the department to rehire her on annual eight-month contracts. Her salary started lower than in the 1930s, and she received no benefits. The department head allegedly told her that a woman would join the permanent staff only over his dead body! She served as instructor until 1978, patiently helping multitudes of second-year students through their organic laboratories.

In the 1960s, in the new Lash Miller Building and under Don LeRoy, permanent staff positions grew in numbers and status. Appointees might deal with hundreds of students in a single course, supervising teaching assistants (demonstrators), setting and marking laboratory tests, and introducing new experiments. TV presentations relating to the day's laboratory experiment(s) became standard in undergraduate laboratories, and preparing quality TV tapes — usually a task for the permanent laboratory supervisor — took a great deal of time. Chapter 7 mentioned earlier personnel. Later individuals such as Colleen Dean, Cecilia Kutas, Betty Leventhal, Myrtel Morgan, Helen Ohorodnyk, and Jackie Yuen spent many hours creating and improving these tapes, writing or rewriting lab manuals, and faithfully helping students in first- and second-year chemistry laboratories for many years.

Lecturers such as Drs. Robin Cox, Doug McIntosh, Stan Skonieczny, and Ates Tanin taught first- and second-year students, sometimes one section of a large course. They soon became senior lecturers.

Of late, post-doctoral fellows have often been lecturers to introductory courses for students in other faculties, such as Nursing and Dentistry.

This arrangement has given them valuable experience and eased pressure on senior colleagues. The department (like most others) has now established a computing laboratory where students can use computers to access teaching programs, course notes, and other general aids.

Stuart Whittington (Chairman, 1985–88): Problems and Prestige

The successor to Keith Yates was Stuart Whittington. During his PhD studies at Cambridge he had worked briefly in 1966 in Toronto with John Valleau, Toronto's senior theoretical chemist. Valleau, Jim Guillet, and Imre Csizmadia asked Don LeRoy to invite Whittington to Toronto, to join the theorists including Malcolm Bersohn (who then also had many other interests). Whittington said a reluctant no in 1969 — he had an unfinished PhD and family concerns. When Acting Chairman Brook approached him the next year, he accepted.

One of Whittington's interests was polymers — computer modelling and analytic studies. He focused on the unusual behaviour of polysaccharides, particularly seaweed alginates. He looked also at percolation theory and at polymer adsorption, where he published an influential paper with John Hammersley of Oxford.[4] More recently he has examined the statistical mechanics of random copolymers, especially the localization transition at the interface between two liquids.

Stuart Whittington.
Courtesy Department of Chemistry, University of Toronto.

When he became chairman in 1985, Whittington inherited problems from Yates. The second year of the chemistry specialist program required a full course in each of physical and organic chemistry, but only a half-course in inorganic chemistry. The inorganic chemists, led by Brice Bosnich, argued that by second year most students were choosing their probable area of specialization. They believed that reduced hours of faculty–student contact led to less interest in their field and demanded that the playing field be levelled, with inorganic chemistry becoming a full course in second year. The department ultimately agreed, also adding a half-course in analytical chemistry.

Whittington faced demand, particularly from some physical chemists, for more democratic faculty meetings. Some faculty members wanted votes on every major departmental decision, which Whittington rejected.

There were compensating events, however — and one still keeps paying dividends! For most department members Wednesday, October 15, 1985, started out as a normal morning. Not so for John Polanyi, who received a telephone call from Stockholm informing him that he was co-winner of the 1986 Nobel Prize in Chemistry. The committee cited him, Dudley R. Herschbach of Harvard, and Yuan T. Lee of the University of California at Berkeley "for their contributions concerning the dynamics of chemical elementary reactions." The media had arrived and were besieging Polanyi's home, seeking comments and interviews. Eventually the laureate managed to reach his university office, where countless colleagues and students offered their congratulations. The excitement lasted throughout the day, finishing with a large dinner celebration at the president's house in the evening. On December 10 in Stockholm, King

John Polanyi and King Carl XVI Gustaf of Sweden.

Courtesy J.C. Polyani.

Carl XVI Gustaf presented Polanyi with his medal and cheque and Polanyi delivered his Nobel lecture, which soon appeared in print.[5,6]

Other Toronto researchers had won the Nobel earlier. In 1923 the prize in physiology and medicine went to Frederick Banting and J.J.R. Macleod for the discovery of insulin. Charles Best had just graduated BA at Toronto in biochemistry in 1921 when he joined Banting for research work that led to the discovery. Banting nearly rejected the Nobel because it omitted Best as a co-winner, and he promised his young colleague half of the award money. Over the years, the award brought prestige, research funding, and research institutes to the university.

Worldwide recognition for Polanyi transformed the department's prospects. The laureate became the first holder of the new John C. Polanyi Chair in Chemical Physics (see Chapter 11). The province of Ontario funded five annual John C. Polanyi prizes, worth $15,000 each, in Sweden's five Nobel Prize fields — chemistry, economic science, literature, physics, and physiology or medicine. The Canadian Society for Chemistry set up the John C. Polanyi Lecture Award, sponsored by the Xerox Research Centre of Canada. Also, the periodic John C. Polanyi Nobel Laureate Lecture Series, in Convocation Hall, allows prize winners to present popular lectures on their specialty to students and the public.

Polanyi's signal honour demonstrated to the university administration the Chemistry Department's extraordinary quality, and more funding followed for new appointments, research equipment, and enhancement of the building. It attracted students, both graduate and undergraduate, and new members of faculty. It probably encouraged alumni and others to be generous to the university (see, for instance, Chapter 11 below). It also was very satisfying for the department, justifying its confidence in and immense support of Polanyi's research over many years.

Michael Dignam (Chairman, 1988–94): Passionate Intensity

Michael Dignam succeeded Whittington as chairman. A Canadian, he had taken both his BA and his PhD (1956) at Toronto under Don LeRoy. He worked for the Aluminum Company of Canada but then returned to the university's Chemistry Department and initiated research on surface effects on metal, using a variety of techniques, some quite original. He was associate chairman from 1969 to 1970 and chairman from 1988 to 1993.

Dignam had a very lively mind, pacing as he spoke or lectured, tossing out ideas. He was an innovator, designing and building novel pieces of equipment to observe and measure details of the surfaces he was studying. With his sons' help, he had built a cottage on an island in Georgian Bay. Later he renovated an old farmhouse near Erin, northwest of Toronto, even adding an indoor pool. For a while he and his wife, Nancy, bred and sold sheep, as well as golden retriever puppies. While he was chairman (1988–93), they would gather faculty members and their families at their farm and hold dinners in their apartment just north of Bloor Street on Huron.

In summers, Dignam would stay in town during the week while his family was up north. Former student Bob Stobie recalls, "I lived at Bloor and St. George streets at the time, close enough to come back after supper, and one night he [Dignam] stayed and talked with Bhim Rao (a post-doctoral student with Dignam) and me until 12:40 a.m. We were curious to see how long he would keep going and deliberately didn't mention how late it was getting." When Nancy was in town, she and her husband would frequently socialize with the students.

Michael J. Dignam.
Courtesy Department of Chemistry, University of Toronto.

Bob Stobie was in fourth-year honours physics and chemistry when he took Dignam's course in physical chemistry, a field called by one professor "everything that is interesting." "I started with MJ's [Dignam's] group in September 1968. My reason for choosing him was that everyone else in the physchem section seemed to be doing some form of gas phase kinetics, and I felt that field was getting over-crowded. MJ was into electro- and surface chemistry, and I thought that might have wider applicability in the 'real' world." Stobie and several classmates chose physical chemistry for graduate school.

Stobie recalled that graduate student Martin Moskovits "studied with Dignam how the optical properties of evaporated silver films were changed by adsorption of various gases.... He and MJ used these results to develop theories of the effect of surface roughness on the spectroscopy of adsorbed species. Every once in a while Martin and MJ would have what is commonly termed in diplomatic circles as a 'frank discussion'. The rest of us would keep our heads down and out of sight." Yet the two men were close friends and would sometimes play recorder duets for the students.

After Dignam stepped down in 1993, he planned to return to research and teaching. He and his wife flew to a conference in Australia to present a paper on his recent research. Sadly he dropped dead of a heart attack shortly after the plane landed in Sydney.

Changing the Guard

The end of the 1980s saw something new for Chemistry — many of its faculty members reached mandatory retirement age (sixty-five) at about the same time, and it had to hire new personnel almost every year. This situation affected every division in the Chemistry Department, and the many appointments reflected the university's high regard for it.

Now a complex search procedure involved advertising each vacancy in several appropriate journals and giving initial preference to Canadian applicants. Invitees would visit the campus for a couple of days for interviews with many potential colleagues in the same area and with the administration. They would present a seminar on their previous research and attend a departmental meeting, which discussed their proposed research projects. Some had also to lecture to undergraduates on an announced topic. This process certainly revealed a lot about applicants — and many current personnel wondered how they would have fared!

Adrian Brook, in organic chemistry, was one of the first retirees, and the department sought a first-rate replacement. It selected Mark Lautens, an organic chemist who had obtained his BSc at Guelph, his PhD at Wisconsin, and done post-doctoral work at Harvard under David Evans. He arrived in July 1987 and was soon lecturing and doing research, particularly in metal-catalyzed reactions leading in many cases to cyclic products, some of which might prove biologically active.

The next three years saw three other organic chemists retire: Peter Yates (1990), Keith Yates (no relation), and Jerry Kresge (1992). George Schmid (1994), Bryan Jones and Stewart McLean (1997), and Imre Csizmadia (1998) followed. Thus in ten years virtually all the organic chemists (except Bob McClelland, Ian Still, and Tom Tidwell) — most on staff since the LeRoy years in the 1960s — left.

New organic chemists included Drew Woolley (PhD, Toronto) in 1983, Rob Batey (PhD, London) in 1984, Rick Friesen (PhD, British Columbia) in 1990 (he soon moved to the pharmaceutical industry), and Andrei Yudin (PhD, Southern California) in 1998. Appointees Andrew McMillan and Scott Taylor, Toronto PhDs, soon went to other universities.

In earlier times the organic group had concentrated on synthetic or physical organic areas, but it now shifted towards bio-organic chemistry, initiated by Bryan Jones and Ron Kluger, then Juta Reed, and later Drew Woolley. Molly Shoichet (PhD, Massachusetts) joined in 1995, cross-appointed from Chemical Engineering; Jik Chin (PhD, Toronto), from McGill, and Deborah Zamble (PhD, MIT) in 2000 also enhanced the bio-organic group.

Similar major changes affected the inorganic, physical, theoretical, and analytical sub-disciplines. In inorganic, Maurice Lister retired in 1982 (he died in 2004), and Brice Bosnich moved to the University of Chicago in 1987. In the late 1980s, the faculty stalwarts, on all three campuses, were Dave Farrar, Bob Morris, John Powell, Tony Poë, Peter Robinson, Jim Thompson, and Alan Walker. Poë retired in 1994, Robinson and Walker in 1998, and Thompson in 2003. Ian Manners (PhD, Bristol) joined in 1990. Michael Denk (PhD, Munich), appointed in 1995, left in 2001.

The physical chemists covered many areas, including polymer chemistry and mass and NMR spectroscopy, and were either experimentalists or theoreticians. By the 1990s Don LeRoy's appointees were retiring: George Burns, Jacques Deckers, Jim Guillet, Alex Harrison, John Polanyi (who moved to the Polanyi Chair), and Bill Reynolds. Michael Dignam had died in Australia, and a car accident in South Africa killed John Dove and his wife. Also, Geraldine Kenney-Wallace and Stephen Wallace, who had joined in 1978, left in

1987 and 2002, respectively.

There were seven new physical appointments: Jamie Donaldson (PhD, Carleton) in 1988, Peter Macdonald (PhD, Alberta) and Cynthia Goh (PhD, UCLA) in 1990, Dwayne Miller (PhD, Stanford) in 1995, Eugenia Kumacheva (PhD, Moscow) in 1996, Jon Abbatt (PhD, Harvard) in 1999, and Michael Georges (PhD, Waterloo) in 2001. Cynthia Goh used atomic force microscopy (AFM) to analyze biological filaments such as collagen and paired helical filaments — features of Alzheimer's disease. She served terms as associate chair for graduate affairs and later undergraduate affairs.

The theoreticians (Chemical Physics Theory Group) lost John Valleau to retirement in 1996 but added Jeremy Schofield (PhD, MIT) in 1997 and Daniel Lidar (PhD, Hebrew University) in 2000.

In analytical chemistry, the 1976 appointment of Michael Thompson had been a big boost, and in 1983 his former student Ulli Krull started teaching at Erindale. Both were very active in research, especially in chemical- and bio-sensors and surface analysis. In 1999 Frank Wania (PhD, Toronto) joined Scarborough College.

Despite the massive turnover, the department was able to offer retirees offices, and sometimes laboratory facilities, so many could continue their research and interact with newer colleagues — a valuable source of continuity and collegiality in an era of rapid personnel change.

Chapter Nine

Chemistry in the Suburbs
(1964–2005)

In the mid-1960s, when demand for higher education skyrocketed, the University of Toronto created two suburban campuses, in Scarborough to the east, and later Erindale in what is now Mississauga to the west. Staff and students in both colleges have long commuted to and from the downtown St. George campus; relations between college and downtown professors, administrators, and graduate students have been quite complex at times.

At Scarborough, which began earlier (1963), the college and department had to build everything — literally and figuratively — from the ground up. Preparing televised lectures was very time-consuming and ultimately backfired. Despite much excellent research, turnover in personnel has remained high. Erindale (1967) was able to learn from Scarborough's example: construction was more piecemeal, and Chemistry was able to put together a substantial research presence on campus.

This chapter looks at the history of Chemistry on both campuses over the last four decades.

Starting from Scratch: Chemistry at Scarborough[1]

The University of Toronto founded its Scarborough campus in 1963. Major investments in higher education were occurring in Ontario, demand was growing rapidly, and employment prospects for graduates were favourable. This new college of the Faculty of Arts and Science was to absorb growing suburban enrolment by postwar baby boomers. It was to present only general (three-year) BSc and BA degrees; courses would be identical to downtown offerings, with the same numbers (for example, CHM110).

The new facility — variously Scarborough College, the Scarborough Campus of the University of Toronto, and most recently the University of Toronto at Scarborough — emerged from a futuristic vision. Its avant-garde building, by architect John Andrews, soon acquired international fame. Striking vistas and scenic vantage points abounded, and the lively central meeting place, from which the wings radiated, focused activity. However, the cold, unfinished-looking concrete construction and fortress-like appearance, not to mention the leaky roofs, shifting foundations, and broken floor tiles, later attracted criticism. Later structures, more utilitarian, have added little aesthetically.

When the building was not ready for the scheduled opening in September 1965, classes met downtown instead, in the old Zoology Building on the southeast corner of the Front Campus. Classes began at Scarborough in January 1966, with the S-wing (Sciences) complete. The chemistry teaching and research laboratories had modern equipment, including NMR and infrared spectrometers, a library with many chemical journals, and shops for machinery, carpentry, and glassblowing. The combined Physical Sciences Division facilitated cross-discipline collaborations. Television was to carry much of the teaching, with heavy investment in developing audiovisual-assisted education. However, students did not respond well to sitting in front of a TV

Scarborough College.
Courtesy Scarborough College.

monitor to receive their lectures, and more conventional lecturing slowly became commonly used.[2]

Chemistry appointees for Scarborough represented the four sub-disciplines: analytical, inorganic, organic, and physical chemistry. The department gave little consideration to potential areas of research and did not base selection of personnel on fields of concentration or specialization. Except for Fred Lorriman, who had taught introductory organic chemistry downtown very effectively for decades, few appointees had lecturing experience, especially for TV. Most had not conducted independent research, although some had done post-doctoral work downtown. There were almost no senior professors to serve as mentors.

The college was inventing itself. Newcomers had not only to prepare lectures and laboratory courses, recruit graduate students, start research programs, and acquire instrumentation — standard tasks — but also to help organize and run the college. Promotion and tenure required performance roughly like that downtown, at a time when universities generally considered research more important than undergraduate teaching.

These expectations now look unreasonable. Few Scarborough chemists obtained tenure, and many departed within the first five years, leaving a changing and insecure remnant. It was only later, with the addition of some senior professors who moved their research groups downtown, that the Scarborough faculty began to coalesce and have an impact on the rest of the university's Chemistry Department.

The first appointee (1965) at Scarborough was Alan Walker, an inorganic chemist who helped launch the subject on the campus. In July 1966, Ron Harris (inorganic), Jim Riddick (physical), and Karen Emery (later Henderson; undergraduate laboratories) joined the faculty. The veteran Fred Lorriman deferred retirement and taught introductory (second-year) organic chemistry. In July 1967, Tom Lynch (organic chemistry) and Marvi Heinola (later Ricker) also signed on. Because TV monitors presented the taped first-year lectures, the course in 1968–69 accommodated even part-time students, who could attend an evening lecture section and a Saturday laboratory.

Collective insecurity vis-à-vis downtown and college and university administrations' differences over funding led to a split at Scarborough in the late 1960s, especially between its science and its humanities and social science faculties. The latter wanted an independent university, or one virtually so, which could teach, organize, and develop as it saw fit. Science saw this as a serious hindrance to research, tenure, and promotion. Scientists usually require graduate students for their research, as well as for demonstrating in undergraduate laboratories, and they also need modern instrumentation for research. A separate university seemed unlikely to attract the best graduate students, and applications for research funding and equipment from NSERC and other granting agencies might be less successful.

Implementation of the university's Hare Report[3] of 1970 on undergraduate education changed Scarborough. First, the college would have its own curriculum, leading to both three- and four-year degrees. Second, like St. George, it would introduce "cafeteria style" programs — i.e., the New Program — and students could take courses in any order, if they had the prerequisites. The Scarborough chemists decided to offer courses different in content from those at St. George.

The college changed its course-designator codes to A, B, C, and D levels from 100- to 400-level courses. Because it lacked enough instructors for fourth-year courses, a student could achieve the same level in discipline content by the end of C level (third year) as those taking St. George courses reached at the end of 300 level. Thus Scarborough students, if they had to move downtown, could blend into the 400-level courses fairly easily. Free bus service linked the two campuses.

As the college developed, Chemistry staffed its four subdivisions — inorganic, physical, organic, and analytical — and hired laboratory personnel.

Inorganic chemistry, taught originally by Alan Walker (PhD, Nottingham) and by Ron Harris (PhD, Toronto), flourished in the college's first decade, until Harris left for Britain in 1976. His replacement was Tom Jack, an inorganic interdisciplinarian, who worked with limnologists on the uptake of manganese in algae; funding was difficult to obtain, and Jack soon left for a government laboratory in Alberta. Bert Allen, former dean of Arts and Science, became principal in July 1976 and began to set up a research laboratory, but he died tragically of a brain tumour on Christmas Day 1976. Chris Cook, a former PhD student of Allen's, had had a brain tumour in 1972, so Allen's was the second from the same laboratory. Were some of the chemicals in their laboratory powerful carcinogens? Ultimately the two cases appeared to have no connection, involving different types of cancer.

For several years, Bob Morris (PhD, British Columbia), a 1980 inorganic replacement, exchanged his second-year Scarborough course with Jim Thompson from downtown so that he could teach a fourth-year course downtown. Eventually the two men switched campuses, and Thompson became chair of the Division of Physical Sciences at Scarborough and taught inorganic chemistry with Alan Walker. Both Thompson and Walker retired about 2000, and Savitri Chandrasekhar replaced them on a contractually limited teaching appointment (CLTA).

Jim Riddick was the first physical chemist at Scarborough but soon became assistant dean. Bob Caton (PhD, Rochester) joined him but left about five years later for a government laboratory. Michael Yealland (PhD, Toronto), a post-doctoral fellow of Jacques Deckers's, lectured to the first-year physical chemistry course for several years. After both Riddick and Caton had departed, Paul Brumer (PhD, Harvard) and Geraldine Kenney-Wallace (PhD, British Columbia) — Toronto's first female chemistry professor — joined in the mid-1970s, but both moved to the St. George campus in the 1980s. Ray Poirier (PhD, Toronto) was a CLTA at this time. John Dove transferred out to Scarborough in the mid-1970s as chairman of Physical Sciences and then went back. Jim Guillet (PhD, Cambridge), a polymer chemist, moved to Scarborough as associate dean for research and then returned downtown. Later appointments included Simon Fraser (PhD, Cambridge) in 1986 and Jamie Donaldson (PhD, Carleton) in 1988.

After the retirement of Fred Lorriman, Scarborough's initial organic chemist, Tom Lynch (PhD, Toronto) became its first young organic chemist, but five years later he transferred to industry. Marvi Ricker (neé Heinola, MSc, Toronto) was an assistant in the undergraduate organic laboratory until 1971, when she became assistant to the principal, and Janet Potter replaced her. Tom Tidwell (PhD, Harvard) joined as an associate professor in 1972. Jerry Kresge (PhD, Illinois) left the

Illinois Institute of Technology to become a full professor at Scarborough. He did his research downtown, as did Tidwell, but kept lecturing at Scarborough until he retired in 1992. Bob McClelland (PhD, Toronto) became assistant professor in 1973; later, as full professor, he carried out his research downtown.

Early on at Scarborough, teaching in analytical chemistry was in the hands of inorganic post-doctoral fellows or term appointees, such as Dave Cash, Kevin Grundy, Ray Hemmings, Dave Johnson, and John Stevens. After Alan Walker retired in 1998, the first trained analytical chemist arrived: Frank Wania (PhD, Toronto) works on environmental problems and has revived chemical research at the college after a ten-year gap.

Scarborough employed a number of people to run and demonstrate in the laboratories. Annette Allen, Lynn Baigrie-Boyd, Janet Potter, Ann Verner, and others played valuable roles in undergraduate instruction.

The 1970s and 1980s brought a golden age for Scarborough Chemistry, with active research in many areas, as we can see from the numerous awards, large enrolments, and optimistic outlook. The faculty's outstanding research — often in St. George laboratories — included isolation of metal complexes of H_2 (Morris) and of other metal complexes (Walker, Harris); studies of fast reactions (Kenney-Wallace); control of chemical reactions with lasers (Brumer); and investigations of organic reaction mechanisms, including flash photolytic generation of reactive intermediates (Kresge, McClelland, Tidwell). The organic faculty ranked with the best in the world in physical organic chemistry for a quarter-century, but all are now retired.

This era of prosperity was brief, as the provincial government thereafter cut back funding to universities. In addition, the college de-emphasized physical sciences: equipment rapidly became obsolete, research space dwindled, and graduate enrolment did not materialize. Essential appointments in analytical and biological chemistry did not occur. Professors moved their research downtown and did well there; by 1990 chemical research had disappeared from Scarborough.

The great turnover of chemists at Scarborough clearly reveals the college's great difficulties in establishing a permanent, resident faculty with the funding, research facilities, and graduate students for meaningful and rewarding research. This is still a continuing problem there. However, new appointments — Barbara Sherwood Lollar, Myrna Simpson (cross-appointed from Geography), Andre Simpson, and Frank Wania — have revitalized chemical research at Scarborough.

Chemistry at Erindale: Building a Critical Mass[4]

The University of Toronto created Erindale College on an estate in what is now Mississauga that it purchased in the early 1960s. In 1965 a small planning team included Peter Robinson (University College, London), an inorganic chemist who had joined the department in 1961 and who rose to become principal of Erindale. The property had no buildings appropriate for university teaching (although the house became a wonderful principal's residence); a "preliminary" building opened in 1967.

Among the college's other early chemists were James J. Rae, a senior organic chemist from downtown, who became registrar; David

Erindale College, South Building.
Courtesy University of Toronto Archives.

Clarke (PhD, Toronto), in physical chemistry; and Ian Still (PhD, Glasgow), an organic chemist. Over the years Erindale made more excellent appointments, including Martin Moskovits (PhD, Toronto), in inorganic physical chemistry; Geoffrey Ozin, in inorganic-nanochemistry; and Mitchell Winnik (PhD, Columbia), in organic polymer chemistry. Both Ozin and Winnik later earned the title "University Professor," and Moskovits became chairman of Chemistry at Toronto and later dean of science at the University of California at Santa Barbara. All of these three eventually moved their research groups to the St. George campus to have access to its graduate students and sophisticated equipment.

In September 1970, Anthony (Tony) Poë (PhD, London), an inorganic specialist, arrived as the campus's first full professor in chemistry. He had been a lecturer at the Imperial College of Science and Technology, London. His wife, Judith, also a chemist, accompanied him. Jacques Deckers (DS, Louvain), a professor of physical chemistry, moved out to Erindale after he finished his work on molecular beams downtown. At that time the new South Building was not complete. Classes took place in the original, temporary North Building. In November 1970, lecture and laboratory classes began in the partly completed South Building, but research laboratories did not become available until later. Thus faculty members had to conduct their research downtown.

By the time Erindale's research laboratories opened in 1973, graduate enrolment downtown had dwindled. Chemistry worried that another department (Geology?) might take over the empty spaces created on the St. George campus when the Erindale graduate students departed for Mississauga. A proposal emerged that research groups should remain downtown. But many Erindale instructors wanted research on that campus and did not want "commuter professors" and travelling teaching assistants ("commuter TAs"), as Scarborough had. However, it became clear that the difficulty of recruiting graduate students would make setting up research groups at Erindale quite problematic. Eventually the department allowed free choice of campus for research, and some research started at Erindale, with all its benefits and problems.

These beginnings for Erindale — early appointment of senior professors and research downtown, with its pool of graduate students — avoided many of Scarborough's early problems. In addition, at the start Erindale had senior administrators knowledgeable about scientific research (see below). For research that depended on the latest instrumentation, however, the new campus seemed deficient; thus some research groups remained downtown. Other groups managed better, and Erindale found ways to subsidize post-doctoral fellows and technical assistants and hire them as TAs.

Research continued in this metastable equilibrium for many years, and on-campus research proved beneficial. Fourth-year research projects, for instance, helped generate a university atmosphere. Students could complete a chemistry specialist program entirely at Erindale, although the department advised most to take some fourth-year courses downtown to broaden their experience. Also, professorial appointments in appropriate areas made research at Erindale more specialized — to the point of creating a critical mass. Currently new appointees must carry out all their research at the college.

This was all part of the university's reasoned attempt to encourage the suburban campuses to define themselves in a way complementary to the St. George campus. Inevitably, perhaps, the gap between central and suburban campuses widened, despite constant efforts by the original faculty to attend seminars and other events downtown and otherwise sustain contacts.

Erindale's research specialization goes back to the 1970s, when it became clear that biological chemistry and analytical chemistry were up-and-coming fields. Judith Poë helped set up and teach the main third-year biochemistry course (CHM360), and the corresponding laboratory course also started. This led to the appointment of biochemist Juta Reed (PhD, Wisconsin) to Erindale and established biochemical research on campus.

The scarcity of available positions inhibited development of analytical chemistry. However, once the department downtown decided that the subject was "really a part of chemistry" and appointed Michael Thompson, the addition of Ulli Krull at Erindale created a strong analytical presence on campus. More recent appointments in environmental, polymer, and solid-state NMR chemistry — namely, Michael Georges (PhD, Waterloo) and Peter Macdonald (PhD, Alberta), both as full professors — have established these specializations, and research at Erindale is now flourishing.

The unexpected departure, through long-term disability, of Jacques Deckers at the end of 1986 heralded a period of relative instability. In organic chemistry, Masad Dahma (PhD, McGill) and Scott Taylor (PhD, Toronto) stayed for five years and then left for McGill and Waterloo, respectively. In inorganic chemistry, Tony Poë and Peter Robinson retired in 1994; Michael Denk (PhD, Munich) started in 1995 but also left after five years for Guelph. In physical chemistry, Peter Macdonald arrived in 1998 as a university research fellow, and more personnel became necessary for undergraduate teaching. Laura Billard (PhD, Toronto) ably filled the role for several years. Juris Strautmanis (PhD, Toronto) did the same in both organic chemistry and biochemistry.

The recent retirements of Juta Reed and Ian Still, as well as planned increases in enrolment, have paved the way for more hirings: Scott Prosser and Jumi Shin (biological chemistry), Ulrich Fekl (inorganic-organic), and David McMillen (physical-biophysics). Since 2003, the chemistry group has been part of a new Department of Chemical and Physical Sciences, with more than twenty members. This expansion, and the money that comes with it, may well ease some of the problems that existed at Erindale in its formative years.

Looking back, Tony Poë recalled, "The early developments at Erindale were accompanied by continuous [administrative and departmental] friction between the St. George and Erindale campuses.... It was felt that the St. George campus took a distinctly imperialist attitude." Some downtown chemists looked down on their Erindale counterparts and students. Yet a number of suburban professors "became outstanding members of the department at the U of T, and other universities." As for students: "Many of the aspersions regarding the quality of Erindale students were confounded by their successes in fourth year and graduate school, and a significant number have now attained professorial status in various universities."

According to Poë, "The sometimes irritating facts of Erindale life have also included the need for frequent intercampus travel for committee work, teaching graduate classes, seminars, etc." But Erindale professors rarely had "the privilege of teaching fourth year and other undergraduate courses on the St. George campus." Teaching loads at Erindale were often onerous, yet professors downtown often took on courses in Mississauga, including Michael Dignam, John Dove, and Stuart Whittington in physical chemistry, Maurice Lister in first-year chemistry, Bob McClelland and Bill Reynolds in organic chemistry, and Michael Thompson in analytical chemistry.

Throughout all this, Erindale remained an essentially "loyalist" part of the department and university, with one of its dedicated founders, chemist Peter Robinson, rising through the administrative ranks to become principal. Other outstanding scientists became senior administrators — most notably, David Strangway (physics, geology, moon rocks) and Tuzo Wilson (physics and geology). Attempts at independence generally found little support among scientists.

Chapter Ten

PROBE AND MEASURE: INSTRUMENTS AND KEEPERS (1960–2005)

In its growth as a science, chemistry has come to rely increasingly on instrumental techniques that can unravel the structures of new compounds that researchers discover or create as well as measure molecular properties of interest. This chapter's seven sections describe the development, especially at Toronto, of instrumentation and procedures that have become routine in any modern chemistry department over the last fifty or so years:

- spectroscopy: ultraviolet, infrared, and nuclear magnetic resonance (NMR);
- mass spectrometry;
- X-ray crystallography and the Advanced Instrumentation for Molecular Structure (AIMS) Laboratory;
- Powder X-ray diffraction (PXRD);
- analytical laboratory for environmental science research and teaching (ANALEST);
- computing; and
- machine, glassblowing, and electronics shops.

SPECTROSCOPY: ULTRAVIOLET, INFRARED, AND NMR

Prior to the 1950s there was little high-tech instrumentation to help chemists determine the structures of compounds or study their reactions. Colorimeters were common, and the Beckmann DU UV (ultraviolet) Spectrometer was standard in North American laboratories. In the 1940s Woodward published his rules[1] for predicting the position of ultraviolet absorption maxima in organic molecules having conjugated systems, and these helped determine organic structure, thus increasing organic chemists' use of UV spectrometers. Over the years, the Chemistry Department at Toronto added other spectrometers, including Bausch and Lomb Spectronic 505, Perkin Elmer 237B, and Unicam SP.800 models. However, as more powerful instrumental techniques became available, scientists used UV spectrometers less to determine structure and more to characterize molecules.

When Adrian Brook was a post-doctoral fellow in 1952–53 at Iowa State College, he learned about the new, commercially available infrared (IR) spectrometers, which inorganic and organic chemists were starting to use to determine structure and identify compounds. On his return to Toronto he found that the department's only IR spectrometer was in Don LeRoy's laboratory. It was a Perkin Elmer 12-C Single Beam Prism Spectrometer — a large salt prism mounted on a circular table and connected by a cable to an electric motor, which had an eccentric "take up" spool attached. The motor adjusted the slit's width as the prism rotated to compensate for the decrease in the globar radiation output with wavelength. The directed diffracted signal fell on an IR detector attached to a recorder. Running a spectrum in the range of 2 to 15 microns (the region of interest to organic chemists) gave several feet of chart and was a slow, time-consuming business, especially since the operator had to run "blanks" to recognize solvent or other non-specific absorptions.

Kenneth Cashion, while studying for his BA and MA degrees with Don LeRoy, used the machine for product studies in his research on the photolysis of hydrocarbons. He and his supervisor essentially split the instrument in two, to facilitate troubleshooting and modification. When John Polanyi joined the faculty in 1956 and began his classic studies that led to the discovery of infrared chemiluminescence (the "iraser" effect),[2] Cashion, now a PhD candidate working with Polanyi, had full-time use of this spectrometer for their chemiluminescence studies, since their modifications made it unusable for other purposes — such as for "organicers" and their routine spectra.

Eventually the organic chemists persuaded the department in 1959 to buy a conventional commercial instrument, a Beckmann IR-5, and soon thereafter a Beckmann IR-8 model and then a Perkin Elmer 237B grating spectrometer. Heavy usage of these, as well as of several department-owned UVs, led to the hiring of a technician to maintain them in a common-use equipment laboratory. The first supervisor was Dianne Jones.[3] Several of the larger research groups eventually purchased UV and IR spectrometers for themselves. Use of infrared spectroscopy declined in the late 1960s as a tool for determining structures, and the department eventually closed the general equipment room.

In 1961 Steven Danyluk arrived at Toronto. His research interests lay in nuclear magnetic resonance, and Chemistry acquired a Varian DP-60 60 MHz broad-line/high-resolution NMR spectrometer for his studies of proton resonances. This device was complex, and general users had only limited access. In the early 1960s, the department obtained a Varian A-60, which it housed in the Lash Miller basement, for organic and inorganic chemists to obtain proton (^{1}H) spectra. NMR spectroscopy became crucial for determining structure and characterizing molecules, particularly when tables appeared such as the Varian Spectra Catalogs[4] of proton frequencies in various structures.

In 1965 Danyluk left for the Argonne National Laboratories, and Bill Reynolds took his place. According to Reynolds, Don LeRoy and Peter Yates hoped that he would interact closely with the organic and inorganic chemists and endeavour to upgrade the NMR facility to assist both his and their research. Thus the department purchased in 1965 a Varian HA-100 (to replace the DP-60 and for use by Reynolds's and other research groups) and in 1967 a Varian A56-60 for obtaining ^{1}H and ^{19}F spectra. Now Toronto chemists could routinely record spectra of nuclei other than protons. Soon the department acquired two reliable, easy-to-use T-60 proton NMR spectrometers, which became the primary source of routine proton spectra.

Varian also began producing commercial NMR spectrometers that used higher magnetic fields. The HR-220 operated at 220 MHz for ^{1}H only. Because it was so expensive, the National Research Council decided to fund only one in Canada. In 1968, it awarded the device jointly to the chemistry departments at Toronto and McMaster. The universities installed the instrument at the Ontario Research Foundation in Sheridan Park, midway between them.

This device served as a national centre, with Toronto's Bill Reynolds on the management committee. However, the commercial availability of the pulse Fourier transform NMR spectrometer with its much higher sensitivity, which made NMR practical for ^{13}C, soon made the HR-220 obsolete. The Medical Research Council gave Toronto's Faculty of

Pharmacy a grant to buy a Varian HA-100. However, the faculty consulted with Chemistry, and the two together received a matching grant from NSERC and together acquired a much costlier Varian XL-100 — Canada's second pulse Fourier transform NMR spectrometer. This instrument, with its massive (five-ton) electromagnet, found a home on the fourth storey of the Pharmacy Building. However, interference from FM radio-station transmitters on the new CN Tower affected its performance for ^{1}H and ^{19}F. It was moved to the Lash Miller basement and provided ^{1}H, ^{13}C, and ^{19}F spectra for another ten years.

In the late 1970s higher-field superconducting solenoid spectrometers became available that operated in pulse Fourier transform mode. Toronto's Chemistry Department and several of its Ontario counterparts set up a regional high-field NMR centre at Guelph, which installed a 400-MHz Brüker WM-400. However, demand for high-field NMR time was growing so fast that the department purchased its own Varian XL-200 in 1980. Although it operated at only half the frequency of the WM-400, progress in hardware and software permitted a much broader range for the new multi-dimensional NMR experiments that were transforming organic structure determination (and subsequently protein NMR).

A Varian XL-400 in 1984 doubled the in-house frequency range and ended Toronto's use of the regional centre. In 1988, Erindale obtained a Chemagnetics CMX-300 broad-line/solid-state spectrometer for Peter Macdonald's biomolecular NMR research. In 1992 the department's high-field NMR capabilities grew further with the purchase of a Varian Unity 500 spectrometer as well as a Unity 40 console to replace the obsolete XL-400 console. Lewis Kay, a joint appointee to Chemistry and Medical Genetics in 1993, set up a protein NMR laboratory in the Medical Sciences Building, with spectrometers ranging from 500 to 800 MHz. In 1995 Chemistry established a solid-state NMR facility, with Brüker DSX-200 and -400 spectrometers.

The department has continued to strengthen NMR research at Erindale and Scarborough. In 2002, Scott Prosser (PhD, Guelph) joined Erindale with research interests in biomolecular NMR. Also, the new Biotechnology Research Centre at Mississauga has installed Varian INOVA 500- and 600-MHz spectrometers, principally for Macdonald and Prosser. Also in 2002, Myrna and Andre Simpson joined the Scarborough faculty, which has purchased a 500-MHz spectrometer with LC accessories for their environmental applications of NMR. The St. George chemists were planning installation of a higher-field (700 MHz) spectrometer and a spectrometer able to sustain very high throughput of samples for biomolecular NMR and combinatorial chemistry.

Over the last four decades the department's NMR facility has changed beyond recognition. While originally it could routinely obtain NMR spectra only for ^{1}H, it can now do so for an incredible variety of magnetic nuclei and carry out sophisticated multi-dimensional NMR experiments. Furthermore, the 60-MHz spectrometers installed by 1965 had a guaranteed signal to noise ratio of 16:1 on a 1.0 percent ethylbenzene sample. Future NMR devices will include a probe for a 600-MHz spectrometer with a ratio of 3,500:1 on a 0.1 percent ethylbenzene sample! As well, in 1965 technicians or staff members and students doing NMR research (six to eight people at most) obtained almost all spectra. Currently almost 250 trained student operators run most of the spectra in all areas of chemical research.

Mass Spectrometry

In 1959 Alex Harrison, a specialist in mass spectrometry, joined Chemistry (see Chapter 7). The department had ordered a Metropolitan-Vickers (later AEI, even later Kratos) MS-2 magnetic-sector instrument. It arrived in November, and Harrison's fourth-year student James Tait began work on gas-phase ions. After the 1963 move to the Lash Miller Building, construction of a magnetic-sector mass spectrometer (MS) for observing ion/molecule reactions was soon completed. In 1973 the department obtained funds for a commercial magnetic-sector instrument to study chemical ionization — a new field. Then, in 1985, a state-of-the-art multiple-sector/quadrupole mass spectrometer in Lash Miller became the centrepiece of the Ontario Regional Ion Chemistry Laboratory. Harrison's research group — and colleagues from Guelph, Queen's, Trent, and Waterloo — used this device until the mid-1990s for basic research in gas-phase ion chemistry.

Mass spectrometry has played a large role in the department. Jacques Deckers and John Polanyi applied it to detection work in their molecular beam experiments, and John Dove used time-of-flight mass spectrometers to follow the fast reactions in shock waves. In addition, mass spectrometry has an important analytical function in environmental chemistry, ANALEST (see the section below) has a dedicated GC/MS, and Scott Mabury and Jon Abbatt have dedicated instruments of various configurations for their research.

It was clear by the early 1960s that double-focusing mass spectrometers (combining magnetic and electric sectors) made possible mass-to-charge measurements accurate within a few parts per million — precise enough to confirm elemental compositions, which reduced organic chemists' reliance on elemental analyses. Such instruments became commercially available within a few years. In 1967 the department installed an AEI double-focusing MS-902 in Room 65 (home of the MS service laboratory) and hired David Priddle to operate it.

Demand increased for mass spectral analyses, and so the laboratory in 1971 added a magnetic-sector instrument for obtaining routine low-resolution mass spectra from electron ionization. Accurate mass measurement with the MS-902 was tedious and time-consuming without a data system, and in 1977 the department added a Kratos MS-30 instrument. This gave way in 1987 to a VG Analytical 70-250S double-focusing instrument, which provided chemical and fast-atom-bombardment ionization as well as of electron ionization in the analytical service laboratory. This last instrument, with a new and improved data system, still generates reliable results.

Service in the MS laboratory suffered during the 1980s; the problem ended when Dr. Alex Young took charge in 1990. The facility added a dedicated GC/MS instrument in 1995 and an electrospray ionization/quadrupole instrument in 1998. In January 2003 it installed an MDS SCIEX quadrupole/time-of-flight MS, which can accurately measure the mass-to-charge ratio of ions produced by electrospray ionization; this instrument is coupled directly to a liquid chromatograph. The facility now does 3,000 to 4,000 analyses each year for the department's research groups and for many non-university clients.

The recent appointments of Rebecca Jockusch, Mark Nitz, and Aaron Wheeler, who all require mass spectrometers for their research in biological and bioanalytical chemistry, created a demand for more space for mass spectrometers. As a result the AIMS Laboratory opened in the summer of 2005, occupying a former undergraduate teaching laboratory. In addition to supporting the analytical needs of the department, the facility provides for the development of new instrumentation, including mass spectrometry and others, and for the investigation of the physical and chemical fundamentals of instrumentation used in the determination of molecular structure.

X-ray Crystallography

X-ray crystallography was first employed in the department in 1947–48 in the hands of Adrian Brook, then a first-year graduate student! Brook worked for George Wright on a problem that sought to establish the stereochemistry of the addition to a carbon-carbon double bond (*cis* or *trans*) in the oxymercuration reaction. Wright had isolated the exclusive product from the reaction with cyclohexene, in the form of 1-chloromercuri-2-methoxycyclohexane. He believed that determining the compound's X-ray crystal structure would provide the answer and assigned the problem to Brook.

"Neither of us," recalls Brook, "knew anything about X-ray diffraction techniques, or how to solve a crystal structure." Wright had purchased an X-ray generator and had it installed in the corridor outside his second-floor office in the Old Chemistry Building, together with powder cameras and a single crystal Weissenberg camera. A pseudo darkroom in the top floor of the old elevator shaft worked fine, as long as users of the shaft's basement and ground floors (A.R. Gordon's students servicing their methanol still) did not open the doors and let light enter, destroying the X-ray film.

Brook began learning how to solve crystal structures. The necessary Fourier summations used cardboard Beevers-Lipson and Patterson-Tunell strips, and undergraduate students assisted in the lengthy calculations with adding machines. After learning the method by practising on a known compound, Brook found that the X-ray structure of the "natural" isomer was the product of *trans* oxymercuration (e,e). This finding gained confirmation when the structure of the second (unnatural) isomer showed that the configuration of the groups in the molecule was *cis* (a,e). Wright later rejected the results because they conflicted with some of his other studies, but in fact the configurations and mode of addition to the double bond of simple alkenes (*trans*) that Brook found were correct, as other researchers have subsequently clearly established.

Few people in the department did much further X-ray work on crystal structures until Stanley C. Nyburg[5] arrived in 1964. He recalls, "At the University of Toronto I was generously supported and purchased a state-of-the art automated four-circle diffractometer, a Picker (which is still going strong). This was initially operated by Hollerith pre-punched cards generated at the University Computing Centre. Over the years automation was changed to a Digital PDP-8e mini-computer running on its own in-house program written in autocode." This set-up could run a service solving crystal structures — about 115 in all — for colleagues. At least two fascinating structures emerged quite early: "the first ever compound to contain the dinitrogen ligand, nitrogenpentammineruthenium (II) dichloride made by Bert (A.D.) Allen and C.V. Senoff"[6] (although *Chemical Communications* rejected the first report!) and "the first ever stable solid silene (silaethylene), prepared in Adrian Brook's group."[7]

Nyburg's pioneering work at Toronto involved explanations of various features observed in some crystal structures as well as collaborations with several colleagues. Nyburg took early retirement in 1987 and returned to England, where he continues to work at King's College, London.

During Nyburg's tenure and beyond, Dr. J.F. Sawyer determined a number of crystal structures for research groups in the department. Dr. Alan Lough succeeded Sawyer in 1990. David Farrar, an inorganic chemist who had taken his BA at Scarborough and his PhD under Nicholas Payne at the University of Western Ontario, had learned the technique at Western. After he joined Toronto in 1981, he determined a number of crystal structures of products from his own research, until he moved into administration.

Alan Lough has described the X-ray facilities in 1990. The laboratory, in the Lash Miller Building, had "a Nonius CAD-4 (four circle) diffractometer controlled by a PDP-8 computer (there were no personal computers [PCs] in the laboratory at that point)." The instrument could "be used to determine the space group and collect accurate data for structure solutions." It operated "at room temperature and produced about 40-50 data sets a year." To handle air-sensitive crystals or those that melted at about room temperature, the department bought low-temperature equipment that helped solve many crystal structures.

By 1993, Siemens was making a faster, more automated diffractometer — the Siemens P_4. A large grant from NSERC paid for the P_4, which had customized low-temperature apparatus. The laboratory now had two diffractometers and could employ them simultaneously to obtain some seventy to seventy-five data sets each year from the P_4.

As demand for crystal structures grew, so did the need for better instruments. In 1997 NSERC gave the department some $240,000 to add a CCD area detector to the P_4. The chemists bought a new Nonius Kappa-CCD, complete with a low-temperature device from Oxford Cryostream. By 2003 this equipment was collecting about three hundred sets of data each year. The department moved it in the autumn of 2002 to the newly renovated X-ray facility in Lash Miller, which also has Pentium PCs for processing data and solving structures. Other university departments, Ontario firms, and foreign companies also use the laboratory.

Powder X-ray Diffraction (PXRD)[8]

In 1991 Geoffrey Ozin's research group needed PXRD equipment to characterize inorganic compounds that it prepared using organic molecules synthesized for use as templates. Ozin, with colleagues Ian Manners, Martin Moskovits, and David Farrar, obtained funds for a Siemens D5000 X-ray powder diffractometer. To operate the device, Ozin hired as a post-doctoral fellow, Dr. Srebri Petrov, who had managed a similar unit at the Ontario Geosciences Laboratory.

The instrument had a solid-state Kevex detector to remove unwanted K-beta components from the diffracted X-ray beam; a high-temperature attachment to analyze in situ structural changes of up to 1,200 °C under different pressures, including vacuum; and a low-temperature attachment that operated down to temperatures close to liquid nitrogen. The new facility needed accessories, and so the laboratory charged users for analyses, which permitted purchase of accessories and supplies and payment for repairs and maintenance. After 1996 it became a self-supporting unit in the department, analyzing as many as 1,200 to 1,500 samples annually — two-thirds of them from Ozin's laboratory and the majority of the others from outside companies.

Ozin's group received $150,000 from NSERC in 1998 to upgrade the equipment. It obtained powerful new software for data processing from Siemens/Brüker AXS and accessories such as an automatic sample changer. In 2000, the facility purchased two diffractometers representing a new generation of equipment from Siemens/Brüker AXS: a versatile, multi-purpose microdiffractometer with a 2D area detector and a unique small scattering diffractometer, which could analyze the degree of ordering of polymer and semi-amorphous nano-materials.

Toronto now had one of the best-equipped PXRD laboratories in Canada, including a fully automated standard Bragg-Brentano focused D5000 Diffractometer for performing high-quality diffraction-phase analyses of single- and multi- component samples; a GADDS D8 Diffractometer with 2D Detector — a versatile, multi-purpose, fast diffractometer; and a NanoStar SAXS Diffractometer — designed for high-quality diffraction data of low-theta regions, which is a fine analytical tool for semi-crystalline, high-molecular-weight compounds and ideal for analyzing the short-range order in polymers.

Analytical Laboratory for Environmental Science Research and Teaching (ANALEST)

At the time the Chemistry Department was recruiting Scott Mabury, Chairman Martin Moskovits informed him that the department was planning a large, up-to-date laboratory for environmental research — ideal for Mabury's work. When he joined the staff he received $20,000 to start implementing this plan. This teaching facility would be accessible to anyone keen to learn how to acquire analytical data on material. Moskovits suggested that Mabury canvas the chairmen of related departments about financial support. Visits to Botany, Geography, Geology, and Zoology ultimately raised $50,000. Physics gave nothing.

Dean of Arts and Science Don Dewees promised to match the pledges. The enthusiastic Mabury next approached Chemical Engineering, with which Chemistry had long had little contact, and it offered $20,000. He then prevailed on Dewees to match the new $120,000, for a total pledge of $240,000! Vice President of Research and International Relations Heather Munroe-Blum then offered to match that pledge!

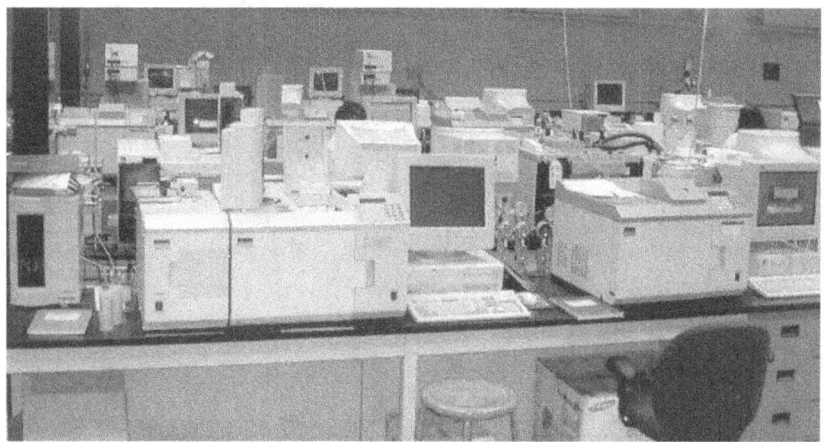

The ANALEST research facility, 2004.
Courtesy A.G. Brook.

Mabury next called on makers of scientific instruments. The Perkin Elmer Corporation recognized a potential showplace to countless students and offered $250,000 worth of equipment, reduced prices in future, twenty days a year of on-site training, and $250,000 cash. It wanted a partnership and negotiated a three-year arrangement, which worked superbly for all parties and has since continued.

The current laboratory consists of an area for instruction, a small lecture room, and a sample preparation room, in addition to the instrument area. The highly trained supervisor, Dan Mathers, has an assistant. Thanks to careful maintenance and excellent training, no instrument has broken down. Computers run all the instruments and have tutorial software for each device. The facility registers 116,000 user-hours per year, especially for Chemical Engineering (37 percent of the total) and Chemistry (34 percent). Other departments — and industry (5 percent) — make up the balance. All users pay for instruction and/or instrument time (a total of about $120,000 per year), with rates differing for original contributors, university non-contributors, and non-university users.

∽ Computing ∽

Second World War inventions that helped break German military codes, and later developments, resulted in primitive electronic computers. The Physics Department in the University of Toronto was a leader in this field.⁹ Computing looked promising for chemists, particularly in theoretical studies, and many used the university computer in the 1950s. A number attended lectures by Professor Pat Hume of Physics about use of the FORTRAN computer language. Entering the program and the relevant data onto punched cards and then submitting them to the computer could be a humbling experience. Some of the theoretical chemists, including Imre Csizmadia, John Valleau, and Stuart Whittington, became heavy users of the university computer.

Over time, the university acquired bigger and faster machines. In 1963 it planned to replace its IBM 7094 computer, and a consortium of chemists and physicists proposed acquiring the 7094 for their own use. In the event the university sold it to them for one dollar, but IBM warned them to service the machine constantly, and for several years they had a very expensive IBM maintenance contract (some $40,000 per year). In a grand gamble, they hired an experienced maintenance engineer, and he performed miracles until the university backed out of the requisite heavy air conditioning in the Physics Building to sustain the instrument.

In the early 1980s the Chemistry Department acquired its own high-performance computer — a Gould machine — mainly for the consortium. The Gould was not very satisfactory, and an Apollo machine replaced it. Mike Peterson, a PhD graduate of Imre Csizmadia's, supervised the Apollo while running the computing facility. Recent huge increases in computers' speed, memory, and computing power have pushed many theoretical chemists towards reliance on desktop PCs, although they have two parallel computers in-house for crunching larger numbers.

The development of PCs has affected all chemists. In the mid-1980s computers were a curiosity. But incredible new software could not only process words but be used to draw chemical structures, keep track of references, perform calculations, and so on. Those powerful factors, together with the computers' speed and general ease of use, soon converted almost everyone to their use. In earlier days a chemist drafted a chemical manuscript, generally by hand, and then had a typist type it onto paper — often a long, slow process, particularly with some people's writing. Errors and changes were awkward to correct and usually involved much retyping. Drawings usually required a draughtsman, and references were a nightmare to retype. Nowadays, with the ability to correct errors easily and to import references and drawings, the professor — often with students' help — generates a much better product faster and much more easily.

Administrators took advantage of PCs. Whereas in the 1970s the department had two or more typists and numerous private secretaries for faculty members, most professors today type their own papers and letters, and there are almost no secretaries. Further, thanks to Chairman Martin Moskovits, e-mail now conveys most communications in the department. For better or worse, faculty members now virtually live at their computers, often on-line.

Machine, Glassblowing, Electronics, and Other Shops

Before 1949, Chemistry had no professional machine or glassblowing facilities and obtained such services from other departments (Physics, Chemical Engineering) or the private sector. The move to the Wallberg Building that year liberated space in the Old Chemistry Building, and Professor George Wright oversaw creation of a machine shop there. He contributed his own watchmaker's lathe and helped to buy second-hand equipment for an English craftsman, Reg Carter, to use in constructing equipment. The shop gradually acquired tools and machinery and added personnel, and a small shop emerged for graduate students. Physical chemists were the major users of the facility.

Later, the Lash Miller Building contained a much larger shop, new equipment, and several machinists, and personnel there could build complex experimental equipment for faculty members. Designing and constructing ultra-high vacuum vessels and miniature equipment became a specialty. More recently, while many professors purchase equipment for their research, the shop, under John Ford, remains busy and is more productive, thanks to procedures that Adrienne De Francesco introduced when she was the department's business manager.

Glassblowing developed in similar fashion, and early on the shop built quite complex pieces of equipment and repaired broken glassware for organic and inorganic chemists. Experienced employees tended to migrate to the better-paying private sector; hence there were high turnover rates. The current facility, also under John Ford, remains active, with two glassblowers who divide their time roughly evenly between repairing and constructing equipment.

The Lash Miller Building initially had a good but small electronics shop; under Wolfgang Panning, it designed and built special research equipment, primarily for the physical chemists. With the development of transistors, devices became much smaller and more complex. Later, the servicing of computers, particularly PCs and their peripherals, became areas requiring expertise. Accordingly, the shop's emphasis moved towards improving and maintaining computer facilities. It facilitates the use of e-mail, removes spam, detects and traps worms and viruses, assists with programming, maintains servers, and services computers, printers, and other computer peripherals; it also answers students' and professors' questions and solves their problems, both complex and trivial. Frank Bures currently runs this important service.

Mention should also be made of the department's chemicals and equipment stores, essential for laboratory work. In the early years (Pike's time) the small quantities of supplies necessary for undergraduate laboratories were maintained and supervised by E.J. Repath, and then his successor R. Fortescue. After the 1950s, when research activities by faculty and graduate students increased dramatically, a series of supervisors including Fred Jones had to provide enormous amounts and varieties of chemicals, glassware, and other equipment to both undergraduate and graduate students.

Ultimately, it became impossible for the department to stock the huge variety of supplies requested by researchers, and responsibility for acquiring their research needs devolved to each research director and his or her group. The current supervisor Ken Greaves is responsible for chemicals, glassware, and equipment needed for undergraduate laboratories, and he also maintains a minimal supply of basic glassware and equipment for researchers, as well as basic needs such as solvents, Xerox paper, and toner cartridges for laser printers. He is also safety officer and conducts safety courses for new research students.

Chapter Eleven

Transforming the Lash Miller Building (1993–2006)

This chapter covers an eventful period in the history of the Chemistry Department, as it expanded and reconfigured its principal home to allow research in exciting new fields. Three chairmen — Martin Moskovits (1993–99), David Farrar (1999–2002), and Scott Mabury (2003–present) — have overseen the physical transformation of the Lash Miller Chemical Laboratories and the addition of the Davenport Research Building. This chapter discusses each chairman and also looks at the department's lively extracurricular activities, traditional and new.

Martin Moskovits (Chairman, 1993–99): Man with a Vision

Martin Moskovits was a challenging, forceful, and ambitious man with a compelling vision. He had graduated in physics and chemistry at Toronto with a BSc and then worked under Michael Dignam for his PhD on surface phenomena. After a brief period with Alcan Canada, he returned to the University of Toronto, initially as a post-doctoral fellow at Erindale with Geoffrey Ozin and then as assistant professor.

His broadly based research centred on spectroscopy, surface chemistry, and heterogeneous catalysis and later involved laser-induced fluorescence, Raman, and resonance Raman spectroscopy of metal atoms and small metal aggregates. Moskovits eventually was able to transfer his research to the St. George campus. He rose quickly and became professor in 1982 and chairman in 1993 — the second time that a professor and his student had been department heads in succession (à la Gordon and LeRoy).

Martin Moskovits.
Courtesy Department of Chemistry, University of Toronto.

Moskovits had lots of ideas about what was good and bad in the department and what it needed for the future. He did not think very highly of most of his predecessors, particularly what he regarded as their autocratic style (typical of the times at many universities), which in his view lacked adequate consultation with the faculty.

During his tenure as chairman, Moskovits introduced environmental chemistry into the curriculum. Scott Mabury (PhD, California) joined the department in 1995 and, in addition to teaching in the new field, established the ANALEST laboratory (see Chapter 10) to deal with the many analytical problems arising from environmental studies. Jamie Donaldson (PhD, Carleton) was part of the environmental group, as was Jon Abbatt (PhD, Harvard) — a 1999 addition.

The department set up Canada's first graduate program in environmental chemistry in 2000, with four professors — Abbatt, Donaldson, Mabury, and Frank Wania. The program has grown rapidly, taking on two more professors — Jennifer Murphy (junior Canada Research Chair) and André Simpson — and two cross-appointees from allied departments. It is now Canada's largest program in the field and one of the most sizeable in any chemistry department in the world.

Its research expertise is wide, ranging from studies of the transport and fate of organic pollutants, through soil chemistry and development of analytical methods, to laboratory and field studies of atmospheric processes. A unifying theme is the study of environmental processes from a fundamental molecular perspective. The program benefits from close collaboration with scientists at nearby governmental laboratories, a number of them adjunct appointees in the department. Growth in environmental studies coincided with similar expansion in materials and biological chemistry, indicative of the rapid changes in the discipline and the department's ability to respond in a timely fashion.

Moskovits recognized that the department required more and more modern space and more graduate students. Its administration needed reorganization and modernization and — as a result of painful cutbacks by the university — additional sources of funding. Moskovits was an eloquent spokesman for Chemistry and courted university administrators to encourage them to help in its development. His persuasion proved extremely successful.

Reorganization and modernization received great impetus from the appointments of Adrienne De Francesco as general manager and of Penny Ashcroft Moore as departmental secretary. The two dynamic additions instituted changes that transformed the running of the department.

Moskovits identified philanthropy as a possible source of substantial new funding — "something that the department and … the university as a whole … had not had a great deal of experience in." Such resources could help provide fellowships: "The dearth in graduate student numbers made it hard to recruit new faculty who require a healthy graduate enrolment to animate their research programs. The Province and the University had, on more than one occasion, instituted attractive matching programs on funds raised externally in support of graduate fellowships…. By raising graduate fellowship funds we could multiply those proceeds three (and in one case six) times."

Endowments from individuals or families or from chemical firms could also fund chairs on a permanent basis and this became the university's premier campaign goal in which the provost provided a highly attractive matching incentive. If the department raised $1 million in endowment, he would commingle that with $1 million in existing endowment, and, if the faculty member appointed to the chair was already teaching at the university, a new junior faculty slot would be granted to the department. Since recruitment of new faculty was important, the department participated enthusiastically.

This led to another crucial appointment. Moskovits wanted a full-time staffer to represent the department to friends and alumni and handle technical issues, including relations with the university's development office. Sue McClelland joined the team — "a remarkable person, a greatly intuitive individual with great compassion and personal skills, not to mention years of experience in the university.... Little would have happened without her."

The first endowed chair came through the generosity of two exceptional, genteel individuals: Roel and Dorothy Buck. Roel was a highly imaginative and successful engineer who had built a spectacular automotive parts business. Chancellor Rose Wolfe introduced him and his wife, Dorothy, to the department, and they became keen to endow a chair in theoretical chemical physics. In 1997 Paul Brumer became the first holder of the Roel Buck Chair in Chemical Physics. The Bucks' generosity also allowed the department to recruit Dan Lidar several years later. To celebrate the couple's gift of 1997, the department sponsored a symposium, "Science in the 21st Century," with speakers Brumer, Ron Kluger, Geoffrey Ozin, and Moshe Shapiro (Weitzman Institute, Israel) and a reception in the University College quadrangle.

More recently NSERC created two categories of chairs to be awarded across the country, one for outstanding researchers and another for highly promising young researchers. At the time of writing, twelve members of Toronto's Department of Chemistry hold chairs: John Polanyi occupies the John C. Polanyi Chair; Paul Brumer, the Roel Buck; Ulli Krull, the AstraZeneca; Mark Lautens, also an AstraZeneca and the NSERC/Merck Frosst Industrial; and Rebecca Jockusch, Dwayne Miller, Jennifer Murphy, Geoffrey Ozin, Eugenia Kumacheva, Gilbert Walker, Aaron Wheeler, and Deborah Zamble each occupy an NSERC Canada Research Chair.

In 1997, at a reception in the university's Rotman Management Centre, Lieutenant-Governor Hilary Weston unveiled a portrait of John Polanyi that the department had commissioned in honour of his Nobel Prize; Polanyi later married the artist, Brenda Bury. The painting temporarily hangs in the Croft Chapter House at University College. Also in 1997, the ANALEST laboratory opened in one of the former undergraduate laboratories in Lash Miller. It was to handle not only the many analytical problems of the environmental chemists but also general analytical problems needing solution by graduates students, faculty members, the university, or members of the public. For details of the facility, see Chapter 10.

In the last few decades of the twentieth century, the university established two new categories of research professor. The first group, with the title "University Professor," had done outstanding research. In Chemistry, the first appointee was John Polanyi (1974), and later came

Peter Yates (1986), Adrian Brook (1987), Bryan Jones (1994), Paul Brumer (1995), Mitchell Winnik (1998), and Geoffrey Ozin (2001).

The university also created endowed chairs for distinguished researchers. While such positions had long existed in Britain and the United States, it was probably the establishment of the John C. Polanyi Chair in Chemistry that initiated the practice at Toronto. Soon after Polanyi won the Nobel Prize, Mary Jackman, acting through the Jackman Foundation, and with the Natural Sciences and Engineering Research Council of Canada providing matching funds, set up the John C. Polanyi Chair in Chemical Physics. Thus the laureate would not need to retire from the university when he turned sixty-five.

The John C. Polanyi Nobel Laureate Lecture Series, another brainchild of Martin Moskovits's, was to have four incarnations — in 1994, 1995, 1997, and 2000. The first celebrated the launch of the Polanyi Chair. Sue McClelland helped organize the lecture series and recalls vividly the events leading to its creation: "The initial idea was to invite Y.T. Lee and Dudley Herschbach, who had shared the Nobel Prize with John, to visit the Department and give lectures." But the idea soon expanded. "On November 3rd and 4th, 1994, we brought together eleven Nobel Laureates to celebrate with us, nine of whom gave lectures over the two days." There were six laureates in chemistry, Dudley Herschbach (1986), Gerhard Herzberg (1971), Max Perutz (1962), George Porter (1967), Ilya Prigogine (1977), and Michael Smith (1993); two in medicine, Christian de Duve (1974) and James Watson (1962); and three in physics, Bertram Brockhouse (1994), Henry Kendall (1990), and Charles Townes (1964).

A gala dinner for 550 people took place at the Four Seasons Hotel, and guests included Deputy Prime Minister Herb Gray and Pierre Trudeau. The Ontario legislature interrupted its sitting to greet the laureates when they visited Queen's Park. Adrienne Clarkson directed a press conference in the Council Chambers at the university's Simcoe Hall, and the university president and the Metro Toronto chairman gave a party in their honour. A volunteer committee included prominent Torontonians such as Bluma Appel, Adrienne Clarkson, Nona Macdonald Heaslip, Helen Vari, and Sis Bunting Weld.

Nobel Laureates at the University of Toronto Lecture Series (1994) honouring John Polanyi. Standing, from left: Max Perutz, Michael Smith, Dudley Herschbach, Bertram Brockhouse, John Polanyi, Christian de Duve, Charles Townes, and Henry Kendall. Seated, from left: Gerhard Herzberg, George Porter, James Watson, and Ilya Prigogine. *Courtesy Department of Chemistry, University of Toronto.*

The lectures — whose theme was "Science and Society" — took place in Convocation Hall and Hart House Theatre and were, according to McClelland, "a smash hit." There was overflow seating available in Hart House Theatre, and a video screen projected the lectures live. Loudspeakers broadcast them outside both venues. Local television stations ran some of the lectures for weeks, and the nationwide press gave them extensive coverage. Dudley Herschbach called the events "the Woodstock of Science." The series placed the department "on the map." Most notably, there were photos of ticket queues — for a series of science lectures!

Publisher House of Anansi produced a book from the lectures, and the department decided to launch it in conjunction with a second lecture series. It invited three Canadian-affiliated Nobel Prize winners to speak on "The Future of Science," particularly in terms of the "brain drain" that had followed cuts in funding for research. Rudolph Marcus (chemistry, 1992), George Olah (chemistry, 1994), and Arthur Schawlow (physics, 1981) had won their prizes as Americans. A splendid reception took place in the University of Toronto Bookroom on November 16, 1995, and the next day the three guests and Polanyi spoke in Convocation Hall. The impressive turnout demonstrated the great public interest in science, despite politicians' reluctance to fund research. A press conference attracted the media, and again the Chemistry Department proved effective in focusing public attention on the need to support advanced research.

The third lecture series — "The Power of Ideas" (1997) — occurred at the same time as the announcement of the Davenports' gift to the department (see below) and the university's launch of its most ambitious capital campaign ever with "A Week of Great Minds." Three Nobel laureates in chemistry — Harry Kroto (1996), Sherwood Rowland (1995), and Y.T. Lee (1986) — as well as medicine winner Joshua Lederberg (1958) and Astronomer Royal Martin Rees were guests of honour at a celebratory dinner on November 29 at the downtown Sheraton Hotel, where John Polanyi spoke on the series theme. Adrienne Clarkson moderated the lectures at Convocation Hall the next day. The audience filled Convocation Hall; Rowland's lecture, about global warming, attracted particular attention from the media, and the press wrote about the events two days running.

The fourth series followed the opening on November 27, 2000, of the Davenport Building; the theme was "Building with Molecules." The four lecturers included two Nobel Prize winners in chemistry, Richard E. Smalley (1996) and Ahmed Zewail (1999), a soon-to-be laureate, Barry Sharpless (2001), and John Meurig Thomas, master of Peterhouse College, Cambridge. The opening of the building took place in a marquee at the south end of the department's undergraduate wing before more than three hundred guests; a luncheon followed in the Davenport Atrium.

The next morning John Polanyi and University President Robert Birgeneau — a distinguished physicist — met with Ontario Minister of Energy, Science and Technology Jim Wilson and his scientific experts. Polanyi observed later, "the message delivered was unmistakable — let the nation's scientists make discoveries where nature permits, rather than where policy dictates." The lectures took place in the afternoon, with a reception following in the chambers of the governing council in Simcoe Hall.

After many years of use, the facilities in the Lash Miller Building had become old and out of date, and the department needed improvements to keep attracting the best people. It required more space for the growing number and size of research groups. The idea of constructing more research space on top of the undergraduate laboratory wing along St. George Street had occasionally been discussed, but the department had done nothing. Moskovits began planning for such an extension.

Moskovits vividly recalls the six breathtaking weeks in August and September 1997 that launched the department's physical renewal. On August 19, with planning for the new structure well underway, he received a phone call from lawyer Barbara Sloan in Florida. Sloan was speaking for an anonymous Toronto graduate who wanted to make a gift — perhaps $500,000 for scholarships — to the university to honour her late husband, also a graduate.

Sloan, on her client's instructions, had first called Chemical Engineering, where the officer who answered had been rather uninformative. When she phoned Chemistry, Armando Marquez — well aware of the chairman's plans for expansion — sought out Martin Moskovits, who spoke with Sloan. He outlined possibilities for scholarships or for a chair or several chairs, or even a new building, which could take the donor's name. When Sloan asked, "What size gift is required to do that?" Moskovits replied, "Ten million." The superbly trained lawyer indicated no surprise and said merely that she would speak to the benefactor's son.

She called again on August 22 to report the son's interest in the building and named the potential donor as Edna Davenport. Her late husband, John L. Davenport, had been a leading figure at Pfizer Corporation. He had grown up in Owen Sound, Ontario, and had been a student in chemical engineering and a pole-vaulter at Toronto, graduating in 1929. He and Edna had met at the university and married in Hart House Chapel. Their children were Peter Davenport and Linda Davenport Spire.

According to Martin Moskovits, Peter too had met his wife, Sylvia, at university — Tufts. When Peter called on August 27, he said that Edna had intestinal cancer, and he was keen to act while she could still celebrate the benefaction. He liked choosing a name for a structure but wondered if the project was real or a spur-of-the-moment idea of Moskovits's. He was assured that this was indeed a high priority and that conceptual plans were available that could be shared with him.

Gary Goldberg, a long-time friend of the department's, had advised Moskovits apropos of fundraising: "You need plans to make the building concrete and visible." He had offered to hire a major architect to prepare conceptual drawings, and the department now had full-colour architectural renderings that it could show to the Davenports.

Moskovits wrote up a virtual tour of the proposed building and sent the package to Peter Davenport. Peter phoned on September 4 to tell Moskovits that he and his sister were thinking seriously about the new structure. Moskovits told him that the third series of Polanyi Lectures would take place on September 28. A celebratory dinner would bring out perhaps four hundred of Toronto's most prominent residents, and Moskovits suggested that it would be incredible if the Davenport gift could be announced at the event in the presence of the Davenports.

Peter grasped the opportunity. He instructed Barbara Sloan to arrange a transfer of about US$7 million in Pfizer stock (about CAD$10 million) to the Chemistry Department to erect the Davenport Chemical Research Laboratories. Moskovits worked with the lawyer to ensure that the chairman of Chemistry had full authority over that money and any interest that accrued.

On September 28, Peter Davenport surprised the gala dinner in the Sheraton Centre Hotel by announcing the massive gift. The four hundred or so guests in attendance rose to their feet and cheered. The publisher of the *Toronto Star* and science reporter Joe Hall were in attendance. The story, together with a photo of a beaming Peter Davenport, appeared on the front page the following day.

To thank the ailing Edna Davenport in person, the university in December sent a small group to Florida, including President Robert Prichard, Vice-President Jon Dellandrea, Professor Mark Lautens, Sue McClelland, and Martin Moskovits. They brought her a gift book of photos and memorabilia from the University of Toronto that she and Jack had known in the 1920s. Mrs. Davenport was elated. She examined each page in great detail and commented on the things she recognized and recalled.

On November 6, 1997, the university's governing council received 100,000 shares of common stock of Pfizer Corporation, worth about $10 million. In the following months, the Canada Foundation for Innovation and the Ontario Innovations Fund matched the gift with $14.5 million more. These funds together allowed the department to construct the Davenport Building and renovate much of Lash Miller. In August 1998, Barbara Sloan informed Moskovits that Edna Davenport's will had left a $2-million endowment to the department, with interest to go to upkeep of the new structure. Moskovits commented, "Such is the special blessing of encountering people of boundless generosity and grace."

Construction began in late 1998 and reached completion in 2000, just three years after Sloan's initial phone call. Martin Moskovits added poignantly, "Although I had the pleasure and privilege of seeing the design phase of the building to its completion, it fell to my successor Dave Farrar to carry out the onerous construction phase. Scott Mabury followed him, completing several renovation projects including significant additional enhancement projects for which he raised additional funds."

In the late 1990s, before and during construction, the users committee for the new building, which included Mark Lautens, had worked hard to ascertain colleagues' needs and wishes and to communicate them to the university committee, which selected the architects A.J. Diamond, Donald Schmitt and Company to design and implement the work. Adrienne De Francesco, an engineer and the department's former business manager, became the department's principal supervisor and coordinator for the construction and the Lash Miller renovations.

The Davenport Building, a two-storey upper addition along St. George Street, opened officially on November 27, 2000. Present for the

The Davenport family, with Peter Davenport and Linda Davenport Spire (front row centre).

Courtesy Department of Chemistry, University of Toronto.

Davenport Building, the top two floors on the Lash Miller Building.
Courtesy Department of Chemistry, University of Toronto.

opening were Peter Davenport and Linda Spire and most of their families, the lawyer Barbara Sloan, Nobel Prize winners (in town to give Polanyi Lectures), and numerous university personnel, including the new chairman of Chemistry, David Farrar, and of course Martin Moskovits.

The Davenports' new laboratories doubled the department's research space. In addition, a small seminar room had the latest electronic technology, and an open atrium became very popular for small receptions and meetings. The beautifully laid out and equipped laboratories could house a number of the department's large and successful research groups — the "organicers," Mark Lautens, Rob Batey, Jik Chin, Ron Kluger, Andrei Yudin, and Deborah Zamble, and the inorganic chemists, Dave Farrar, Ian Manners, and Bob Morris. As well, the new addition housed the vast and totally up-to-date A.D. Allen Chemistry Library, rededicated in June 2002. Librarian Patricia Meindl facilitated Internet access for the faculty, staff, and students using PCs, which made available invaluable research tools such as Scifinder and Beilstein and other programs and databases, including the university library and virtually every chemistry journal published.

Mark Lautens recalls the old laboratories, where he had worked for thirteen years: "Built in the 1960s and never really upgraded, they stood as a symbol of all that had changed in the field of organic chemistry over the past forty years." In contrast, the new labs were "safer, functional, cheerful, bright and beautiful." Research, he feels, improved vastly in the new quarters. "In-house nitrogen and in-house vacuum systems, dedicated equipment rooms and solvent distillation rooms are just a few of the new features we have grown to enjoy." The suite for each faculty member also includes a "lunch/computer/group room."

Martin Moskovits served six years as chairman and then in 1999 returned to academic ranks. Shortly thereafter he joined the University of California's Santa Barbara campus as dean of science.

◦ David Farrar (Chairman, 1999–2002): ◦ Ongoing Transformation

David Farrar obtained his BSc and MSc degrees at Toronto and his PhD at the University of Western Ontario, where he became an expert in determining X-ray crystal structures, especially of inorganic molecules.

David Farrar.
Courtesy Department of Chemistry, University of Toronto.

He joined the Toronto faculty in 1981 and rose to full professor. Farrar, more reserved than Moskovits, established a great rapport with students. During weekends he worked and maintained a farm that he owned near Sarnia.

Moskovits had masterminded funding and planning of the Davenport Building. Farrar saw to its completion, planned the very demanding renovation of upper-floor undergraduate laboratories that took place while the laboratories below were in use, and shepherded the department into its magnificent new home. Again, he and his committee

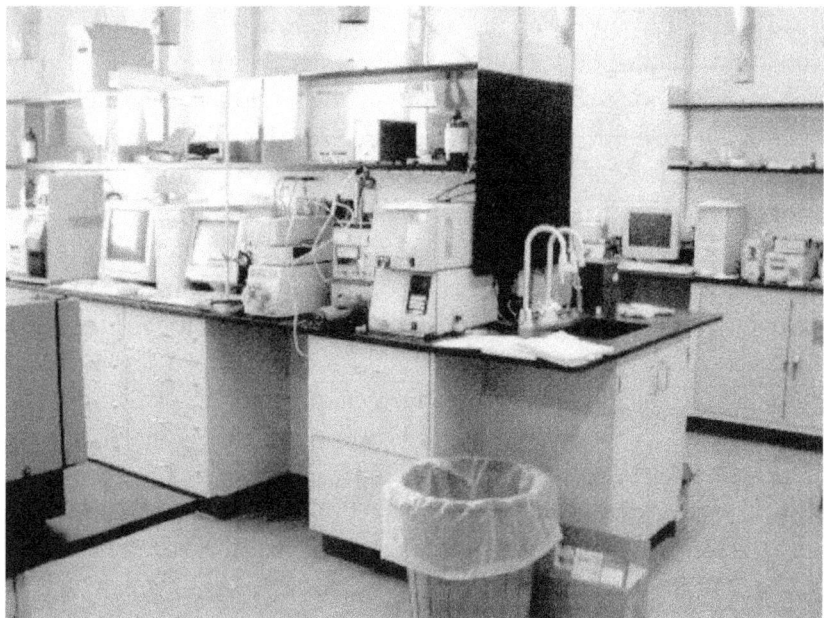

Renovated Research lab in Lash Miller Building.
A.G. Brook Collection.

made every effort to respond to the needs and hopes of all the building's varied constituencies.

Throughout late 2002 and much of 2003, major renovations were in progress in the Lash Miller research wing, with money from the Davenports, the university, and the province. Farrar helped plan the renovation of the many laboratories and offices, which involved complex temporary moves of personnel to other locations. Farrar's research group had to move three times! Erection of a temporary building named "LOMO" outside Lash Miller's northwest corner provided a substitute lecture/seminar room for some of the nomads. The process was modernizing the whole building, making it much more attractive and useful. Much credit goes to Farrar for the relatively smooth transitions.

Computer monitors, unknown in laboratories before 1980, became ubiquitous. People now use computers to run experimental equipment, to record the results of experiments, to write papers, to communicate results and information, and to read the literature. The experimentalist, who earlier sometimes had to work through the night to record results, now leaves it to the computer and leads a more normal life.

During Farrar's terms as associate chairman and chairman he sought to appoint outstanding academics (as chairman he hired ten) and to modernize the undergraduate curriculum to reflect twenty-first-century chemistry. Cynthia Goh, as associate chair for undergraduate affairs, also played a major role. The department now offers specialist programs in chemistry, biological chemistry, environmental chemistry, and materials chemistry. One of the early changes in curricula introduced organic chemistry into first year, which greatly helped to raise students' interest in chemistry; the general chemistry component, which high school had already covered and which generated less interest, shrank accordingly. Students performed organic laboratory experiments on a micro scale; this reduced costs for chemicals and glassware, increased safety, and permitted a number of interesting experiments. The department started redesigning the chemistry content of other undergraduate laboratories — a task that Scott Mabury completed. So by early in the twenty-first century, students at Toronto could participate in the excitement of modern chemistry.

In the 1990s the Faculty of Arts and Science introduced a tenure-track position entitled "Lecturer." This post (with a familiar name but new responsibilities) was for individuals who wanted to teach and to develop better methods of presenting lectures and laboratories. In Chemistry, the first such appointment was Scott Browning (PhD, Toronto), who did much of the teaching in first-year general chemistry. Later Andy Dicks (PhD, Toronto) became lecturer for the first-year organic chemistry component; he recently won a Faculty Teaching Excellence Award. Helen Ohorodnyk, a member of the department since 1971 and long involved with first-year laboratories, as well as other administrative responsibilities, is currently a senior lecturer; she recently received the inaugural Department Staff Excellence Award. Armando Marquez won the award in 2006.

Farrar's leadership on student projects, and on the renovations, so impressed the university administration that in late 2002 it persuaded him to become vice-provost (students). To fill the sudden gap, Stuart Whittington, chairman from 1985 to 1988, returned as acting department head for a year. In 2003 the search committee chose Associate Professor Scott Mabury as the next chairman. Subsequent events proved this to be a splendid selection, as will be seen below.

Historical Distillates

~ Life Outside the Classroom ~

Various activities have enriched the department's extracurricular life. The banquets, skits, and sales that the venerable Chemistry Club sponsored; a new, annual weekend get-together; and a recent centennial celebration have been among the highlights.

The University Chemical Club (the "Chem Club") has played an important role in the lives of chemistry students for many decades. At times its activities have been primarily for undergraduates, but in other eras graduate students have run it, with minimal involvement of undergraduates. There is mention of the University Chemical Society, an undergraduate organization, meeting in the early 1900s in the evening to discuss various chemical subjects. By the 1940s and 1950s the club was meeting monthly with invited speakers, often a faculty member, and one- to three-day field trips took members to chemical companies or organizations like NRC and Chalk River. The activities were crowned by the annual banquet and skits, mentioned earlier, funded by membership fees and from the sale of lab coats. The skits "roasted" faculty members, with Andy Gordon and George Wright favourite targets. Some of the undergraduate skits were fairly simple, but on occasion a brilliant script emerged — for example, the fourth-year presentation in 1956 of Rod Anderson's *Ye Tragedies of Macbeth*. In later years the banquets were abandoned, being replaced by departmental Christmas parties where songs about the faculty were sung. Some of the skits and songs from these affairs appear in the Appendix.

At one time the Chem Club also served as the student section of the Toronto branch of the Chemical Institute of Canada (CIC). The health of the club diminished during the late 1960s and the 1970s, the period of student apathy toward involvement in most university affairs. However, in the early 1980s Michael Powell, a graduate student, was elected president. Powell revolutionized the club's financial operations by setting up a business model for the club involving the sale of lab coats, safety glasses, and old exams to chemistry undergraduates. Graduate student volunteers were to run the club stores, and the financial profits would be used to bring in speakers and for picnics and parties. A street vendor who set up a truck to sell lab coats in competition one year was bought out by the club under the condition that he would never return. His inventory served the club's needs for several years and overall cost the club less than its usual provider.

This entrepreneurial action revitalized the club, which continues to be very active and successful to this day.

Christina Schwarz, a member of the club's executive for 2003–04, observed that the society still has several functions. It sells lab coats, goggles and gloves, old examinations, notebooks, and manuals for most undergrad courses. In 2003–04 it had some 2,500 customers. Over the years it has used the profits to organize a summer student-research poster session and offered a cash prize for the best poster. In 2003–04 it gave $10,000 to the university endowment fund toward funding a summer scholarship for an undergraduate to do chemical research. Subsequent contributions have raised the funds to $50,000, which when matched by other funds created an endowment of $150,000 to support the scholarship. A graduate scholarship has now been similarly funded through another gift of $50,000, leading to a second $150,000 endowment. The club used some of its profits to bring a visiting speaker to the department (Professor George Whitesides of Harvard in 2003). In 2005 it began the organization of annual mini symposia with changing themes and two invited speakers (Professors Warren Piers and Janine Cossy in 2006, with metathesis as the subject).

The club continues to organize social events. Currently popular social gatherings are coffee and doughnuts on Friday afternoons and the December and spring parties. The club also puts on movie nights and each year operates a curling bonspiel, barbeques, monthly cultural events, and a trip to Canada's Wonderland north of Toronto.

During the 1990s a series of weekend events excited many physical chemistry students. As a result of a stimulating meeting of faculty members and students at a Chemical Physics Weekend at the University of Waterloo, Professor Cynthia Goh and some Toronto students decided to organize a similar event. After much planning, in May 1991 the first Annual Physical Chemistry Weekend Retreat took place at Hart House Farm, chaired by graduate student St. John Dixon-Warren. The farm, on the Niagara Escarpment near Caledon, was the idea of Nicholas Ignatieff in the late 1940s, when he was warden of Hart House.

Goh recalls the event's history. The first year saw about sixty participants, and almost everyone contributed. The setting was rustic: "We brought our own food, sleeping bags, chairs, overhead projectors, and we knew there were no showers." A well-equipped kitchen, however, allowed some early risers to prepare fresh muffins each morning! The invited speaker was Professor John Hepburn from the University of Waterloo, and participants started a tradition by giving him a used flange from one of John Polanyi's ultra-high vacuum chambers with their names engraved on it.

By its fourth year, the group dropped "Physical" from its title and opened the weekend to the entire department. "Freshly baked muffins were essential, as well as kegs of beer and dips in the cold pond at the farm in lieu of showers." One time, Martin Moskovits displayed his pizza-making ability.

In October 2001, group members again attended the Chemical Physics Weekend in Waterloo. They decided to resuscitate the weekend, but now in April, and with a focus on "the confluence of chemistry, physics and biology." The first Chemical BioPhysics Symposium (CBP), in 2002, attracted 120 guests and speakers from across the continent. The event, now limited to 150 attendees, has continued annually, becoming very popular with an international community.

In 2003 the Chemistry Department celebrated the one-hundredth anniversary of the university's granting of the first PhD to a woman (and Chemistry's second-ever PhD). Clara C. Benson obtained her doctorate in 1903 under the direction of William Lash Miller with her thesis, "The Rates of the Reactions in Solutions Containing Ferrous Sulphate, Potassium Iodide, and Chromic Acid." She became professor of physiological chemistry in the Faculty of Household Science and eventually dean of that faculty, which had quarters in the Lillian Massey Building at University Avenue and Bloor Street. The university named the women's athletic centre at Huron and Harbord streets the Benson Building in her honour. The Lillian Massey later housed a store and provincial offices; the Benson facilities are open to men.

For the centennial, the Chemistry Department, the Faculty of Arts and Science, and the Faculty of Physical Education and Health jointly sponsored the day-long celebration. Lectures included two on chemistry by Professors Deborah Zamble ("Metals in Biology") and Cynthia Goh

("From Molecular to Macroscopic: Hierarchical Assembly and Design Principles from Nature"); other speakers addressed women's involvement in Physical Education and Health. An exhibition of documents and mementos relating to Benson and her era were on display in the Lash Miller Atrium, where lunch took place. In addition, there was a re-enactment of Benson's PhD thesis defence. Graduate student Christine Braban portrayed Benson; Professor Stuart Whittington, examiner Lash Miller; and Professor Jamie Donaldson, department head Professor William Lang.

The final lecture — "Undergraduate Chemistry of the Future," by Scott Mabury — described what the renovated undergraduate laboratories at Lash Miller would look like. In particular, they were to have a fume cupboard for every student, and groups of sixteen students would work in separate, colour-coded "pods," each under the supervision of a teaching assistant. The facilities would make full use of the latest techniques, including electronic notebooks that could access the chemical literature or course notes on the Internet, as well as downloading the TA's "chalk talk" about each experiment. Mabury's address was so exciting, it almost made the listener want to go back and take the lab course again!

Scott Mabury (Chairman, 2003– Present): Entering the New Century

Scott Mabury was an American who had obtained his PhD at the University of California in environmental chemistry; he joined the department in 1995. He has a farm east of Toronto that he works on weekends. Early in his term as chairman several events helped set the tone for the start of the new millennium. The department completed the renovation of the undergraduate laboratories mentioned above and built a facility to explore the new frontier of the "nano-world." Under Mabury's leadership, fully redesigned and rebuilt undergraduate laboratories in the Lash Miller Building reached completion in November 2003 — in record time, under budget, and without interrupting the undergraduate students working in adjacent laboratories.

In mid-term, happy groups of undergraduates taking first- and second-year organic chemistry occupied the new facilities. The laboratories complemented the new first-year curriculum that David Farrar, Cynthia Goh, and others had developed. The official opening occurred on

February 25, 2004. Scott Mabury, the enthusiastic initiator, supporter, and planner of the laboratories, served as master of ceremonies at the event, which Sue McClelland organized beautifully.

Also, the department gained a new underground laboratory for its Centre for Nanostructured Polymer and Inorganic Material, built with part of a major grant for materials research from the Canadian Foundation for Innovation (CFI) and the Ontario Innovation Trust (OIT). Grass now covers the large hole excavated for construction between the Lash Miller Building and Willcocks Street. This 1,700-square-foot facility houses three of the finest microscopes in Canada: a field-emission scanning electron microscope, from Hitachi; a super-high-resolution scanning transmission electron microscope, also from Hitachi; and a laser confocal scanning fluorescence microscope, from Leica. As well, microtomes and sample preparation space allow very high-resolution investigation of the detailed structures of solid materials.

The CFI and OIT funds came as part of a $10.7-million grant that the department used to obtain forty-two pieces of state-of-the-art instrumentation. Mitch Winnik was the leading principal investigator, doing much of the writing, cajoling of colleagues, and negotiating of company involvements in the development of the grant application; other principal investigators were Eugenia Kumacheva, Ian Manners, Geoffrey Ozin, Molly Shoichet, and Andrei Yudin, along with David James in Mechanical Engineering. Manners returned to England in 2006.

Lately an anonymous donor has presented the department with $1.5 million to convert the outside area to the west of the undergraduate laboratories into a courtyard garden with trees and plants. The garden, dedicated to Edna Davenport, opened officially in mid-November 2005 after a major named-tree planting in the morning by faculty,

Scott Mabury.
Courtesy Department of Chemistry, University of Toronto.

The Davenport Garden Opening.
Courtesy Department of Chemistry, University of Toronto.

staff, and students, and a well-attended barbeque followed.

The garden became accessible by a new door from an impressively redesigned Lash Miller lobby in the spring of 2006, again accompanied by a barbeque.

And so the Chemistry Department, which began in 1843 in simple quarters in the parliament building at Front Street near John Street with one faculty member — Henry Croft — has changed almost beyond recognition. Like the university and Toronto, the worlds of chemistry have also changed and grown, and the department has expanded through its various eras and homes. The Lash Miller–Davenport complex on St. George Street is today the base for scores of professors, academics, and support staff. In the last two years, the department has appointed several new faculty members to the three campuses, including Vy Maria Dong, Rebecca Jockusch, Jennifer Murphy, Mark Nitz, Andre and Myrna Simpson, Datong Song, Mark Taylor, Gilbert Walker, and Aaron Wheeler. With completion of its renovations and additions, with its distinguished faculty, top-rate staff, and excellent students from all over the world, and with its dazzling array of instruments and equipment to support research, the department's future indeed looks bright.

Appendix

Chemisty Club Skits and Songs

The following are some skits and songs that were presented by undergraduate or graduate students at various banquets of the Chemistry Club and other departmental events in earlier years, from the 1940s to the 1960s. Texts of a number of skits and songs presented by students over the years are stored in the University of Toronto Archives, A77-0025/box 004.

Ye Tragedies of Macbeth

A skit presented by the fourth year class of 1956, at the King Edward Hotel, February 1956.

The characters: **A**, A. (Andy) R. Gordon; **G**, G. (George) F Wright; **DJ**, D. (Don) J. LeRoy.

KCR, King Cole Room, a popular beverage room in the Park Plaza Hotel at Bloor and Avenue Roads; **Q, H, S, TdS, PdV,** Thermodynamics symbols.

Scene: A cavern. In the middle, a boiling cauldron.
(Thunder. Enter three witches).

A: Thrice the brindled cat hath mew'd

G: Thrice, and once the hedge pig whined.

DJ: Harpier cries, 'Tis time, 'tis time.'
A: Round about the cauldron go;
        In the poison'd catalyst throw.
        Now toss in our backwards Q,
        S will muddle students too.
G: You know S, entropy, S—

A: Problem, test, and lab report,
     We can flunk them just for sport.

All: Double, double, toil and trouble;
     Students burn, and cauldron bubble.

G: Ruptured bonds of complex strange
     In the cauldron rearrange
     Throw the text-books in this slime;
     A theory is a waste of time.

DJ: The molecules never knew it,
     Let George do it,—

G: Gummy stench and vapours loose,
     Vats of sick tobacco juice,
     Guts of inorganic fools,
     Burnt-out souls of molecules.
     For a charm of powerful trouble,
     Like a hell-broth boil and bubble.

All: Double, double, toil and trouble;
     Fire burn, and cauldron bubble.

DJ: Here we have some Glauber's Salt
     Noblest chemical in our vault.

G: Well I'm from where the corn grows tall,
     And so I swear by furfural

DJ: Lizard's leg and blind-worm's slobber,
     Nothing, sister, is like Glauber.
     Phase rule fancy by the mole;
     Activation is our goal.
     Coefficients of transmission,
     Fudging factors in collision,
     dH dagger squared and less
     The sum of QRVES.

Historical Distillates

        I'm sorry, I seem to have a sign wrong here somewhere—

All: On the double, toil and trouble;
        Students burn and cauldron bubble.
        Right is wrong and George is Wright,
        Hover through the filthy night.

G: Cool it with a graduate's blood,
        Then the charm is firm and good.
        But hold. By the furan on my thumbs,
        Something wicked this way comes.
        Open, locks,
        Whoever knocks!

Enter Macbeth

Mac: (aside)
        O foul stench! Hell is mercurial.
        All the perfumes of Arabia
        Could not sweeten this filthy lab!
        How now, you secret, black, and midnight hags!
        What is't you do?

All: A deed without a name.

Mac: I conjure you by that which you profess,
        O dark professors of black witchcraft lore,
        Though some strange evil alchemy you invite
        To bring the dreaded answer to my plight,
        Though you unleash your most malevolent spells
        In fabricating vile ungodly smells,
        Though you make the surface region vanish
        Though you lie about election smears,
        Though you irradiate with J.J. Rays
        And racemize the rancid liquid phase,
        Even till your lectures sicken; answer me
        To what I ask you.

A: Speak.

G: Demand.

DJ: We'll answer.

A: Say, if thou'dst rather hear it from our mouths,
      Or from our masters'?

Mac: Call 'em; let me see 'em.

A: Pour in hydrofluoric that hath eaten glass,
      Grease extracted from the smouldering acid bath
      Throw into the flame.

All: Come, high or low;
      Thyself and office deftly show!
              (Thunder. First Apparition on oscilloscope.)

Mac. Tell me thou unknown power, 'fore it is too late,
      What must I do to graduate?

App: Macbeth! Macbeth! Macbeth! Beware Wetmore;
      Beware the thane of activation overpotential.
      Dismiss me; enough.
              (Descends)

Mac: Whate'er thou art, for thy good caution, thanks;
      Thou hast harp'd my fear aright; but one word more,—

A: He will not be commanded; here's another,
      More potent than the first.
              (Thunder, Second Apparition, skull, with sign "I did not
              do my problems")

App: Macbeth! Macbeth! Macbeth!

Mac: Had I three years, I'd hear thee.

App: Be bloody, bold, and resolute; laugh to scorn
The power of Wright; for none of organic born
Shall harm Macbeth.
    (Descends)

Mac: Then live, Wright: what need I fear of thee?
But yet I'll make assurance double sure,
And take a conjugated bond of fate: thou shalt not live;
That I may tell pale-hearted fear it lies,
And sleep in spite of resonance-hybrids.
    (Thunder. Third Apparition, silk hat and rabbit.)
What is this
That rises like a rabbit from a hat
And wears around his wondrous magic ribs
The sacred air of Saint J. Willard Gibbs?

All: Listen, but speak not to't.

App: Be lion-mettled, proud, and care not who
Say essays, tests, and lab reports are due:
Macbeth shall never fail until dE
Exceeds TdS minus PdV. (Rabbit goes back into hat)

Mac: That will never be:
Who can impress our Gordon, bid the chief
Unfix Lash Miller's firmly planted root?
Then failure's head rise never till the heresy
Of Guggenheim arise and our Macbeth
Shall quaff in KCR two months of beer
Until examination time appear.
Yet tell me, if your art can so much say,
What questions must I fear from old D.J.?

All: Seek to know no more.

Mac: I will be satisfied: deny me this
And an eternal curse fall on you and
Reactions, one and all, miscarry: let me know

Shall it happen that I get my year? (More thunder)
What stinks that cauldron? And what noise is here?

A: Show!

G: Show!

DJ: Show!

All: Show his eyes and grieve his heart;
Come like shadows, so depart!
    (Large placard slowly rises.)

Mac: Thou art too like my mark in Physics, down!
That 0 doth sear mine eyeballs. And the next
That other round goose-egg is like the first.
A third is like the former. Filthy hags!
Why do you show me this? A fourth! Start, eyes!
What will the line stretch out to the crack of doom?
Another yet! A seventh! I'll see no more:
And yet the eighth appears and many more.
Horrible sight! Now I see 'tis true.
For the mark pinching breakdown leer upon me
And points at them for his. (Apparition vanishes.)
What, is this so?

G: Ay, sir, all this is so; but why
Stands Macbeth this amazedly?
Come sisters, cheer we his dejection,
Which weights his quantized mean complexion.
Circle we before this king,
In a Kekulean ring,
That this unlucky sap may know
The three weird sisters told him so.
    (Music. The witches dance and then vanish.)

Mac: Where are they? Gone? Let this pernicious hour
Stand aye accursed. Beware the Ides of May!

To be or not to be without BA. ?
(Exit)
(Also Fini).

Faculty referred to were D.J. LeRoy, A.R. Gordon, G.F Wright, F.E. Wetmore, and J.J. Rae.

Cast: Macbeth, Jim McIntyre. Witches: DJ, Jim Martin; Andy, Duncan MacKillop; George, Rod Anderson. Rod Anderson wrote most of the script.

* * * * * *

A Chemist's Mikado

The Graduate Skit at the Chem Club Banquet, March 29, 1951, sung to the well-known songs in *The Mikado*.

ACT I

As the skit opens three chemists come on the stage wearing signs saying "Organic, B.A.", "Inorganic, B.A." and "Physical, B.A." They stare around them in wonderment.

Org.: Quite a place, isn't it?

Phys.: Sure is.

Inorg.: I wonder if there is anyone who can show us around here?

(Enter Chorus in lab coats)

All 3: Who are you?
Chorus: If you want to know who we are,
    We are grads at the U of T,
We are smarter than you by far,
    We work for an advanced degree;
We demonstrate for our pay,

Research is not for the day,
At night we still slave away.

Org.: Could you people tell us a little about this place?

1st Graduate Student: A pleasure, young man.
(Tenor Solo)
A graduate student I,
    I have no income status,
    I do my research gratis,
And very often sigh.
My days are very long,
    Include some lecture courses;
    To work Professors force us,
We do it, right or wrong.

Phys.: Can you tell us a little about the Faculty?

1st Grad. Student: That's quite a job. There's an awful lot of them around here. They don't do much to affect us. We just ignore them. There's LeRoy, Wetmore, McBryde, McCasland, Lorriman, Rae, Lister. And probably a couple of dozen others. I never stopped to count them. And then of course there's Dr. Gordon, the Mikado himself. This fellow can probably tell you more about him; he works for him.

2nd Grad. Student: Well here's a little I can tell you.
(Solo) Our great Doc Gordon, virtuous man,
When he to rule our labs, began,
    Resolved to try
    A plan whereby,
Chemists might best be steadied;
And he decreed to all he saw,
That Willard Gibbs'us word was law,
Unless someone could find a flaw.
    No one has yet objected
        Objected, obje———cted,
    No one has yet objected.

Chorus:
>   And you'll allow, as I expect,
>   That they were right to not object;
> And I am right
> And you are right
>   And everyone is quite correct
> Quite correct.

Solo:
This great decree which we now had
Caused great dismay throughout the lab
>   From basement men,
>   To third floor, then,
Were equally affected.
Organicers said nasty words,
Of Willard Gibbs some had not heard
And worried on the smelly third
>   That they might be ejected,
>   Ejected, eje————————cted
>   That they might be ejected.

Chorus:
>   And they were right you must agree
>   To worry so for a degree
> And I am right
> And you are right
>   And everyone is quite correct
> Quite correct.

Inorg.: This is most absorbing; tell us more.

1st Grad. Student: Well, we haven't mentioned "it" yet, and I suppose we should. Oh-oh: It won't be necessary; here he comes now. (Enter Dr. Wright, white hair and pipe as per usual.)

Chorus:
Behold the Lord High Executioner:
>   A personage of noble rank and title.

As head of the organicers,
    His functions are particularly vital.
        Defer, defer:
To the Lord High Executioner,
        Defer, defer;
To the noble Lord High Executioner.

Dr. Wright: Gentlemen, I am much touched by this reception. I understand that one of these lowly persons intends to <u>work</u> (you'll note I stress that word, young man) to <u>work</u> for me.

Org.: Yes, your Lord High Executionership.

Dr. Wright: If so, you must, learn a few of my ideas about discipline. (Solo)
My object all sublime,
I shall achieve in time,
To make the punishment fit the crime,
The punishment fit the crime;
And make each prisoner pent
Unwillingly represent
A source of innocent merriment
Of innocent merriment.
All chemists who think that they know it all
And have nothing more to learn,
    Must quietly listen
    To students who glisten
In my lab every Saturday morn.
A student whose work gives him much lower yields
Than the ninety percent required,
    Shall give it ten tries,
    He'll work till he cries,
And then he shall prob'ly be fired.
All chemists who write on a monthly report
For several days at a time,
    Shall get sharp retorts
    On these same reports
And for each day will pay me a dime.

A man who's allowed to work in my lab
And burns it in gratitude,
    Shall clean off my rack
    And put it all back,
Before I get back my good mood.
My object all sublime
I shall achieve in time,
To make the punishment fit the crime
The punishment fit the crime;
And make each prisoner pent
Unwillingly represent
A source of innocent merriment
Of innocent merriment.
And that's enough wasted time. Come on new student. Get the hell upstairs to work.

CURTAIN (End of Act I)

ACT II

Two years later. Throughout this act several grad. students may cross the stage shooting squash bottles. One student is asleep on the floor and others stand around. Our three heroes(?) enter.

All three: (Trio)
Three little M.A.'s now are we
Filled to the brim with chemistry
Starting to work for our Ph.D.
    Three little M.A.'s now.

Org.: Chemistry is a source of fun,

Phys.: Half of the job has now been done,
Inorg.: Life is a joke that's just begun

All three: Three little M.A.'s now.
Three little M.A.'s, learn<u>ed</u> very,
Filled to the jowls, with chemis<u>ta</u>ry,

Plugged with the genius tutelary,
    Three little M.A.'s now,
    Three little M.A.'s now.

Org.: Well, let's get to work now. On to the Ph.D.!

(Exit the three. Several grad. students enter and one sits on a stool waving a Bunsen burner under an imaginary flask.)

3rd Grad. Student: (Solo)
On a rack, in a chem lab, a reaction sat,
    Going "Burble, burb-burble, burb-burble".
And I said, "Oh reaction, now what are you at
    Going "Burble, burb-burble, burb-burble".
"You are not very helpful, reaction," I cried,
"Don't you think that you might now react, if you tried?
"But instead of reacting it just up and died
With a "Burble, burb-burble, burb-burble."
(Exit 3rd Grad. Student with a sigh and looking dejected.)

(Enter Organic and Physical M.A.'s, the former carrying a few sheets of paper.)

Phys.: Where are you off to?

Org.: Just going to write my report. A monthly report is merely corroborative detail intended to give artistic verisimilitude to an otherwise bald and unconvincing narrative.

Phys.: How very clear you are.

(Enter the chorus in bunches, mumbling: "The Mikado is coming."
"Here comes Dr. Gordon" etc.
Enter Dr. Gordon lighting a cigarette. The students line up in front of him, bowing.)

Dr. Gordon: (Solo)
From every kind of man

Obedience I expect,
As Emperor here I can
Make everyone be correct,
Everything that is run,
Is very well done
By an Emperor who's select.

Chorus: Bow! Bow:
To an Emperor who's select.
Bow: Bow!
To an Emperor who's select.

Dr. Gordon: Well, gentlemen. Everyone hard at work? All of you feeling thermodynamically stable? I hope so. I don't relish disciplinary action but I have been making a list in case I find a victim.

(Solo)
As some day it may happen that a victim must be found,
I've got a little list, — I've got a little list
Of chemical offenders who might well be underground,
And who never would be missed — who never would be missed:
There's professors on this Faculty who sleep in seminars,
All people, who against my wish, smoke in the corridors,
All students who with water fights, get all the floors so wet,
And those who start big fires, that might be burning yet.
But it really doesn't matter whom you put upon the list,
For they'd none of them be missed — they'd none of them be missed.

Chorus: You may put 'em on the list — you may put 'em on the list,
And they'll none of 'em be missed — they'll none of 'em be missed.
(Exit Dr. Gordon and most of the students. Two grads come to the centre of the stage.)

4th Grad. Student: Well, spring is nearly here. My orals are over. Nothing but a thesis to write. Wonderful, isn't it?

5th Grad. Student: Spring, bah: Spring means damned exams, no work done.

4th Grad. Student (Solo)
>   The flowers that bloom in the spring tra, la,
>   Will bring a degree that is mine,
>   Car and a wife and a ring tra, la,
>   Are some of the things it'll bring tra, la,
>   In a summer of roses and wine,
>   In a summer of roses and wine.

And that's what we mean when we say that a thing
Is welcome as flowers that bloom in the spring.
>   Tra la, la la la la,
>   Tra la, la la la la,

Is welcome as flowers in spring.

5th Grad. Student:(Solo)
>   The flowers that bloom in the spring, tra, la,
>   Have nothing to do with the case,
>   For exams are all it will bring tra, la,
>   A thought that does not make one sing, tra, la.
>   I hope I have stated my case,
>   I hope I have stated my case.

And that's what I mean when I say or I sing,
Oh bother the flowers that bloom in the spring,
>   Tra la, la la la 1a,
>   Tra la, la la la la,

Oh bother the flowers of spring.

CURTAIN (End of Act II)

ACT III and Finale

Enter all the cast. The three students now wear signs which say Ph.D. in addition to their other degrees.

Chorus:
>   For they've got their Doctor's degree, degree,
>   So do not be wary,
>   Just let us be merry,
>   And join their expression of glee, of glee,

For they have their Doctor's degree.

FINALE — ALL
Then let the throng
    Our joy advance,
With laughing, song,
    And merry dance,
With joyous shout and ringing cheer,
Inaugurate our new career.

CURTAIN

* * * * * *

UNIVERSITY OF TORONTO CHEMICAL CLUB

Third-Year Skit presented at the Banquet February 21, 1952

Lyrics: Eric Channen and Helen Shemilt
Pre-Dinner Music: The bagpipes assisted by Al Westland.
Piano Accompaniment: Mavis Reid (Vic.)
Jokes (?): Owen Funnell
Ad-Libs: John Moffat
Rehearsals: Joan Stewart's, Marg Blackstock's, Helen Shemilt's (Annesley)
Typing mistakes: Bert Blevis.

Cast / Members of the class

<u>Physics and Chemistry</u>
Margaret Blackstock
Bert Blevis
Eric Channen
Mike Dignam
Owen Funnall
Bob Graham (Vice Pres.)
Sel Marks
Joan Stewart

<u>Chemistry</u>
George Atkinson
John Moffat
Helen Shemilt
Al Westland

"Souse Specific"

Bob: (In front of curtain with handful of notes) Ladies and gentlemen (pauses uncertainly, looks through notes) Ah yes — and members of the faculty. This evening we will be treated to selections from the sensational new musical comedy — "Souse Specific".

If you sit quietly and listen attentively you will hear a performance of xtraordinary beauty and taste. However, since no one sits quietly, we don't give a damn. So I'll turn you over to our M.C.

Curtain Raised

Bert: (John enters, walks around and in front of the M.C. carrying an electric cord) Good evening, folks — (stops and watches John angrily) Say, what are you doing here?

John: (Gives an extemporaneous speech, followed by:) Oh friends, Oh yes! Someone told me to put a plug in for the third year skit.

Bert: The first thing we will <u>render</u> is in sympathy with the graduate students.

<u>SOME DARK AND HAUNTED EVENING</u>
    (Music: Some Enchanted Evening)
(Sung by John and Al, and interrupted frequently with ad libs).
Some dark and haunted evening,
You may see a stranger — walking through the Wallberg,
Across a murky room.
And somehow you know, you know even then,
Somewhere you'll see him, again and again.
Some dark and haunted evening,
You may hear him laughing, you may hear him laughing,
A fearful note of doom.
And night after night, as strange as it seems,
The sound of his laughter will haunt all your dreams.
You can't escape him,
Even though you try.
A demon to torment you,

'Till the day you die.
Some dark and haunted evening,
You will see this stranger, you will see this stranger,
Across a murky room;
With shackles, that bind, in prison you'll be,
Since ghosts of the Wallberg will never be free.

Bert: Our next number, ladies and gentlemen, is— (enter Joan hurriedly; whispered conference on stage). Ladies, and Gentlemen (continuing in emotionless C.B.C. voice), I regret to announce that there has been an explosion in the Wallberg Building. The building will henceforth be known as the "Berg" building, — no wall!

Bert: Our next selection from. "Souse Specific" is dedicated to — (looks at script, scratches out something., shakes head and says "Oh, no!!" as if afraid to say what is written.)

BLOODY GUFFY
   (Music: Bloody Mary)

Girls:	Bloody Guffy is the man we love, Bloody Guffy is the man we love, Bloody Guffy is the man we love,
Male Chorus:	Now ain't that too damn bad.
Girls:	Bloody Guffy's drinking ethanol, He is always drinking ethanol, Bloody Guffy's drinking ethanol,
Chorus:	Now ain't that too damn bad.
Girls:	Bloody Guffy smokes a smelly pipe, Bloody Guffy smokes a smelly pipe, Bloody Guffy smokes a smelly pipe,
Chorus:	And he don't use Pepsodent.

Girls:	His hair is whiter than an angel's robe,
	His hair is whiter than an angel's robe,
	His hair is whiter than an angel's robe,
Chorus:	And he don't use Fitch shampoo.
Girls:	Bloody Guffy is the man we love,
	Bloody Guffy is the man we love,
	Bloody Guffy is the man we love,
Chorus:	Now ain't that too damn bad.
All:	Now ain't that too damn bad.

(M.C. approaches front of stage. George who has been looking at Glasstone during the song looks up).

George: Say Sel, when a man's had twelve beers, is it steady state or equilibrium?

Sel: With respect to what process?

George: How should he know after twelve beers?

Bert: (Exasperated) Our next number is a charming ditty, we hope most of you will enjoy.

HUNDRED-AND-ONE POUNDS OF FUN

All: Hundred-and-one pounds of fun,
That's our little honey bun.
Get a load of honey bun tonight. (unfortunately absent)
A trifle bald, but quite spry,
Only sixty inches high
Every inch is packed with dynamite
In the classroom, he's a killer—
He always quotes Lash Miller;
His quips are pips — they cut like whips.

> Oh, what a thriller!
> Problems are another trap,
> If you do them, you're a sap,
> We are caught and we don't want to run,
> cause we're having too much fun with honey bun.

Helen: Believe me sonny,

All: He's a cookie who will cook you till you're done.

Sel: Say Mike, does your brother work?

Mike: No, he's a demonstrator.

Bob: (After laughter from audience has subsided, bursts out in a fit of laughter) NO WALL

Bert: Our final number is the theme song of "Souse Specific"

THERE IS NOTHING LIKE A BEER
    (Music: There is Nothin' Like a Dame)

Male chorus:
> We got benches hard as rocks,
> We got tall revolving stools,
> We got pencils, pens, and slide-rules, and a lot of other tools;
> We got Chemical Club lecturers that come from far and near
> What ain't we got? We ain't got beer.
> We got fancy apparatus for experimental show,
> We got Beilstein writ in German, none of us will ever know
> We got every sort of gadget that would make a chemist cheer:
> What ain't we got? we ain't got beer.

Recit:
> We got nothin' to make us root for —
> What we want is what there ain't no substitute for —

Chorus:	There is nothin' like a beer, nothin' in the lab. There is nothin' that will cheer like a great big bottle of beer. We got lots of dandy labs, We got demonstrators too, We get counsel from professors and a lot of it is true, We got lectures full of boredom and examination fear— What ain't we got? We ain't got beer.
Recit:	We have been doing research all term, but brother— In spite of many attempts to synthesize with 85% yield There is still one thing in this world that is in No way shape or form like any other—
Chorus:	There is nothin' like a beer, nothin' in the lab. There is nothin' that can cheer like a great big bottle of beer
Finale:	There are no books like a beer, And nothin looks like a beer, There are no drinks like a beer, That attract like a beer.

* * * * * *

A Chemistry Professor's Christmas Carol
presented at the Chem. Club Christmas Party, December 1964

On the first day of Christmas my Chairman sent to me,
A large raise in <u>salaree</u>,

On the second day of Christmas my Chairman sent to me,
Two Xmas trees and a large raise in <u>salaree</u>,

On the third day of Christmas ray Chairman sent to me,
Three travel grants, two Xmas trees and a large raise in <u>salaree</u>,

On the fourth day of Christmas my Chairman sent to me,

Four Post Doc's, three travel grants, two Xmas trees
and a large raise in <u>salaree</u>,

On the fifth day of Christmas my Chairman sent to me,
Five Old Deans, four Post Doc's, three travel grants, two Xmas trees
and a large raise in salaree,

etc.

Two Xmas Trees,
Three Travel Grants
Four Post Doc's
Five Old Deans
Six Memoranda
Seven Lab Assistants
Eights Taps A-Leaking
Nine Grads A-Sleeping
Ten Typists Typing
Eleven Demis Deming
Twelve Months Notice   NB Stop Dead Here Without
                              Going Through Sequence

* * * * * * * *

Another song, presented at the University Chemical Club Christmas Party, December 1966

Tune — Old Black Joe
Start on middle C
To be sung *a capella*.

Folk Song

Gone are the days when the Chemist's chin was bare;
Gone are the years when he sported lots of hair;
Gone, from the lab to a world of pen and ink;
I hear Administration calling — "Leave that stink!"

Chorus- (To be sung with feeling after each verse except the last)

>They're going! They're going!
>The Department's getting thin.
>I hear Administration calling
>"Come-on-in!"

Why should we weep when he goes to heights above?
Why should we sigh when he's Prexy's hand in glove?
Now he's a Dean, and there's stuffing in his shirt;
Hear Administration calling — "Good-old-Bert:"

Peter's the next for departure from the fold;
Grads he'll forsake; they'll be orphans in the cold;
Off to the west, in the fields and pastures green,
I hear the pipes of Erin calling— "Be-Our-Dean;"

Grads, mourn no more; there are better days ahead.
Here comes a Dean, with assistance, in his stead;
Keith soars aloft, and he's a right before the gates;
I hear Administration calling — "Come-In-Yates."

"Who'll count the kids?", do I hear a College cry;
"Who'll keep the roll of the ones that qualify?
"Who'll cheer the staff with a fresh yarn every day?
I hear Administration calling, "Send-us-Rae!"

Last chorus-
>We're coming! We're coming!
>And our step is full of beans,
>With help for the Establishment,
>And Three Grand Deans

With special reference to Professors Bert Allen (to become Dean of Arts and Science), W.A.E. (Peter) McBryde (to become Chairman of the Chemistry Department, University of Waterloo), Keith Yates (to become Associate Dean, School of Graduate Studies, U of T), and Jim Rae (to be Registrar at Erindale College).

Notes

Acknowledgements
1. For brief accounts of the University of Toronto's Department of Chemistry, see L.E. Westman, "The Department of Chemistry," *University of Toronto Monthly* 21 (1921): 253, and F.R. Lorriman, "The Department of Chemistry, University of Toronto," *Chemistry in Canada* (reprint, October 1959).

Introduction
1. Bruce West, *Toronto* (Toronto: Doubleday Canada Ltd., 1967), 1–21; Katherine Hale, *Toronto: Romance of a Great City* (Toronto: Cassell and Co. Ltd., 1956), 37–8.
2. J.G. Hodgins, ed., *A Documentary History of Education in Upper Canada* (Toronto: Warwick and Rutter, 1894–1910), I, 11–2; W. Stewart Wallace, *A History of the University of Toronto* (Toronto: University of Toronto Press, 1927), 2; W.R. Riddell, *The Life of John Graves Simcoe* (Toronto: McClelland and Stewart Ltd., 1926), 339–40.
3. J.L.H. Henderson, *John Strachan* (Toronto: University of Toronto Press, 1969), 3–16, 40–9, 70–1, and 76–80; J.L.H. Henderson, ed., *John Strachan: Documents and Opinions* (Toronto: McClelland and Stewart Ltd, 1969), 183–99, also letter to Lefroy, 231; T.A. Reed, *A History of the University of Trinity College, Toronto* (Toronto: University of Toronto Press, 1952), 3–22, 33–49; Wallace, *History*, 1, 1–19, 20–59.
4. A.G. Croal, "The Teaching of Science in Ontario 1800–1900" (DPaed thesis, University of Toronto, 1940), 13.
5. Wallace, *History*, 15.
6. Hodgins, *Documentary History*, IV, 202–209.
7. J. Ross Robertson, *Landmarks of Toronto* (1894; reprint, Belleville: Mika Publishing, 1974), I, 351–9; III, 317–22.

Chapter 1
1. Garrison Creek flowed into Lake Ontario near the western entrance to Toronto harbour, just east of Fort York. Later, like Taddle Creek and various small waterways in the city, it was diverted underground into a sewer. At the time referred to there was no eastern entrance to the harbour. See Robertson, *Landmarks*, III, 93.

2. D.C. Masters, *The Rise of Toronto* (Toronto: University of Toronto Press, 1947), 9.
3. Charles Dickens, *American Notes* (London: William Collins and Sons, 1850), 310–11.
4. L. Pearce Williams, *The Selected Correspondence of Michael Faraday* (New York: Cambridge University Press, 1971), 309. Mitscherlich's law of isomorphism links similar crystal forms of substances to similarities in their chemical composition. He also investigated dimorphism among minerals, whereby two substances of identical chemical composition crystallize in different forms. However, his achievements were wide-ranging; see *Dictionary of Scientific Biography* (New York: Charles Scribner's Sons, 1974), IX, 423–6. He earned a doctoral degree in Oriental languages before he took up the study of medicine, from which he strayed into chemistry. With such a versatile preceptor, Croft readily became proficient in several scientific disciplines.
5. Williams, *Selected Correspondence*, 175–7, 645, 653–4.
6. From 1851 to 1859, Tavistock House was Charles Dickens's London residence, site of numerous soirées and minor theatrical performances.
7. John King, *McCaul, Croft, Forneri* (Toronto: Macmillan Co. of Canada Ltd., 1914), 117–25. King (MA, Toronto, 1865) sat for years on the university senate. He was the father of William Lyon Mackenzie King, long-time prime minister of Canada. A good deal of the material on Croft originally appeared in the *Varsity* 1 (1880–81): 87, 122. Notwithstanding the flowery language of King's memoir, it appears to contain a few errors of fact.
8. *Chemical Gazette* 1–17 (1842–59). The firm was successively Richard and John E. Taylor, Richard Taylor, then Taylor and Francis. On its history, see Allan Ferguson, *Natural Philosophy through the Eighteenth Century* (London: Taylor and Francis, 1972).
9. For further details of Croft's coming to Toronto see J.G. Slater, *Minerva's Aviary* (Toronto: University of Toronto Press, 2005), 25–7. For details of letters from Sir Charles Bagot concerning Croft's appointment to Chemistry see J.G. Slater, *Letters from the Papers of Sir Charles Bagot* (University of Toronto Archives, deposited 1998), 28–9, 32–4, 39, 61–2, 67–70.
10. Kingston was serving as capital of the Province of Canada. See Robertson, *Landmarks*, I, 351–9; III, 317–22.
11. W.J. Alexander, ed., *The University of Toronto and Its Colleges* (Toronto: Librarian, University of Toronto, 1906), 175; see also J.P. McMurrich, "Recollections of an Old Boy," *University of Toronto Monthly* 8 (1908): 103.
12. W.F.A. Boys, "Early Days at the University," *University of Toronto Monthly* 2, Supplement (1901): 33.
13. George Kennedy, "Recollections of an Old Boy," ibid. 8 (1908): 103.
14. Rev. N. McNish, "Acadian Reminiscences", ibid. 4 (1904): 220.
15. W.J. Loudon, *Sir William Mulock* (Toronto: Macmillan Co. of Canada, 1932), 30.
16. W.J. Loudon, *Studies of Student Life* (Toronto: Macmillan Co. of Canada, 1926), III, 63–9.
17. A.G. Croal, "The Teaching of Science in Ontario 1800–1900" (DPaed thesis, University of Toronto, 1940), 41, 52; see also Robin D.S. Harris, *A History of*

Higher Education in Canada, 1663–1960 (Toronto: University of Toronto Press, 1976), 34.
18. Hodgins, *Documentary History*, IV 238, 297; V, 33–4, 132, 138.
19. Croft and his wife married in an earlier structure of St. James Cathedral; John Strachan was rector, but his assistant performed the ceremony. On Aeneas Shaw and his family in early York, see Robertson, *Landmarks*, I, 541–3. See also W.R. Riddell, *The Life of John Graves Simcoe* (Toronto: McClelland and Stewart Ltd, 1926), 389–91.
20. King, *McCaul*, 138–9. Because of Croft's early ability at the piano, the blind king of Hanover offered him a position as court pianist. See also E. Henderson, *Ontario Historical Society Papers and Records* 26 (1929): 456.
21. Ibid., IX, 122.
22. Wallace, *History*, 100; quotation from Daniel Wilson's diary.
23. Wallace, *History*, 70–1.
24. Copies of these examination papers were found under the floor of Croft Chapter House during renovations in 1972. Principal A.C.H. Hallett of University College sent them to Professor A.G. Brook, then chairman of the Department of Chemistry, 23 June 1972.
25. Harris, *Higher Education*, 203–30, 454–61.
26. Henry Scadding and John Charles Dent, *Toronto: Past and Present; Historical and Descriptive* (Toronto: Hunter, Rose and Co., 1884), 228.
27. D.C. Masters, *The Rise of Toronto*, 56–61, 67–73; G.P. deT. Glazebrook, *The Story of Toronto* (Toronto: University of Toronto Press, 1971), 106–10.
28. See Douglas Richardson, with J.M.S. Careless, G.M. Craig, and Peter Heyworth, *A Not Unsightly Building: University College and Its History* (Toronto: Mosaic Press, for University College, 1990).
29. John Langton, *Early Days in Upper Canada* (Toronto: Macmillan Book Co. of Canada, 1926), 291–2; Elizabeth Hulse, "'A Long and Happy Life': Daniel Wilson with Family and Friends," in Marinell Ash, *Thinking with Both Hands, Sir Daniel Wilson in the Old World and the New*, ed. Elizabeth Hulse (Toronto: University of Toronto Press, 1999), 260–1.
30. Eric Arthur, *Toronto: No Mean City*, 2nd ed. (Toronto: University of Toronto Press, 1974), 134–42. See also Hodgins, *Documentary History*, XII, 293–4.
31. *Globe* (Toronto), October 6, 1856.
32. Henry H. Croft. The original owners of the copies in the Thomas Fisher Collection at the University of Toronto were (first edition) H. Miller, Galt, and then Rob Miller, Toronto School of Medicine (almost certainly W. Lash Miller's uncles Henry and Robert), and (second edition) W.H. Ellis.
33. James Loudon, "Memoirs," unpublished, University of Toronto Archives, deposited 1964, 7.
34. See Loudon, *Mulock*, 39–40.
35. The university senate in 1874 resolved to make laboratory work obligatory in the undergraduate science course. James Loudon's report of 1875 to the minister of education concerning the School of Practical Science (SPS) (see Hodgins, *Documentary History*, XXVII, 87–9) recommended provision of instructional

36. laboratories. Funding of the SPS building, completed in 1878, did allow for teaching labs in chemistry, mineralogy and geology, and biology.
36. William Odling, who briefly succeeded Faraday at the Royal Institution, became Waynflete Professor of Chemistry at Oxford. See R.T. Gunther, *Early Science at Oxford*, XI (London: Dawsons, 1937), 293; also *Dictionary of Scientific Biography* (New York: Charles Scribner's Sons, 1974), X, 177–8.
37. *Canadian Journal*, 2nd series, 1 (1856): 13–19. *Philosophical Magazine*, 3rd series, 21 (1842): 355.
38. See Hodgins, *Documentary History*, IV, 293.
39. W.H. Ellis, "Henry Holmes Croft D.C.L.," *University of Toronto Monthly* 2 (1901): 29–32; Marjorie Freeman Campbell, *A Century of Crime* (Toronto: McClelland and Stewart Ltd., 1970), 28, 56, 58, 61–2; W. Stewart Wallace, *Murders and Mysteries* (Toronto: Macmillan Co. of Canada Ltd., 1931), 267–8, 281–8.
40. "The Yorkville Poisoning Case," *British American Journal* (ICS) 2 (1861): 85–91; C.W. Orono, *The Life and Trial of Wm. H. King, M.D. for Poisoning his Wife at Brighton [Ont.]* (Stewart and Vosper, 1859). For a more modern discussion of this case see Michael Corbett, "Henry Holmes Croft D.C.L., F.C.S., First Canadian Forensic Chemist and Toxicologist," *Distillations* (2005): 23.
41. R.A. Huber, review of *The Life and Trial of Wm. H. King for Poisoning his Wife at Brighton*, by C.W. Orono, *Canadian Society of Forensic Science Journal* 8 (1975): 1–7.
42. Arthur Conan Doyle, *A Study in Scarlet* (1887). Holmes made this remark allegedly in 1881. See W.S. Baring-Gould, *The Annotated Sherlock Holmes* (London: John Murray, 1967), I, 141–51.
43. G.A. Purdy, *Petroleum: Prehistoric to Petrochemicals* (Vancouver: Copp Clark Co., 1957), 20–6. On J.M. Williams, see *Dictionary of Canadian Biography*, XI (Toronto: University of Toronto Press, 1982), 929.
44. *Leader* (Toronto), 3 June 1859; *London Free Press*, 15 September 1859.
45. Masters, *The Rise of Toronto*, 135–6.
46. *Globe* (Toronto), 30 September 1874.
47. Minute Books 1848–1851, Mechanics Institute (York, later Toronto), Toronto Reference Library. Also *Guide to the Manuscript Collection in the Toronto Public Libraries*.
48. Minute Books, (Royal) Canadian Institute, Toronto, *Transactions of the Canadian Institute* 6 (1899): 8–9.
49. Ellis, "Henry Holmes Croft," 30.
50. E. Horne Craigie, *A History of the Department of Zoology at the University of Toronto* (Toronto: University of Toronto Press, 1965), 5, 7.
51. "Rev. Charles James Stewart Bethune MA, D.C.L. FRS," *Canadian Entomologist* 42 (1910): 2–3; A.W. Baker, "A Short History of the Entomological Society of Ontario," ibid. 71 (1939): 14–20, 26.
52. *Canadian Journal* (ICS) 7 (1862): 525.
53. W.W. Judd, *Early Naturalists and Natural History Societies in London, Ontario* (London, ON: Phelps Publishing Co., 1979), 1, 6, 16–9.
54. See King, *McCaul*, 148.

55. P.H. Bryce, *University of Toronto Monthly* 2 (1901–2): 150–4; C.C. James, "The Ontario Agricultural College," ibid. 3 (1902–3): 297–303.
56. F.E. Gattinger, *A Century of Challenge* (Toronto: University of Toronto Press, 1962); also Ontario Veterinary College, *Annual Reports* (University of Guelph Archives).
57. See Hodgins, *History*, v 90–1; King, *McCaul*, 141; Loudon, *Mulock*, 52–5. The third of these accounts tells of the presentation to Croft of a tray and set of silver by the men of No. 9 Company early in 1863, in appreciation of his fine leadership.
58. Ellis, "Henry Holmes Croft," 29–32.
59. Two university participants wrote accounts of the engagement at Ridgeway. That of W.H. Ellis, who was taken prisoner, appears in the *Canadian Magazine* 13 (1899): 199–203; that by Dr Adam Wright, later professor of surgery at the university, in *University of Toronto Monthly* 21 (1921): 392–6.
60. C.R. Young, *Early Engineering Education in Ontario* (Toronto: University of Toronto Press, 1958), 22–55.
61. Ontario Sessional Papers (1881), xiii, Part 3, No. 13, pp. 392–3.
62. Robertson, *Landmarks*, i, 398–9.
63. J. Loudon, "The Origin of Technical Education in Ontario," *University of Toronto Monthly* 1 (1900): 148.
64. Minute Book, Board of sps, 23 December 1879, and 1 March and 20 April 1880.
65. Minute Book, Toronto Entomological Association, now in the possession of the Royal Canadian Institute.
66. W.H. Ellis in "Review of Historical Publications Relating to Canada," W. Briggs, ed., 19 (1915): 213.
67. Henry J. Morgan, *Biblioteca Canadensis* (1867; reprint, Detroit: Gale Research, 1968), 85–6. Concerning Chaveau, see *Dictionary of Canadian Biography*, xi, 225.
68. Maurice Hutton, *Memorials of Chancellor W.H. [Edward?] Blake, Bishop Strachan, Professor H.H. Croft, and Professor G.P. Young, University of Toronto; 13 January 1894* (Toronto: Rowsell and Hudson, 1894). The "occasion" was Strachan's funeral. See W.H. van der Smissen, "McCaul: Croft: Forneri," *University of Toronto Monthly* 16 (1915): 138–9.
69. Ellis, "Henry Holmes Croft," 31–2.

Chapter 2
1. Masters, *The Rise of Toronto*, 165.
2. Scadding and Dent, *Toronto: Past and Present*, 265.
3. West, *Toronto*, 173–6.
4. Glazebrook, *Toronto*, 120.
5. Aaron J. Ihde, *The Development of Modern Chemistry* (New York: Harper and Row, 1964), 404–10.
6. Ibid., 333–8, 454–64.
7. H.H. Langton, *Sir Daniel Wilson: A Memoir* (Toronto: Thomas Nelson and Sons, Ltd., 1929), 98.
8. Ibid., 98.

9. W.H. Pike, Curriculum Vitae, University of Göttingen (in Latin in his own handwriting), Department of Chemistry Archives, University of Toronto.
10. For a good account, see P.A. Dunae, *Gentlemen Emigrants* (Vancouver: Douglas and McIntyre, 1981), 117–20, 122, 224–5.
11. A copy of the thesis is in the University of Toronto Archives.
12. Information from Roger Highfield, librarian, Merton College, Oxford.
13. Foster, *Alumni Oxonensis*, III (1715–1886).
14. *Varsity* 1 (1880–81): 49, 86, 138.
15. C.R. Young, *Early Engineering Education at Toronto* (Toronto: University of Toronto Press, 1958), 71.
16. *Annual Report, Board of S.P.S., 1880–81*, 393–6.
17. Wallace, *History*, 170–1; Young, *Engineering*, 89.
18. Loudon, "Memoirs," 48.
19. Wilson did not become chairman until October 11, 1880.
20. See Application and Testimonials of W. Hodgson Ellis, Candidate for the Chair of Chemistry in University College, 1879, pamphlet, University of Toronto Archives.
21. *Annual Report, Board of S.P.S. 1883–84*, 199.
22. Ibid. 1886, 168; 1887, 249; 1891, 292–3.
23. "In 1877, the candidate for an Honour degree in Natural Sciences was required to take each of the three subjects: Biology, Chemistry, Geology and Mineralogy throughout his course; but the curriculum of 1885 not only introduced a greater amount of Physics into an early part of the course, but recognized three divisions in the Fourth Year, in each of which one of the three sciences was a major subject, and the other two minors. In 1891, by the introduction of laboratory work into the First Year, further specialization was made possible; the Honour department of Chemistry and Mineralogy made its appearance; and in the Natural Science Course the student in his Fourth Year was allowed to devote himself wholly either to Biology or to Geology." Alexander, *University*, 90–1.
24. *Annual Reports of the Council of University College*, 1882–83 and thereafter.
25. Peter N. Ross, "The Origins and Development of the Ph.D. Degree at the University of Toronto" (EdD thesis, University of Toronto, 1972), 49.
26. University of Toronto Calendars, 1889–90 and 1892–93.
27. "The real beginning of serious post-graduate work may be dated from the year 1882, when the present President of the University [Loudon] suggested the Fellowship system, mainly with a view to affording tutorial assistance, but also in the hope of encouraging research among the graduates.... As a natural complement to research, and the Fellowship system, Professor (now President) Loudon pressed for the institution of the Ph.D. degree, and committed the Senate to an approval of such a course in 1885. It was not, however, until 1897 that, by the instrumentality of Professor Macallum, the course was actually laid down." Alexander, *University*, 92.
28. Ostwald received the degree in absentia. However, he did visit the university during the summer of 1904 en route to the International Congress of Arts and Science in St. Louis. See W.L.M., "The Congresses at St. Louis – Professor Oswald at Toronto," *University of Toronto Monthly* 5 (1904): 20.

29. *Annual Report of the Councils of the University of Toronto and University College, 1889–90*, 362.
30. E.M. Pomeroy, *William Saunders and His Five Sons* (Toronto: Ryerson Press, 1956), chapters 3 and 4. The youngest brother, F.A., graduated in mathematics and physics in 1895 and then earned a PhD in physics at Johns Hopkins. Later, with H.N. Russell, he discovered the Russell–Saunders coupling of angular and spin momenta of electrons in gaseous atoms.
31. E.S. Archibald, "Frank Thomas Shutt," *Transactions of the Royal Society of Canada* 3rd series 34 (1940): 121–4.
32. See "The Late Professor E.B. Kenrick," *University of Toronto Monthly* 5 (1905): 174.
33. See ibid. 8 (1908): 125; *American Men of Science*, 2nd ed. (1910).
34. *Annual Report of the Councils of the University of Toronto and University College 1889–90*, 361.
35. J.G. Hodgins, *The Establishment of Schools and Colleges in Ontario 1792–1910*, III (Toronto: L.K. Cameron, 1910), 53–4.
36. A.E. Hamilton, "The Literary and Scientific Society — A Fiftieth Anniversary," *University of Toronto Monthly* 4 (1904): 136.
37. John Cooper, "Professor William Herbert Pike MA, PhD," ibid. 3 (1903): 124–5.
38. W.H. Pike, "German Science," *Varsity* 1 (1880): 12.
39. W.L. Miller in H.M. Tory, ed., *A History of Science in Canada* (Toronto: Ryerson Press, 1939), 28.
40. W.H. Ellis, "Inaugural Address," *Varsity* 2 (1881): 88; "University College News," ibid. 99; *Globe* (Toronto), 12 April 1882.
41. T.A. Reed, *The Blue and White* (Toronto: University of Toronto Press, 1944), 148–9, 268.
42. City of Toronto, Office of Land Titles. Balliol made significant contributions to research and teaching in chemistry from 1851 on. Pike may have done some of his lab demonstrating at Oxford in the famous No. 16 laboratory at Balliol College. See Sir H. Hartley, *Studies in the History of Chemistry* (Oxford: Clarendon Press, 1971), 225–8.
43. Pike to Miller, 27 April 1900, University of Toronto Archives.
44. Cooper, "Pike," 124–125.
45. Langton, *Wilson*.
46. Loudon, "Memoirs," 62.
47. L.F. Barker, *Time and the Physician: The Autobiography of Lewellys F Barker* (New York: Putnam, 1942), 6–7. Professor R.S. Harris kindly provided this reference.
48. Cooper, "Pike," 124–125.
49. *University of Toronto Monthly* 21 (1921): 311; remark attributed to "a colleague" (probably Miller).
50. Cooper, "Pike," 124-125.

Chapter 3

1. Avogadro's hypothesis had been known since 1811, but it was not until the Karlsruhe Conference in 1860 that Cannizzaro outlined how to use it to define

key atomic weights. Uniform notation in chemical formulae emerged quickly and paved the way for advances such as the periodic law.

2. David P. Mellor, *The Evolution of the Atomic Theory* (Amsterdam: Elsevier Publishing Co., 1971), 148.
3. C.F.W. Everitt, "James Clerk Maxwell," *Dictionary of Scientific Biography* (New York: Charles Scribner's Sons, 1974), xix, 198–230.
4. This paragraph is based mainly on Lang's application (University of Toronto Archives) and on information kindly provided by Michael Moss, archivist, University of Glasgow.
5. Of the nine publications that Lang listed in 1899, only five at most involved experimental research; two of these (one in English and one in French) describe the same investigation made in Paris with a collaborator.
6. Anon., *The Curious Diversity, Glasgow University on Gilmorehill: The First Hundred Years* (Glasgow: University Press, 1970), 23.
7. Ferguson's writings include "Bibliographical Notes on Histories of Inventions and Books of Secrets," "Bibliographical Notes on the Witchcraft Literature of Scotland," and *Biblioteca Chemica* — a two-volume catalogue (more than a thousand pages) of the alchemical, chemical, and pharmaceutical books in the collection of the late James Young. James Maclehouse and Sons, of Glasgow, published the compendium in 1906 "for private distribution." Young was the pioneer in Britain of the industrial-scale distillation of coal to produce, among other things, illuminating oil.
8. John Read, *Humour and Humanism in Chemistry* (London: G. Bell and Sons, Ltd., 1947), 80. Read himself was a highly respected contributor to the history of chemistry and alchemy.
9. From a testimonial on behalf of W.R. Lang supplied by Professor William Ramsay, University of Toronto Archives.
10. Application and Testimonials on behalf of W.R. Lang for the chair of Chemistry at the University of Toronto 1900 — handwritten copy by W.L. Miller, University of Toronto Archives.
11. W.R. Lang and A. Rigaut, "The Composition and Tensions of Dissociation of the Ammoniacal Chlorides of Cadmium," *Transactions of the Chemical Society* (1899), 883–7. See also *Comptes Rendus* 129, no. 5 (1899): 294–6.
12. William Ramsay was professor of chemistry 1884–1912 at University College, London. His most famous work, with Lord Rayleigh, led to the discovery of the "inert" gases. Ramsay himself had been tutorial assistant in the Chemistry Department at Glasgow from 1874 to 1880. See *Dictionary of Scientific Biography*, xi, 277–84.
13. Wallace, *History*, 134–5, 164–5. G.W. Ross, long-time Liberal minister of education under Oliver Mowat, became premier in 1899 and named Richard Harcourt as minister. There was a change of government soon afterwards.
14. Frederick Soddy (1877–1956) attained many scientific honours, including the Nobel Prize in Chemistry in 1921.
15. Muriel Howarth, *Pioneer Research on the Atom* (Oxford: privately published, 1958), 40–56.

16. Frederick Soddy, "Reminiscences of McGill 1900–1902," *Old McGill, McGill University* 36 (1933): 16–21.
17. Leo Yaffe, *History of Department of Chemistry, McGill University* (Montreal, 1978), 10–16.
18. T.J. Trenn, *The Self-Splitting Atom* (London: Taylor and Francis, 1977). A history of the Rutherford–Soddy collaboration.
19. Loudon, "Memoirs," 262–3. Loudon discusses the "slanderous" attack in the *Globe* in the spring of 1904 and his subsequent interview with the editor. See also *Globe* (Toronto), 8 April 1904.
20. *Varsity* 20 (1900): 3.
21. Lang and Miller to Loudon, Loudon to Lang and Miller, and Memorandum of Agreement, December 1900, University of Toronto Archives.
22. "Glasgow University Magazine", *Varsity* 20, 27 November 1900. Comments about Lang from *Glasgow University Magazine*.
23. R. Falconer, "Colonel W.R. Lang Given Military Funeral," *University of Toronto Monthly* 26 (1925): 130–1. An appreciation by Sir Robert Falconer of W.R. Lang at his funeral service, 23 November 1925.
24. Popular articles by W.R. Lang: "Poisons," *Royal Engineers Journal*, pre 1900; "Alfred Nobel and the Development of High Explosives," *Transactions of the Philosophical Society of Glasgow* (read March 8, 1899); "A Century of Chemical Progress," *University of Toronto Monthly* 1 (1901): 169, 194; "Chemistry in the Nineteenth Century," *Varsity*, 15 January 1901; "Conceptions of Matter — Ancient and Modern," *University of Toronto Monthly* 5 (1905): 90–5; "Lord Kelvin," *University of Toronto Monthly* 8 (1908): 161–4.
25. "The Chemical Museum," *Varsity*, 21 January 1903.
26. Ontario Sessional Papers 1903, Sec. IV, No. 12, p. 182.
27. *British Association for the Advancement of Science, Report of the 76th Meeting, Toronto, Canada 1897* (London: John Murray, 1898).
28. "Visit of Sir William Perkin," *Varsity*, 26, November 1906: 8.
29. W.R. Lang, *Outline of Qualitative Analysis* (Toronto: University Press, 1907), 2nd ed., 1910. W.R. Lang and Alfred Tingle, *Outline of Quantitative Analysis* (Toronto: University of Toronto Press, 1911).
30. W.R. Lang, personal diaries. His daughter, Dr. Janet K. Ross, kindly permitted access to them and reproduction of certain comments.
31. H.H. Langton, *James Loudon and the University of Toronto*, pamphlet (Toronto: University of Toronto Press, 1927).
32. Alan Bowker, "Truly Useful Men — Maurice Hutton, George Wrong, James Mavor, and the University of Toronto 1880–1927" (PhD thesis, University of Toronto, 1975), 6–12.
33. Wallace, *History*, 152–6.
34. *Globe* (Toronto), 8 April 1904, 6 (editorial); 13 April 1904, 13 (Loudon's reply); 13 April 1904, 6 (editorial). *Saturday Night*, 10 December 1904, 2 (letter to editor). Yves Gingras, "Loudon, James," in *Canadian Encyclopedia*, 1036.
35. *Saturday Night*, 7 January 1905, 2 (re 1851 Exhibition scholarships).
36. "The Summer Session," *University of Toronto Monthly* 7 (1907): 151, 223–4.

37. J. Loudon, "Some Steps Forward," ibid. 6 (1906): 57; ibid, "University of Toronto Summer Session," 168.
38. W. Lash Miller, *The New Requirements in Chemistry for Junior Matriculation and for the Departmental Examinations of the Province of Ontario* (Toronto: Published by the University of Toronto, 1905).
39. A.B. Macallum was professor of physiology and later of biochemistry at the university. He left Toronto in 1916 to become first chair of Canada's National Research Council. See *Dictionary of Scientific Biography*, VIII, 583–4.
40. Peter N. Ross, "The Origins and Development of the Ph.D. Degree at the University of Toronto" (EdD thesis, University of Toronto, 1972), 50–1.
41. W.R. Lang, *Proceedings of the Royal Society of Edinburgh* 21 (1895–97): 278; *Transactions of the Philosophical Society of Glasgow* (1899); *Journal of the Society of the Chemical Industry* 18 (1899): 238.
42. Accounts of the formation of the Canadian Section, Society of Chemical Industry: W.R. Lang, *University of Toronto Monthly* 5 (1904): 44–5; "Electrolyte Manufacture of Caustic Soda and Bleaching Powder at Sault Saint Marie Ontario," *Journal of the Society of the Chemical Industry* 20 (1901): 677; ibid. 21 (1902): 449–51.
43. W.R. Lang, "The Chemical Industries of Canada Chairman's Address to the Canadian Section, S.C.I.," *Journal of the Society of the Chemical Industry* 22 (1903): 527–37; "The Chemical Industries of the Dominion," *Transactions of the Canadian Institute* 8 (1905): 151–90; also *Industrial Canada*, March, April, and May 1905; Public lectures at the University of Toronto 1903, 1905; "Chemical Industry in British Columbia," *Journal of the Society of the Chemical Industry* 26 (1907): 237–9; "Chemical Industry in British Columbia," *University of Toronto Monthly* 7 (1907): 81–7.
44. H. Croft, *Philosophical Magazine*, 3rd series, 21 (1842): 355–7.
45. "Natural Science Association," *Varsity*, 18 February 1902.
46. Anon., *The Curious Diversity, Glasgow University*, 30.
47. Lang to Falconer, 1908, University of Toronto Archives.
48. Ian Montagnes, *An Uncommon Fellowship* (Toronto: University of Toronto Press, 1969), 17–8, 26–7; this book marked Hart House's fiftieth anniversary. Thirty years later Montagnes contributed "The Founder and the Animator" to David Kilgour, ed., *A Strange Elation: Hart House: The First Eighty Years* (Toronto: Hart House, 1999), 5–17.
49. Lang, *diaries*.
50. *Globe* (Toronto), 21 November 1925, 15; *Toronto Daily Star*, 20 November 1925, 1.
51. Falconer, *Monthly*, 130-1.
52. "Sudden Death of Colonel Lang Beloved Commander of the C.O.T.C. Deeply Mourned by University," *Varsity*, 23 November 1925, 1, 3.
53. W. Lash Miller, "William Robert Lang," *Journal of the Chemical Society* (1926): 1024–5.
54. Allan to Falconer, 1925, University of Toronto Archives.
55. Yaffe, *History*, 10–16

Chapter 4

1. John T. Stock, *Ostwald's American Students* (Concord, NH: Plaidswede Publishing, 2004). Chapter 7 describes Miller's experiments.
2. Miller to Harrington, 5 June 1900, McGill University Archives, Dawson Collection.
3. Wilder D. Bancroft and Joseph E. Trevor, both editors of the *Journal of Physical Chemistry*, which Bancroft founded. Since 1896 Miller had been its chief of staff of reviewers.
4. Miller to Harcourt, 7 July 1900, University of Toronto Archives.
5. D.J. LeRoy, "Lash Miller and a History of Chemistry at the University of Toronto," address to the University Chemical Club, 6 February 1963. See p.7 regarding Burwash, who spoke probably about 1900.
6. W.L. Miller et al., *History of Science in Canada* (Ottawa: Royal Society of Canada, 1939).
7. Jack Mitchell to W.A.E. McBryde, 31 October 1989.
8. W.L. Miller, "The Second Differential Coefficient of Gibbs, Function ζ," *Journal of Physical Chemistry* 2 (1897): 633.
9. W.L. Miller and F.B. Kenrick, "On the Identification of Basic Salts," *Transactions of the Royal Society of Canada* 3 (1901): 35.
10. T.R. Rosebrugh and W. Lash Miller, "Mathematical Treatment of the Changes of Concentration at the Electrode, Brought About by Diffusion and Chemical Reaction," *Journal of Physical Chemistry* 14 (1911): 816.
11. W.A.E. McBryde, "Miller, William Lash," in *The Canadian Encyclopedia*, 2nd ed. (Edmonton: Hurtig Publishers, 1988), 1133.
12. Jack Mitchell, "Some Memories of Professor Lash Miller," *Distillations* 1 (1999): 28. *Distillations* is the Chemistry Department's in-house publication.
13. Louise Elder, "Reminiscences of the Chemistry Department in the 1930's," *Distillations* 10 (spring 1997): 12; continued in *Distillations* 12 (1999): 30.
14. Letter to Hon. Richard Harcourt, Minister of Education, 7 July 1900, University of Toronto Archives.
15. Agreement between Dr. Lang and Dr. Miller, 17 December 1900, University of Toronto Archives.
16. W.A.E. McBryde, *William Lash Miller: Canada's Unique Chemist*, undated manuscript, Department of Chemistry Archives, is a source for much of this chapter. See also Mel Thistle, *The Inner Ring* (Toronto: University of Toronto Press, 1966), 59.
17. Correspondence submitted to the Council of the Faculty of Applied Science and Engineering by J.W. Bain (October 1931) and W.L. Miller (November 1931), University of Toronto Archives, A68-0006 (box 31).
18. *Saturday Night*, 7 January 1905; W.E.K. Middleton, *Physics at the National Research Council of Canada* (Waterloo: Wilfrid Laurier University Press, 1979).
19. C.V. Raman, "A New Class of Spectra Due to Secondary Radiation. I.," *Indian Journal of Physics* 2 (1928): 1.
20. McBryde, *William Lash Miller*.
21. L.E. Westman, "The Department of Chemistry," *University of Toronto Monthly* 21 (1921): 253.

22. D.J. LeRoy, "William Lash Miller," *Dictionary of Scientific Biography*, IX, (New York: Chas. Scribner's Sons, 1974), 393.
23. W.A.E. McBryde, "William Lash Miller," in *Electrochemistry, Past and Present*, ACS Symposium Series No 390 (Washington, DC: American Chemical Society, 1989).
24. L.E. Westman, "William Lash Miller," *Canadian Chemistry and Process Industries* (September 1940).
25. Frank B. Kenrick, "William Lash Miller," *Journal of the Chemical Society* 64 (1942): 334–6.
26. Wilder Bancroft, "William Lash Miller," *Journal of the American Chemical Society* 63 (1941): 1.
27. J. Watson Bain, *Transactions of the Electrochemical Society Inc.* 78 (1940): 10.
28. Frank B. Kenrick, "William Lash Miller," *Transactions of the Royal Society of Canada*, series 3, 35 (1941): 131.

Chapter 5
1. John T. Stock *Ostwald's American Students* (Concord, NH: Plaidswede Publishing, 2004), chapter 14.
2. F.B. Kenrick, "Determination of the Surface of Powders," *Journal of the American Chemical Society* 62 (1940): 2838.
3. F.B. Kenrick, "The Scattering of Light. Note on Wolski's Paper on Optically Empty Liquids," *Journal of Physical Chemistry* 26 (1922): 72.
4. F.B. Kenrick, "Are We Teaching the Right Chemistry?" *Canadian Chemistry and Metallurgy* 14 (1930): 45.
5. F.B. Kenrick, "Sour Taste of Acids," *Transactions of the Royal Society of Canada*, 3rd series, 25 (1931): 2227.
6. F.B. Kenrick, C.S. Gilbert, and K.L. Wismer, "Superheating of Liquids," *Journal of Physical Chemistry* 28 (1924): 1299.
7. R Fawcett, *Liquids, Solutions and Interfaces* (Oxford University Press, 2004).
8. F.B. Kenrick, *Zeitschrift für Physikkalische Chemie* 19 (1896): 625. For a further description of one of the crucial experiments see reference 1.
9. D.J. LeRoy, undated autobiography, Chemistry Department's Archives.
10. F.B. Kenrick, *An Introduction to Chemistry* (Toronto: University of Toronto Press, 1932).
11. The *F* in George F Wright is not an abbreviation and hence needs no period after it. Custom in his hometown (Council Bluffs, Iowa) distinguished the many local males of that name by letters, not numbers. The absence of a period used to drive editors wild!
12. Henry Gilman and George F Wright, "Nuclear Substitution and Orientation in Furan Types," *Chemical Reviews* 11 (1932): 323.
13. D.C. Downing, "A Memoir to Professor George F Wright," *Chemistry in Canada*, March 1983, 32.
14. For other descriptions of Wright, see A. Rodgman, "Reflections of Dr. George F Wright," *Distillations* (2000): 34, and J.C. Bond, "More Recollections of George F Wright," *Distillations* (2001): 40.
15. Donald H. Avery, *The Science of War* (Toronto: University of Toronto Press,

(1998), 106–21.
16. F.B. Kenrick, "Daybook," University of Toronto Archives, A77-0025, box 2, file 09.
17. L.H. Cragg, "Frank B. Kenrick," *Distillations* (Spring 1997): 14.
18. A.R. Gordon, *Proceedings of the Royal Society of Canada*, 3rd series, 46 (1951): 91.

Chapter 6
1. W.L. Miller and A.R. Gordon, "Numerical Evaluation of Infinite Series and Integrals Which Arise in Certain Problems of Linear Heat Flow, Electrochemical Diffusion Etc.," *Journal of Physical Chemistry* 35 (1931): 2785.
2. A.R. Gordon, "The Free Energy of Steam and of Carbon Dioxide," *Journal of Chemical Physics* 1 (1933): 308.
3. Byron Lane, "An Appreciation of Andy Gordon," *Distillations* (2002): 29–35.
4. C.T. Bissell, *Halfway Up Parnassus* (Toronto: University of Toronto Press, 1974).
5. W.L. Miller was a Canadian, but he was never formally appointed as Head, although he ran the department for several decades.
6. D.J. LeRoy, from an undated autobiography in the departmental archives.
7. U of T archives, A1977-0025/002.

Chapter 7
1. D.J. LeRoy, undated autobiography, Chemistry Department Archives.
2. From the citation for the degree doctor of science, *honoris causa*, University of Toronto, 1978, awarded to D.J. LeRoy.
3. The department faculty had four professors: F.E. Beamish, A.R. Gordon (head), L.J. Rogers, and G.F Wright; four associates: D.J. LeRoy, F.R. Lorriman, R.L. McIntosh, and F.E. Wetmore; four assistants: M.W. Lister, W.A.E. McBryde; G.E. McCasland, and J.J. Rae; and lecturer E.V. Eastcott.
4. For more on this spectrometer, see Chapter 10.
5. D.J. LeRoy, undated autobiography, Chemistry Department Archives.
6. S.C. Nyburg, *x-Ray Analysis of Organic Structures* (New York: Academic Press, 1961).
7. Copy of a letter by William Lash Miller, provided by Robin Harris from his records to W.A.E. McBryde.
8. W.J. Dunlop, "The University's Greatest Need," *University of Toronto Monthly* 38 (1938): 99.
9. D.J. LeRoy, undated autobiography, Chemistry Department Archives.
10. A.D. Allen and C.V. Senoff, "Nitrogenpentammineruthenium (II) Complexes," *Chemical Communications* (1965): 621.
11. On the serendipitous discovery see C.V. Senoff, "The Discovery of $[Ru(NH_3)_5N_2]^{2+}$," *Journal of Chemical Education* 67 (1990): 368.
12. R.O. Harris, extracts from letter to Scott Mabury, 2004, in Chemistry Department archives.
13. The Faculty of Arts became the Faculty of Arts and Science in 1960.
14. R.O. Harris, extracts from letter to Scott Mabury, 2004, in Chemistry Department archives.

Chapter 8

1. Faculty of Arts and Science, "Planning Statement," May 1982, Department of Chemistry Archives.
2. "A White Paper on the Status of the Science Departments, Faculty of Arts and Science, University of Toronto," March 1983, Department of Chemistry Archives.
3. Esther Sleep, "The Alma Sleep Story," *Distillations* (2001): 39.
4. J.M. Hammersley, G.M. Torrie, and S.G. Whittington, "Self-avoiding Walks Interacting with a Surface," *Journal of Physics* A15 (1982): 539.
5. J.C. Polanyi, "Some Concepts in Reaction Dynamics," *Science* 236 (1987): 680.
6. C. Sadowski, "Meeting John Polanyi," *Distillations* (2001): 35.

Chapter 9

1. Much of this section derives from Professor Tom Tidwell's submission to the author. His assistance was of enormous help.
2. On Scarborough College and its problems, see M.F. Friedland, *The University of Toronto: A History* (Toronto: University of Toronto Press, 2002), 452–5.
3. "Report of the Presidential Advisory Committee on the Status and Future of Scarborough College," University of Toronto, 1970–71, University of Toronto Archives, LE3 T7924T6, RB51001.
4. Much of this section derives from a very useful submission by Professor Anthony Poë.

Chapter 10

1. R.B. Woodward, "Structure and Absorption Spectra of α,β-Unsaturated Ketones," *Journal of the American Chemical Society* 63 (1941): 1123. (1942); "Structure and Absorption Spectra. III. Normal Conjugated Dienes," ibid, 64 (1942): 72; "Structure and Absorption Spectra IV. Further Observations on α,β-Unsaturated Ketones," ibid, (1942): 76.
2. J.K. Cashion and J.C. Polanyi, "Infrared Absorption for the Gaseous Reaction, Atomic Hydrogen Plus Chlorine," *Journal of Chemical Physics* 29 (1958): 455.
3. Diane Jones is the wife of Professor J.B. Jones of the Chemistry Department.
4. N.S. Bhacca, L.F. Johnson, and J.N. Shoolery, *NMR Spectra Catalog*, Varian Associates 1962, and Volume 2, 1963.
5. Nyburg is currently an honorary senior research fellow in King's College, London.
6. F. Bottomly and S.C. Nyburg, "Molecular Nitrogen as a Ligand. The Crystal Structure of Nitrogenpentammineruthenium (II) Dichloride," *Chemical Communications* (1966): 897; "Molecular Nitrogen as a Ligand. The Crystal Structure of Nitrogenpentammineruthenium (II) Dichloride and Related Salts," *Acta Crystallographica* B24 (1968): 1289.
7. A.G. Brook et al., "Stable Solid Silaethylenes," *Journal of the American Chemical Society* 104 (1982): 5667; S.C. Nyburg, A.G. Brook, F. Abdesaken, G. Gutekunst, and W. Wong-Ng, "Structure of 2-(1-Adamantyl)-2-Trimethylsiloxy-1,1-bis(Trimethylsilyl)-1-Silaethylene," *Acta Crystallographica* C41 (1985): 1632.
8. Much of this information comes from Dr. Srebri Petrov.
9. Friedland, *University*.

Index

Abbatt, Jon, 163, 190
A.D. Allen Chemistry Library, 136, 199
Advisory Committee on Academic Planning, 148
Agriculture program at U of T, 45
AIMS Laboratory, 180
Allan, F.B., *100*, 59, 73, 74, 81, 98-100, 105
Allen, A.D. (Bert), *143*, 137, 143-46, 152, 168, 182; Dean of Arts and Science, 144
Allen, Annette, 169
American Chemical Society, 1907 meeting, 72; and Miller, 89
American Electrochemical Society, 89
ANALEST, *185*, 184-85, 190, 192
Analytical chemistry, 58, 98, 152-53, 158, 163, 169, 172
Analytical Laboratory for Environmental Science Research and Teaching (ANALEST), 184-85, 190, 192
Anderson, Rod, 203, 215
Apotex Lecture Series, 150
A.R. Gordon Distinguished Lecture Series, 149
Atomic theory, Miller's aversion to, 21, 85, 87, 98
Averill, Harold, 15
Austin, George, 119

Baker, Eleanor, 119
Baigrie-Boyd, Lynn, 169
Bancroft, Wilder, 89
Banting, Frederick, Nobel Prize, 159
Banton, Bill, 117
Barnes, Colin, 111
Barradas, Remi, 153
Batey, Rob, 151, 162, 199
Beamish, Fred, *119*, 89, 107-08, 121, 152-53
Benson, Clara, 118, 205-06
Bersohn, Malcolm, 137
Best, Charles, 159

Billard, Laura, 173
Biochemistry and Chemistry (B and C), 155
Biological chemistry, 133, 151, 172, 180, 191, 202
Biological chemists, 151
Biological Museum (in UC), 44
Bio-organic chemistry, 162
Biotechnology Research Centre, Mississauga, 178
Bios, 92, 101
Bissell, Claude, on A.R. Gordon, 112, 113
Blackburn, Robert, 141
Boehringer Ingelheim Lecture Series, 150
Bondrup-Nielsen, Kaj, 142
Bosnich, Brice, 149, 152, 162
Bottomley, Frank, 144
Bray, W.C., 59, 100
Brereton, Mary, 139
Brook, Adrian, 14, 121-22, 140, 147-48, 150, 151, 161, 176, 181, 182, 193
Brown, James, 18
Browning, Scott, 202
Brumer, Paul, 152, 168, 169, 192, 193
Buck, Roel and Dorothy, 192
Buckland, George, 45
Bunting, John, 137, 151
Bures, Frank, 188
Burns, George, 137, 152, 162
Burt-Gerrans, J.T., *92*, 91-2, 98, 99-100, 115
Bury, Brenda, 192

Canadian Foundation for Innovation, 197, 207
Canadian Institute, 43, 44, 48, 51, 71-2
Canadian National Exhibition, 50
Canadian Officers Training Corps (COTC), 78, 80, 108
Canadian Society for Chemistry (CSC), 90, 144, 159
Carter, Reg, 187
Cashion, Kenneth, 133, 176
Caton, Bob, 149, 168
Centre for Nanostructured Polymer and Inorganic Materials, 207
Chadwick, Bert, 116, 119
Chairs, holders in department, 192-3
Charter for university in 1827, 17-8, 19; amended, 32
Chemical BioPhysics Symposium, 205
Chemical Institute of Canada, 75, 203
Chemical Physics Theory Group, 152, 163
Chemistry (discipline), status in 1842, 28; in 1859, 39; in 1879, 51-2; in 1900, 67
Chemistry Building (also known as "Old", also "new building of 1895"), *61*, 22, 60-63,

65, 87, 104, 106, 107, 117, 181, 187; organic laboratory, *121*; private laboratory, 70-1, 95; small explosives factory accident, 107

Chemistry and Mining Building, see Mining Building

Chemistry Club (Chem Club), skits and songs, *124*, 209-28; banquets, 122, 203, 209; functions, 203-4; scholarships, 204

Chemistry Department, 22, 73, 87, 114-18, 121, 134-40, 142, 143, 146, 148, 149, 151-3, 155-7, 159, 161-3, 175-88, 189-93, 201-2, 205-8; apparatus in 1954, 38-9; colloquia and seminars, 136, 151; discipline divisions, 150; 1858 examination papers, 36-8; homes (locations), 22; Staff Excellence Award, 202

Chemistry faculty, in 1890, 98; in 1894, 87; in 1900, 108; in 1921, 98; in 1932, *99*; in 1944, 108; in 1949, 121; appointments, in 1950s, 121; in 1960s, 137; in 1969-74, 149; in 1990s, 162-3; fellows in 1880, 57, 58; growth from 1960 to 1969, 137-9; new appointments criteria, 161; retirements after 1989, 161-2

Chemistry laboratory, first, 30-1; in roundhouse, 40-1; at SPS in 1870s, 41; in 1890, 56; renovated Lash Miller lab, *201*

Chemistry Professor's Christmas Carol, 228-9

Chemistry program, in 1840s, 35; in 1850s, 35, 57; in 1870, 57-8; in 1889, 58; in 1893, 58; in 1930s, 97-8; in 1940s, 114-17; changes in inorganic chemistry, 158; in physical chemistry, 146; fourth-year research, 58, 87; graduate studies, 124; in New Program, 144-7; specialist programs in 2002, 202; in environmental chemistry, 190; revised first year curriculum in 2000s, 202, 206-7;

"Chemist's Mikado" (skit), 215-23

Chin, Jik, 162, 199

Christmas Party (Dep't) 1953, *123*; names of faculty, 123

Clarke, Dr. David, 171

Colleges (new), staffing, funding and tenure, 143

Committee on University Government (CUG), 144

Computing, 185-87, 188; for students, 157; 7094 computer, 186; current uses, 201

Cook, Chris, 137, 149, 168

Corry, Madeline, 134

COTC, 108; organization by Lang, 78

Cox, Dr. Robin, 156

Croft, Henry Holmes, *31*, 20, 27, 32, 34, 47, 49; background, 29, 30, 33; botany and entomology interests, 44; Chairman of the Board of SPS, 48; inaugural lectures, 31; involvement with Agricultural and Veterinary Colleges, 45, 46; laboratory manual, 41-42; lectures, 43; obituaries, 49; petroleum work, 42-3; professor of chemistry and experimental philosophy, 20; toxicology and forensic work, 42, 48, 152; University Rifle Corps and Fenian Raids, 45-6; Vice-Chancellor of U of T, 33

Croft Chapter House, *41*, 22; description, 40-1, naming, 49

Csizmadia, Imre, 137-8, 162, 186

Dahma, Masad, 173

Danyluk, Stephen, 137, 145, 154, 177

Davenport Chemical Research Building, *199*, 197-200

Davenport Garden, *208*, 207-8

Davenport, Edna, John, Peter and Linda, *198*, 196, 197, 199, 207
Dean, Colleen, 156
Deckers, Jacques, 137-8, 152, 162, 171, 173, 179
Deckers' Molecular Beam apparatus, *138*, 138
de Francesco, Adrienne, 142, 187, 191, 198
Delury, Don, 134
Demonstrators, lecturers, tutors, essential personnel, 156
Denk, Michael, 162, 173
Department of Chemistry Christmas Party, 1953, *123*
Department of Military Studies, 79; Lang as Director, 79, 80, 88
Dickens, Charles, description of Toronto (York), 28
Dicks, Andy, 202
Dignam, Michael, *160*, 137, 140, 148, 153, 159-61, 162, 173,
Distillations, 15
Divisional seminars, 151
Donaldson, Jamie, 163, 168, 190
Dong, Vy Maria, 208
Dove, John, 137, 139, 152, 162, 168, 173, 179
Downing, Doug, description of Wright, 106
Duncan, Robert Kennedy, 60, 100
Dundas, Henry, 18
Dushman, Saul, 100

Eastcott, Dr. Edna, 104, 121
Elder, Dr. Louise, 95, 118
Electrochemistry, 28, 75, 91-92, 99, 111, 115, 116, 130; sub-department, 91
Electronics shop, 188
Ellis, W.H., 22, 48, 95; dispute with Pike, 55-6, 71; forensic chemistry, 152; role in Chemistry Department history, 46, 47, 49, 55, 91;
Emery, Karen, 166
Enlightenment (Scottish), 20
Entomological Society of Canada, 44
Environmental Chemistry, specialization in chemistry, 190, 202
Erindale College (UTM), *170*, history, 142, 170-4; relations with St. George campus, 173, 174; sites of faculty research, 171-2; St. George staff teaching at Erindale, 173-4
Exhibition of 1851, 21; Scholarships, 21, 59, 73, 96
Experimental Philosophy (part of Croft's title), 20, 35
Experimental Reaction Dynamics, faculty, 138, 152

Faculty of Arts and Science, 145; Planning Statement 1982, 154
Faculty of Science, feasibility studies for separate, 155
Faculty retirements and replacements after 1989, 161-3, 173
Farrar, David, 14, 152, 162, 182, 183, 198, 199, 200, 202; renovations of Lash Miller, 200-1; revision of undergraduate chemistry curriculum, 202; Vice-provost (Students), U of T, 202; work on Davenport Building, 200-1

Fawcett, Ronald, 15, 103
Fekl, Ulrich, 173
First-year laboratory in 1940s, 104
Folk Song (Chem Club party), 229-30
Ford, John, 187, 188
Forensic chemistry, 42, 48, 122; U of T tradition, 152
Fortescue, R., 63, 104, 119, 188
Fourth-year research, 58, 87
Fraser, Simon, 152, 168
Friesen, Rick, 162
Funnell, W.S., 77-8, 99, 117

Gamble, Marnee, 15
Gardiner, Fiona, 15
Gas Phase Kinetics Apparatus, *131*
Georges, Michael, 163, 172
Gibbs, J. Willard, and his thermodynamics, 51, 52, 86, 91, 94, 110, 113, 114
Glassblowing, 74, 103, 116; shop, 187-88
Goh, Cynthia, 15, 152, 163, 202, 204, 205-6, 206-7
Goldberg, Gary, 196
Gordon, A.R., *111, 131,* 107, 110, 125, 131; administrator, 113, 134; description by Bissell, 112, 113; description by Lane, 113; Distinguished Lecture Series, 149; as lecturer, 110-11, 114; research, 111-12; views on contract research, 113, 124; views on women graduate students, 118
Gortner, R.A., 100
Graduate studies, 124, 143
Graduate Studies Committee (GSC), 134
Greaves, Ken, 188
Gregson, Myrna, 139, 150
Guillet, J.E.G. (Jim), 137, 138, 152, 162, 168
Gulens, Julie, 139
Gwynne, William, 32

Haist Rules, 22, 125, 132
Hanlan, Ned, 50
Hare Report, 167
Harris, Ron, 137, 144, 145, 150, 166,   167, 169
Harrison, A.G. (Alex), 15, 123, 137, 148, 153, 162; mass spectrometry, 152, 153, 179
Harvard's Chemistry Library, 141
Haylock, Bridget, 150
Heinola, Marvi, 166, 168
Henderson (neé Emery), Karen, 166
Herschbach, Dudley, 149, 158, 194
Hiatt, Richard, 122
Honours Program, introduction of fourth-year research in 1890s, 58, 87

Infrared spectroscopy, history at St. George campus, 133, 176-7
Inorganic chemists, 158; faculty (1970s), 152
Introduction to Chemistry, textbook written by Kenrick, 97, 104, 108

J.C. Polanyi, 1986 Nobel Prize in Chemistry, 158
Jack, Tom, 167
Jervis, Robert (Bob), 112, 152
Jockusch, Rebecca, 180, 192, 208
John C. Polanyi Chair in Chemical Physics, 159, 192, 193
John C. Polanyi Lecture Award, 159
John C. Polanyi Nobel Laureate Lecture Series, 159, 193-5
John C. Polanyi Prizes, 159
Jones, J. Bryan, 15, 133, 137, 138, 151, 162, 193
Jones, Diane, 177
Jones Fred, 188
Jones, Ken, 15

Kapral, Raymond, 149, 152
Kay, Lewis, 178
Kenney-Wallace, Geraldine, 162, 168, 169
Kenrick, F.B., *102*, 70, 73, 74, 87, 90, 91, 93, 96-9, 102-04, 108; glassblowing, 103; *Introduction to Chemistry* textbook, 97, 104, 108; obituary for Miller, 101; obituary by Lawrence Cragg, 108-9; obituary by A.R. Gordon, 109; research, 103
King's College, *34*, 17, 19, 20, 22, 23, 27, 30, 33, 34; inaugural lectures, 20, 31
Kluger, Ron, 15, 149, 151, 162, 192, 199
Kresge, Jerry, 149, 151, 162, 168-9
Krull, Ulli, 153, 163, 172, 192
Kumacheva, Eugenia, 163, 192, 207
Kutas, Cecelia, 156

Laboratory, (undergraduate), 1900s, *62;* 1950s organic, *121;* renovated Lash Miller, *201;* apparatus in 1854, 38-9; Wright's graduate lab, 120
Ladies Educational Association of Toronto, 43
Lane, Byron, description of Gordon, 15, 112-3
Lang, W.R., *78,* 81, 88; background, 65, 67-9, 70-3; Director of Department of Military Studies, 79-80, 88; lectures, 71; military matters, 69, 77-9, 81; research, 68, 75-7; space disagreement with Miller, 70-1
Lang's "gang", 79
Lash Miller Chemical Laboratories, *141,* 129, 138; building committee, 140; labs for the 2000s, 206; library, 141; renovated Lash Miller lab, *201;* temperature and humidity control, 141
Lautens, Mark, 15, 151, 155, 161, 192, 197, 198-9; description of Davenport Building facilities, 199-200
Lavery, Sally, 139
Lecture series, 149, 150

Lecturer, revised status, 202
Lee, Yuan T., 158
LeRoy, Donald J., *129*, 10, 89, 114-5, 118, 121, 130-2, 148, 152; assistance with Polanyi's research, 133; as chairman, 134-9, 141; comments re chemical kinetics teaching, 114-5; Mathematics and Chemistry course, 134; Vice-President (Scientific) at NRC, 147
LeRoy, Robert J., 134
LeRoy, Don and Lillice, faculty dinners at their home, 133
Leventhal, Betty, 156
Levere, Trevor, 15
Library issues, 136, 141
Lidar, Daniel, 163, 192
Lister, Maurice, 120, 121, 122, 139, 152, 162, 173
Lollar, Barbara Sherwood, 170
Lorriman, Fred, 114, 121, 122, 156, 166
Lough, Dr. Alan, X-ray laboratories, 15, 182
Lundell, Dr. William, 124
Lynch, Tom, 137, 166, 168

Mabury, Scott, *207*, 15, 184-5, 190, 198, 206-7
Macallum, A.B., 74, 95
Macdonald, Peter, 152, 163, 172, 173
Machine shop, 187
Manners, Ian, 152, 162, 183, 199, 207
Marquez, Armando, 15, 196, 202
Martin, W. Howard, 96, 98
Mass spectrometry, 152; history at St. George campus, 179-180
Massey family, gifts to U of T, 51; Hart House, 78-9
Materials chemistry, 152, 190-1, 202, 207
Mathematics and Chemistry course (M and C), 134
Mathers, Dan, 185
McBain, James, 59, 100
McBryde, W.A.E. (Peter), *13*, 13, 14, 94, 97, 120, 121, 140, 153
McCasland, G.E., 121
McClelland, Bob, 149, 151, 162, 169, 174
McClelland, Sue (neé Licence), 15, 150, 191-2, 193-4, 207
McIntosh, Dr. Douglas, 156
McIntosh, R.L. (Bob), 120, 121, 140
McLean, Stewart, 15, 123, 135, 151, 162; reminiscences of LeRoy and Yates, 135-7
McLennan, J.C., 73, 96
McMaster Building, *115*, 22, 66, 114, 115, 118
McMillan, Andrew, 162
McMillen, David, 173
Mechanics Institute, 43, 46; Croft lectures to, 43
Meindl, Patricia, 15, 199

Menzinger, Michael, 149, 152
Merck Frosst, Lecture Series, 150; Industrial Chair, 192
Meresz, Otto, 137
Miller, William Lash, *88*, 13, 21, 22, 57, 59, 64, 69, 70, 79, 81, 88, 89, 101; background, 85-7; associations with Societies, 89-90; Bios research, 92; disputes, 70-2, 95-6; high school course of studies, 98; obituaries, 101; research, 90-2; research with Ostwald, 86; stories relating to Physics Department, 73, 96; teacher and educator, 93-5; Universal Measuring Machine with Kenrick, 93; version of chemistry, 87, 97
Miller, Dwayne, 163, 192
Miller's gang, 73
Mining Building (a.k.a. Chemistry and Mining Building), *116*, 22, 65, 75, 78, 91, 98, 100, 111, 116, 117, 118, 140, 153
Mitchell, Jack, 94
Molecular beam apparatus, *138*, 138
Moore, Penny Ashcroft, 15, 191
Morgan, Myrtel, 156
Morris, Bob, 152, 162, 168, 169, 199
Moskovits, Martin, *190*, 15, 149, 152, 161, 171, 183, 184, 189-191, 199, 200, 205; creation and funding of the Davenport Building, 196-8
Moss Hall, 35
Murphy, Jennifer, 190, 192, 208

Nanochemistry, 149, 171
Nanostructured Polymer and Inorganic Materials Centre, 207
National Research Council (NRC), Postdoctoral Fellowships, 123, 124; funding of research, 121, 143, 177
Natural philosophy, equipment to illustrate principles, 19
Natural Science and Engineering Research Council (NSERC), funding of equipment, 178, 183, 184; funding of research, 143; holders of Chairs, 192
New Program, replacement for Honours program, 140, 142, 144, 145-7, 167
Nitz, Mark, 180, 208
Nobel laureates, *194*
Nobel Prizes, 1901-04, 66; 1986, 158, 194, 195
Nuclear Magnetic Resonance (NMR), history at St. George campus, 136, 145, 152, 154, 177-9
Nyburg, Stanley, 15, 137, 139, 182

O'Brien, Ross, 152
Odell, Ann, 139
Ohorodnyk, Helen, 149, 156; Departmental Staff Excellence Award 2004, 202
Olah, George, 125, 194
"Old Chemistry Building", *61*, see Chemistry Building
Ontario Innovations (Trust) Fund, 197, 207
Organic Chemistry third-year laboratory, *121*, 115-6
Organic faculty in 1970s, 151

Ostwald, Wilhelm, 86, 89, 97; his U of T PhD graduates, 59
Ozin, Geoffrey, 149, 152, 171, 183, 184, 192, 193, 207

Page, John, 122, 153
Panning, Wolfgang, 188
Parliament buildings (first), use by University of Toronto, *30*, 20, 30, 34, 51, 208
Parry, John, 16
Particulate theory of matter, views of Ostwald, Miller and Kenrick, 86-7, 97
Perkin Elmer Corporation, ANALEST partner, 185
Peter Yates Memorial Lecture Series, 150
Peterson, Dr. Mike, 186
Petrov, Dr. Srebri, 15, 183
Physical chemistry, and Biochemistry, 155; birth of, 51, 86; faculty in 1970s, 152; third-year laboratory, 116
Physical Chemistry Weekend Retreats, 204-5
Physical chemists, 152, 155, 162
Physical organic chemists, 151
Pike, William Herbert, *53*, 22, 53-6; controversy with Ellis, 55-6; introduction of undergraduate research, 57, 59, 87; investment authority, 63
Plooard, Pauline, 139
Poë, Anthony (Tony), 15, 149, 152, 162, 171, 173
Poë, Judith, 171, 172
Poirier, Ray, 168
Polanyi, John C., *132, 158*, 10, 15, 122, 123, 132, 133, 152, 159, 162, 176, 179, 192, 193, 194, 195; 1986 Nobel Prize, 158; portrait by Brenda Bury, 192; research 133, 176
Polymer chemists, 138, 152, 157, 171
Polymers and Materials, 152, 157, 184
Porter, Ron, 117
Potter, Janet, 168, 169
Powder X-ray diffraction, 183, 184
Powell, John, 137, 152, 162
Powell, Michael, 203
Priddle, David, 142, 180
Prosser, Scott, 173, 178

Queen's Park, U of T site in 1854, 19, 20, 34, 35

Rae, James J., 117, 121, 170
Rao, Dr. Bhimasena, 160
RDX, Wright's wartime research, 105, 106, 107
Redman, L.V., 100
Reed, Juta, 151, 162, 172, 173
Repath, E.J., 62, 64, 188
Research chairs in chemistry, list, 192
Research instruments and services (departmental), 175-88

Reynolds, Bill, 15, 137, 152, 153, 162, 174; NMR instrumentation in Chemistry Department, 177-9
Ricker (née Heinola), Marvi, 166, 168
Riddick, Jim, 166, 168
Robinson, E.A. (Peter), 137, 162, 170, 173, 174
Roel Buck Chair in Chemical Physics, 192
Rogers, Jocelyn (Josh), 98, 121; forensic chemistry, 122, 152
Roundhouse (UC), 22, 30, 40, 47, 60; renaming in 1915, 49
Royal Society of Canada, 90

Safian, Frank, 150
Sawyer, Dr. Jeff, 182
Scarborough College (UTSC), *165*, 142-3, 149, 163, 164-70; chemistry curriculum, 167-9; faculty, 166-70; funding, staffing, and tenure problems, 143, 165; an independent university?, 167; Physical Sciences Division, 165; relations with St. George campus, 167; teaching by television, 165-6
Schiff, Daphne, 118
Schmid, George, 137, 162
Schofield, Jeremy, 163
School of Practical Science (SPS), *47*, 22, 30, 41, 45, 46, 47, 54, 55, 56, 60, 65, 87
Schwarz, Christina, 15, 204
Science Department Chairmen, white paper on the Status of Science Departments, 154-5
Scottish Enlightenment, 20
Seminars, divisional, 136, 151
Senoff, Caesar, 144, 182
Sharples, Rollie, 134
Shin, Jumi, 173
Shoichet, Molly, 152, 162, 207
Simcoe, John Graves, 17, 18
Simpson, Andre, 170, 178, 190, 208
Simpson, Myrna, 170, 178, 208
Skonieczny, Dr. Stan, 156
Sleep, Mrs. Alma, 156
Sloan, Barbara, 196, 197, 199
Society of Chemical Industry, 72, 75,   90
Soddy, Frederick, 69-70, 81
Song, Datong, 208
"Souse Specific" (skit), 224-8
Specialist program(s), 146, 147; requirements, 155, 158; as replacement for Honours program, 145; in 2000s, 202
Spectroscopy, 175-9; specialists, 152
SPS, *see* School of Practical Science
Steacie, E.W.R., 115, 121; president of NRC, 121; research funding by NRC, 121; work with Don LeRoy, 130
Still, Ian, 137, 162, 171, 173

Stobie, Bob, 15; reminiscences of Mike Dignam and research group, 160-61
Storeroom keepers, *119*
Strachan, John, 17, 18, 19, 20, 31, 32, 33; first president of King's College, 19
Strangway, David, 174
Strautmanis, Juris, 173
Student riots in the 1960s and 1970s, 144
Synthetic and Structural organic chemists, 151, 162

Tanin, Dr. Ates, 156
Taylor, Mark, 208
Taylor, Scott, 162, 173
Television, at Scarborough College, 164, 165, 166; use at St. George Campus, 140, 156
Tenure at Scarborough College, 143, 166
Thermodynamics of Gibbs, 51, 86, 91, 94, 110, 114
Thompson, Jim, 137, 154, 162, 168
Thompson, Michael, 153, 163, 172, 174
Thomson, Mrs. M.A. (Robin), 10, 122, 150
Tidwell, Tom, 15, 149, 151, 162, 168, 169
Todd, Alexander (Lord), 105
Toronto, 27; census and description in 1834, 27-8; in 1861, 39; in 1881, 50; in 1901, 65
Toxicology (by Croft), 42
Twigg, Fred , 104

Ultraviolet spectroscopy, history at St. George campus, 175-6
Undergraduate Curriculum Committee, 155
Undergraduate Laboratory, renovation in 2003, *201*, 201
Undergraduate research, in 1892, 58-9
Universal Measuring Machine, *93*, 93
University Chemical Club (Chem Club), 203-4
University Chemical Society, 72
University College, 22, 35, 39, 40, 43, 46, 47, 49, 54, 57, 65
University College roundhouse, 22, 30, 40, 47, 49, 60
University of Toronto, agriculture professor, 45; creation 1850, 33; new buildings in 1990s, 65; wartime campus, 108
University of Trinity College, 33
University Professor, chemistry awardees, 171, 192-3
University Rifle Corps, 45

Valleau, John, 15,124, 137, 152, 153, 157, 163, 186
Van Loon, Jon, 149, 153
Verner, Ann, 169
Veterinary College, 45

Walker, Alan, 137, 162, 166, 167, 168, 169
Walker, Gilbert, 192, 208

Wallace, Stephen, 162
Wallberg Building, *120*, 22, 60, 110, 118-20, 131, 140, 145, 153, 187
Wania, Frank, 163, 169, 170, 190
Water fights, 117-18
Webster, Rob, 15
Wetmore, F.E.B. (Frank), 107, 114, 115, 116, 117, 121, 139, 153
Wheeler, Aaron, 180, 192, 208
Whittington, Stuart, *157*, 15, 149, 152, 157-8, 173, 186, 202
Williams, James, 42-3
Wilson, Daniel, 33-4, 40, 49, 52, 55, 75
Wilson, Tuzo, 174
Winnik, Mitchell, 149, 152, 171, 193, 207
Woolley, Drew, 151-2, 162
Wright, George F, *105*, 105-06, 111, 113, 120, 121, 122, 134-5, 154, 181, 187, 203; Downing's description of Wright, 106; RDX research, 105-7, 117, 135; teacher, 114, 115, 116-7

X-ray crystallography, history at St. George, 181-3; powder X-ray diffraction, 183-4
Xerox Research Centre, 159

Yates, Keith, *153*, 15, 137, 151, 153, 154, 162; issues with Chemistry vs. Biochemistry and Chemistry programs, 155
Yates, Peter, *135*, 135, 136, 141, 151, 153-4, 155, 162, 193; McLean's assessment, 135-7
"Ye Tragedies of Macbeth" (skit), 203, 209-15
Yealland, Michael, 168
York (town), 17, 19, 27
York University, 124
Young, Dr. Alex, 180
Yudin, Andrei, 162, 199, 207
Yuen, Jackie, 149, 156

Zamble, Deborah, 162, 192, 199, 205

www.ingramcontent.com/pod-product-compliance
Lightning Source LLC
Chambersburg PA
CBHW050349230426
43663CB00010B/2049